Prince Among Slaves

Terry Alford

Prince Among Slaves

Harcourt Brace Jovanovich

New York and London

Library of Congress Cataloging in Publication Data

Alford, Terry.
Prince among slaves.

Includes bibliographical references.
1. Ibrahima, Abd al-Rahman, 1762–1829.   2. Slavery
in the United States—Mississippi.   3. Slaves—
Mississippi—Biography.   I. Title.
E.444.I25A78   301.44'93'0924 [B]   77-73109
ISBN 0-15-174250-2

BCDE

To the children of Ibrahima,

wherever time may have scattered them

Contents

Acknowledgments   ix

Why   xvii

1. The White Turban   3

2. Across the Broad Casamance   20

3. "A Common Slave"   39

4. *Annus Mirabilis* and After   66

5. "Unbroken in Body and Mind"   85

6. A Northern Campaign   112

7. "The Almoner of His Bounty"   142

8. A Single Plank   165

Epilogue   184

Appendix   189

Genealogies

Map of West Africa
in the 1780s

Notes   197

Illustrations

between pages 108 and 109

Ibrahima in 1828

A caravan at Timbuktu

View of Timbo

The great mosque at Timbo

Street scene in Jenne

Plan of the town of Timbo, Futa Jalon

Diagram of the slave ship *Africa*

Deed of sale for Ibrahima, 1788

Natchez, Mississippi, 1796

William Rousseau Cox

Andrew Marschalk

Thomas H. Gallaudet

Deed of conveyance for Ibrahima, 1828

New York African Free School

Notice of the loading of the *Harriet*

The colony at Monrovia, Liberia

Acknowledgments

Research for this biography, delving into many different places, peoples, and periods of time, often led me to seek information or opinions from scholars, archivists, and other interested parties. While I cannot thank by name all persons or institutions who helped me in the last seven years, I would like to acknowledge those who were generous in supplying assistance. They are C. Richard Arena, Whittier College, Whittier, California; James C. Armstrong, Boston University; D. W. Arnott, School of Oriental and African Studies, London; Oumar Ba, Institut Fondamental d'Afrique Noire, Dakar; William A. Baker, M.I.T., Cambridge, Massachusetts; Maxine Tull Boatner, West Hartford, Connecticut; Eleanor Brown, Pine Ridge, Mississippi; J. B. Cain, Washington, Mississippi; John G. Clark, University of Kansas, Lawrence; David Dalby, SOAS, London; Leland Donald, University of Victoria, B.C., Canada; Florence LeC. Eisele, Natchez, Mississippi; R. Brent Forman, Natchez; David Gamble, San Francisco State University; Connie G. Griffith, Tulane University, New Orleans; P. E. H. Hair, University of Liverpool; Laura D. S. Harrell, formerly with the Mississippi State Department of Archives and History, Jackson; Thomas Henderson, Greenwood, Mississippi; The Historical Society of Pennsylvania, Philadelphia, particularly Peter Parker; G. Douglas Inglis, now in Seville, Spain; William L. Joyce, American Antiquarian Society, Worcester, Massachusetts; Byrle Kynerd, State Historical Museum, Jackson, Mississippi; Alexander Peter Kup, Simon Fraser University, B.C., Canada; Waldo P. Lambdin, Natchez; The Library of the

American Philosophical Society, Philadelphia, particularly Whitfield J. Bell, Jr., Murphy Smith, and Carl F. Miller; Verbie Ann Lovorn, University, Mississippi; David Lowenthal, University College, London; M. Stone Miller, Jr., Louisiana State University, Baton Rouge; John H. Morrow, Rutgers University; Carolyn C. Nugent, Natchez; Sulayman Nyang, Howard University, Washington, D.C.; Abd al-Rahman Ousman, Islamic Center, Washington, D.C.; Lucille Peacock, Evans Memorial Library, Aberdeen, Mississippi; Walter B. Posey, Atlanta, Georgia; Nan Foster Schuchs, Natchez; G. Terry Sharrer, Smithsonian Institution, Washington, D.C.; Mrs. Albert D. Williams, Lake Forest, Illinois; and Charles Cooney, Harrisburg, Pennsylvania.

I was fortunate that a number of people made an effort beyond that of courtesy to assist me in my work, either by way of research or of encouragement. I wish to acknowledge Mrs. William A. Adams, Natchez; Caroline Allen, Mississippi State Department of Archives and History, Jackson; S. A. W. Boyd, Roseau, Dominica; Merton L. Dillon, Ohio State University, Columbus; Janet Q. Eichacker, East Setauket, New York; T. J. Foster, Natchez; John R. Kemp, Louisiana State Museum, New Orleans; Thomas Kramer, Franklin, Louisiana; Joan McDaniel, Washington, D.C.; Neil McMillen, University of Southern Mississippi, Hattiesburg; Mamadou M'Daw, Dakar; Charles Poland, Northern Virginia Community College, Annandale; R. Proesmans, Pointe Michel, Dominica; Charlotte Quinn, now in Prague; Lillian B. Quinn, Setauket, New York; Demetra Tsiatsos, Springfield, Virginia; and Samir Zoghby, Library of Congress, Washington, D.C.

Four scholars read this book, either in whole or in part. They are Christopher Fyfe, University of Edinburgh; Jack D. L. Holmes, University of Alabama, Birmingham; D. C. James, Mississippi State University, State University; and Bertram Wyatt-Brown, Case Western Reserve University, Cleveland, Ohio. Each took the time to make lengthy and important criticisms that caused me to rethink and, in some sections, to rewrite the text. Though I have not followed all of their advice, their questions, reflections, and suggestions have made this a better book, and I appreciate their help.

A special note of thanks must go to Thierno Diallo, University of Dakar, for the hours and hours he spent with me discussing Ibrahima and his relationship to the history of Futa Jalon. His courteous manner and disinterested aid convinced me that Ibrahima's people have not lost their most admired characteristics.

There are a few friends for whom the appearance of this book will bring a personal satisfaction. They believed Ibrahima's story was an important one and they thought I could write it, and since I began the work, their support has never failed. My warm appreciation goes to Mary Postlethwaite of Natchez; Bill and Martha Lum of Port Gibson, Mississippi; Wendy Weil, my agent, of New York; Daniel Okrent and Eugene R. Stone, my editors, of the same place.

In conclusion I would like to acknowledge my mother, Bess Alford, for her steady support over the years. Lastly, I wish to remember my wife, Jeanette, who, more than anyone else, knows the sacrifices this book demanded. She helped in the research and supported my work in a hundred other ways. She got to know Ibrahima, and she wanted the book finished. A simple "thank you" would not only be inadequate, it would be inappropriate, too. For her, as for myself, the true satisfaction will be in the telling of his story at long last.

The boy sets sail on the ocean of life
with a fleet of a thousand ships.
The old man reaches the shore at last,
rescued on a single plank.
—Friedrich von Schiller

Why

The incredible story of this book begins in the spring of 1968, when I was a graduate student in American history at Mississippi State University. It was a time of political and emotional turmoil. The Tet Offensive, the murder of Dr. Martin Luther King, a near-riot at the University, and a full-fledged one at Mississippi Valley State College, a nearby school where I was teaching, had overwhelmed me, and I decided to take a few days off and drive down to the southern part of the state. Since southwest Mississippi is an old plantation area, I had the excuse of thinking I could work on a seminar paper on slavery that I had coming due.

I remember little about the drive itself. Meadville, Liberty, Woodville—the small towns were merely a succession of red-brick courthouses, old men at country stores, and cheerless rooming houses. But the uneventfulness of the drive was in complete opposition to the nature of the discovery awaiting me in Natchez. For it was in the courthouse in Natchez that I first became aware of the person who was to influence my own future. I was working in the county deed records, buried in giant cloth-bound volumes of laminated pages, when I found a letter written in 1828 by Henry Clay, then Secretary of State. It concerned the freedom of a slave who was said to be a Moorish prince. I had not heard of this particular individual before, although I knew that from time to time African princes and kings had wound up as slaves, so I wasn't surprised. What did surprise me was the full report of the man's life I received later that day from Miss Mary Postlethwaite, a Natchez antiquarian.

The fact of this person's royal heritage was, presumably, well known, since records showed that the man was called "Prince" while a slave at Natchez. But his true name was Abraham, or, as it would be pronounced among his own people, who were African Muslims, Ibrahima. He claimed to have been born in Timbuktu, the son of a powerful monarch, and educated there and elsewhere in Africa in the way common at the time to Islamic communities throughout the world. I learned that in 1788, when he was twenty-six and a colonel in his father's army, Ibrahima had been defeated in a war, captured, and sold to a slave-ship captain who brought him to the West Indies. During the summer of that year he was purchased by a Natchez farmer named Thomas Foster, and for the next four decades he was Foster's slave on a plantation near the city. Despite his extreme misfortune, Ibrahima adhered to a strict, self-imposed code of conduct throughout that time, never drinking, stealing, or being found guilty of a breach of confidence or trust.

I became intrigued with the prince's story when Miss Postlethwaite told me that after the prince had been a slave about fifteen or twenty years, a most uncanny and remarkable event took place. One day, while he was selling some vegetables in a village in the county, he saw a white person he had known in Africa, a man who owed his life to Ibrahima and his father. The white man recognized him, lept off his horse, and embraced him. This started a chain of events that led ultimately to Ibrahima's freedom. The prince was manumitted by his owner and returnd to Africa, dying shortly after his arrival.

Miss Postlethwaite's story intrigued me. When I returned to the university, I researched the topic briefly, discovering only one published account of Ibrahima's life. That was an article by Charles S. Sydnor entitled "The Biography of a Slave," which appeared in the January, 1937, number of the *South Atlantic Quarterly*. His article confirmed Miss Postlethwaite's remarks, and, although it lacked footnotes or bibliography, it was evidently factual. His text itself suggested sources where I might find additional information on Ibrahima.

Other things, however, prevented me from pursuing the story then. It was 1970 before I could consider an attempt at writing his life.

As I mused over the idea at that time, I realized I was dealing not only with an unusual story, but a remarkable man as well. The drop from freedom to slavery was staggering for anyone to take. It was too difficult for some, as the numerous suicides on slave ships and plantations are witness. But Ibrahima survived the fall. And, unlike many fellow Africans, he fell, too, from wealth, from power, from the world of formal education and ideas. How did he manage to withstand it? Why weren't his character and pride broken, if not his mind? Quite simply, how did he keep himself together and manage to come out at life's end with some dignity and self-respect? I wanted the answers to those questions, and the Library of Congress seemed to me to be the best place to get them. So, in late May, 1970, my wife, Jeanette, and I packed everything we had in our car and moved to Washington, D.C.

Within a week of commencing my research in the primary sources, I came upon new and unpublished material on the African. I worked on through the summer of 1970, principally in the manuscripts of the American Colonization Society, whose members had befriended Ibrahima late in his life. Numerous letters and a pamphlet written about him turned up. There was a moment of great satisfaction for me that year when I found the engraving of the prince reproduced here. I also began to investigate Thomas Foster, his owner, in hopes that I could understand the milieu of the plantation on which Ibrahima had been held a slave.

Ibrahima, I soon learned, had given autobiographical accounts to several people who knew him in his old age. They were Cyrus Griffin, a young attorney; R. R. Gurley, secretary of the Colonization Society; and Thomas H. Gallaudet, the father of deaf-mute education in the United States. All three men had published short biographies of his life in 1828. As best as was possible at the time, each had attempted to evaluate Ibrahima's remarks about himself in the light of travel accounts and second-party interviews. I subjected the facts he gave them to further scrutiny by checking them against contemporary and historical accounts of Ibrahima's era. Less traditional accounts about him, like the Natchez folklore that I discovered, also had value, though subject to use with greater caution.

By September, 1970, the obvious sources had been worked, yet the volume of information I had amassed was distressingly low. There were lacunae in Ibrahima's story that had to be filled. Research at the Library of Congress had brought to my attention important manuscript and newspaper collections in other cities. They needed checking. It was also clear that the Natchez records needed a careful combing. Descendants of Thomas Foster should be located and interviewed. Research in British archives would be necessary to identify the slave ship that brought Ibrahima to the New World and to illuminate that period of his life. African scholars, as well as the *awlube* (the traditional historians of Ibrahima's country), could also contribute to my work. What had seemed in May to be a simple project now swelled like a Christmas goose. The work would have to be continued in libraries and historical societies in dozens of places, at a great cost in time and money.

That, almost, was the end of the book. I had the time but not the money. Despite a flurry of letters I was unable to obtain foundation or grant support. Still, I was unwilling to begin writing with my research so incomplete or to abandon the idea of a biography altogether for a mish-mash of truth and fiction. I did not want a book that people could read and think upon concluding it, "It's interesting that this *could* have happened." I wanted a book that people could put down, thinking, "It's amazing that this *did*."

So it was that I drifted away from the library to some part-time jobs to help support the family. During 1970–71 I worked as a typist, a maintenance man at the Watergate, a Xerox-machine attendant, and a clerk at a bookstore. I kept on falteringly with Ibrahima, going to the library when I found the time, but that wasn't very often. Jeanette and I did agree, however, that we would finish the book no matter how long it took.

A teaching position in the fall of 1972 was pivotal in reviving things. A salary and a schedule I could live with gave me the opportunity to work intensely on Ibrahima again. I haunted the library anew, so familiar a sight by now that I was referred to jokingly as a "Reader Emeritus." My wife and I made trips to Mississippi—usually two a year from 1972 on—working in courthouses and archives, and interviewing people. I visited the old Foster plantation site numerous times and photographed it extensively. In 1973 a stipend from the National Endowment for the Humanities greatly facilitated the appearance of this book by allowing me to spend time in libraries in New York, New England, and the South, researching Africans as immigrants to North America.

During the summer of 1974 one of the last steps in the work was taken when I traveled to Europe and Africa. The manuscripts in the Public Record Office in London were extraordinarily informative. On my first day there I discovered the name of the ship that brought Ibrahima to the Western Hemisphere, and with it a giant piece of his puzzle fell into place. Having come so far and so long with him, I don't think anything could have elated me more. I was gradually pulling Ibrahima from obscurity.

The British Museum was also helpful, as were libraries and scholars at London University and in Edinburgh and Paris.

One of my regrets in writing this book is that I was not permitted to visit Futa Jalon. The Republic of Guinea does not allow Western social scientists to run loose in the interior, hampering the national integration of its ethnic groups by recalling their past divisiveness. However sound this policy may seem to Guineans, it is ironic in view of the reputation Ibrahima's people have always had for hospitality. But Ibrahima's people are a minority in the Republic and are not proportionately represented in its government. One hopes that national self-assurance and internal democratization may in time lead to a change of the present policy. While that may benefit future researchers, I prepared this work under restrictions that prevented investigations in Ibrahima's homeland.

Fortunately, the Institut Fondamental d'Afrique Noire at Dakar in neighboring Senegal has a splendid collection of historical and literary documents from African sources relating to the history of Futa Jalon. I worked extensively with these during the summer and enjoyed the benefit of conversations with Senegalese, Gambians, and Guineans there about Ibrahima. The latter were especially interested in him and helpful to me.

Upon my return from Africa, I began at last to write the text. Now, nearly three years later, I have finished.

It is the spring of 1977, and Ibrahima and I are about to go our own ways. Mississippi State University is just a fading memory for me. The Vietnam war is over and Dr. King long gone. Most of the men and women I teach today don't even remember L.B.J. But, at least, Ibrahima is out of time's shadow. He required a nearly unique synthesis of Africa and America, and I did the best I knew how.

In bringing him back, I not only learned a great deal about him, I learned a great deal from him, too. And I hope that this book, like a stone thrown in still water, can send out that knowledge in ever-widening circles of understanding.

April, 1977
Fairfax, Virginia

Prince Among Slaves

The land of living water, of fruit trees,
of faith, and of liberty.

—Pullo saying

1. The White Turban

This tale of an American slave called "Prince" is an extraordinary story of an intelligent and courageous human being who, born a prince, lived his life a slave and died in freedom. Like some other African kings and princes, "Prince" had been enslaved when defeated in a war. The events surrounding his discovery, in a small Southern American town, of a white man whom his father, an African king, had once befriended, and his being finally set free, were incredible events in themselves. However, the full story of his life, his origins among a Muslim people in Africa, and his development into the unusual human being he was is one of the most powerful and moving tales of that time.

The story begins with another name, which was "Prince's" Muslim name, Ibrahima. This translates literally as Abraham. Ibrahima's father was king of a cattle-raising people, who, in their wanderings in West Africa, had found themselves in a series of wars with the farmers on whose land they had settled. It had been, in the beginning, a friendly invasion, and the farmers, known as the Jalunke, had been glad to have the dairy products and meat from the people known as the Fulbe.*

However, difficulties between the two people soon developed, based on the great differences in their approach and understanding of how the world worked and what forces governed it. The

* In the singular, Pullo. These people are better known by the names that others have given them, such as Fula or Fulani. Writers of Ibrahima's time often called them "Foulah's," "Poulas," or variants thereof.

farmers were animistic, they worshiped many gods. To them the prosperity of their country, which was commonly known as Futa Jalon ("the land of the Fulbe and Jalunke"), was made possible by appeasing the traditional spirits and maintaining a time-honored relationship between the land and the people who lived on it. The Fulbe, the cattle herders, were mostly Muslims. That they prayed to one god, and an invisible one at that, created a tension with the Jalunke that grew to the extent that the Jalunke at last forbade the Fulbe to pray in public, and even forced them to hide their holy books in caves. These restrictions were intolerable. The noted Muslim cleric, Karamoko Alfa, raised a cry for a holy war, known as a *jihaad,* to establish the realm of Islam. God, he wrote in a circular letter, promised success to the faithful. But the Fulbe were in need of a military as well as a religious leader for this war, and Karamoko Alfa, their spiritual head, was not a general.

It was Ibrahima's father, Sori, a man known for his ambition, boldness, and love of life, who finally led the Fulbe into w; r. In a traditional story still cherished in the mountains of Guinea, Sori, in one swift, dramatic act, slashed open the great ceremonial drum of the farmers, thus beginning the war. The Muslims were few in number, compared to the Jalunke, but with Sori's leadership, and the zeal their religion supplied them, they went from victory to victory. By 1730 the Muslim supremacy was established.

The victors created a theocracy, administered by Karamoko Alfa until his excessive religious practices drove him mad in 1748. Though he did not die until three years later, exigency required that his replacement be found straightaway. Sori, extremely popular with the army, was chosen and given the title of *almaami,* "he who leads the community in prayer." He was the people's choice. A ten-day festival at Fugumba, where Sori received the white turban of office, preceded a fifteen-day fête at Timbo, traditional seat of Sori's family. The meat of two thousand cattle was distributed among the people at that time.

As *almaami,* Sori quickly showed the aggressive spirit that had earned him his reputation during the *jihaad.* In the 1750s he led regular campaigns on the northern and eastern frontiers of Futa. He enjoyed the habit of success, and his presence with the army gave it confidence and nerve. In time the expression "as brave as Sori" became common. Once, when attacking a town, Ibrahima said of his father, Sori "found it close shooting and fell down as if dead. The [enemy] king came and danced around him, according to the custom of the country. [Sori], having only feigned death, watched for an opportunity, drew his knife, slew the king, and put his head on a pole and carried it to the city." The defenders were so unnerved that they fled, leaving the town to the Fulbe.

The Fulbe recount the epic stories of their people in historical chronicles known as the *tarikhs,* documents often naming each country with which Sori went to war. Dynastic and military in content, these histories by themselves give a misleading view of the society as a whole. One would conclude from them alone that the Fulbe were either on a battlefield or on the way to one every day. Raiding did play a part of undeniable importance in the nation's economic and religious life, but it was only one aspect of "the land of living water, of fruit trees, of faith, and of liberty," as the Fulbe called their home.

"[They] are handsome men, strong and brave; they are intelligent, they are mysterious and prudent," wrote Antoine Golbery, a Frenchman living on the coast during Sori's reign. In armed caravans of hundreds the Fulbe would appear at the river settlements bearing oblong baskets on their heads. They came to the coast to trade ivory, rice, hides, livestock, and gold, the latter hammered into rings carried about the waist. These items, and slaves who had been taken as prisoners of war, were exchanged for salt and European goods. "They [say that they] could not get any European articles without slaves, and they could not get slaves without fighting for them," an Englishman wrote. "The people with whom we go to war do not pray to God," a brother of Ibrahima explained. "We never go to war with people who do God Almighty service." These trips to the waterside, made from a land not visited by Europeans, brought much attention to the Fulbe. Even in Karamoko Alfa's lifetime the land known as Futa had the reputation of being one of the richest interior nations. On the coast the Muslim Fulbe were orderly and abstentious, quite a contrast to the quarreling degenerates living at the slave factories. Europeans were impressed.

The town called Timbo was to assume first rank in political life during Ibrahima's lifetime. Set on a rolling plain, the town was shouldered on the east by the mountains known as Great and Little Helaya. Six years after *almaami* Sori's death, the population of the town was estimated at seven or eight thousand. The houses were mud-walled and circular, with conical roofs and low, projecting eaves. "They are remarkably neat in their houses," James Watt wrote in 1794, "and have always everything clean and in order." Rooms were large, and wide doors made them seem airy. Each establishment with its courtyard was usually surrounded by a hedge higher than a man so that anyone traveling the narrow streets and culs-de-sac could mind his own business without effort. The mosque, set among orange trees, was the most prominent structure in town, and the second oldest place of worship in Futa. Built in the shape of a great cone, it was supported internally by wooden pillars sunk into a pressed clay floor. The faithful worshiped on sheepskin mats placed in rows three feet apart. Prominent families such as Sori's had rural residences near Timbo and were often there. There was also a two-furlong track outside the town where the Fulbe indulged their chief passion, racing the small horses of the country. The slopes, fields, and groves about Timbo were fed by tributaries of the Senegal River. Town and province imparted together the impression of a settled country of estates, prosperous herds, rural comfort.

"Considerable attention is devoted to the acquirement of knowledge, particularly with the higher class," the American Cyrus Griffin wrote in 1828. Schools associated with clerics at the mosques taught reading, writing, arithmetic, and languages. Manuscript texts of the Qur'an, the Pentateuch, and other works were circulated. Individual libraries on religion and jurisprudence were common, and books and writing paper were prized gifts. Most young Muslims, spurred by a teacher's ferule if all else failed, had read the Qur'an several times and copied it at least once by age twelve. Additional study in Islamic law was available to those who wished it. Many students and teachers came from outside Futa, and Fulbe left in equal numbers to pursue an education or a career in another land. These comings-and-goings, together with the visits of merchants, kept the Fulbe in touch with the Islamic world and informed of events throughout West Africa. Pilgrimages to Mecca, both across the Red Sea and over the isthmus, were performed by some; traveling mendicants from as far away as Morocco and Egypt came to Futa on occasion. Thus was the defeat of the Spanish at Gibraltar in 1782 known in this part of Africa forty days after it occurred. Mungo Park, while exploring the Niger River ten years later, learned similarly of the loss of the English Mediterranean convoy in 1795 during the wars of the French Revolution.

"The male Foulahs have a beauty of form which almost equals that of the women," wrote the slave trader Theodore Canot, "and in fact the only fault I found with them was their feminine delicacy. However, they made up in courage what they lacked in form." Fulbe men ordinarily dressed in full-sleeved, loose-fitting robes and wore turbans or embroidered skullcaps. They kept their hair long, dangling in braids to the shoulders. Sandals were worn or the feet were left bare. Often a leather amulet containing an inscription from the Qur'an was hung about the neck as a charm. Women, covered only from waist to knee in brightly colored cloth, wore gold earrings and elaborate coiffures. "Females were constantly busy over their cotton and spinning wheels when not engaged in household occupations; nor were the men less thrifty," Canot continued. "I never saw man or woman bask lazily in the sun." Silversmithing, weaving, leatherworking, and fabricating products from iron bars went on daily in their towns. The Fulbe pastoral influence was seen, however, in the lack of large markets or bazaars, peddlers alone being present.

Although the victory of the Fulbe made them the rulers, they still retained a traditional contempt for farmers, the old herders' disdain for those who grub the earth. That work was done by the Jalunke, who fed themselves and provided much of the food for their masters, too. Their condition in this period is imperfectly known. It has been called everything from chattel slavery to a loose form of serfdom. One source states that the Jalunke were free to do their own labor after midday prayers; another, that they had two working days a week for their own fields. In time some *modi vivendi* were reached, like that under which a person born in the country would not be sold out of it except as a penalty for criminal conduct. Still, it was thralldom, and the Jalunke, always the majority, were slow to accept their servitude as the final state of affairs. The Muslims knew this, and a law required them to go armed in anticipation of a revolt.

A massive one occurred in 1756, when thousands of Jalunke rose up and left the country in great force. Sori, unable to stop them, felt his hold on power slip with this defeat. Every difficulty now rushed to throw itself upon him. His wealth gave birth to jealousy, especially among those who had lost their slaves in the exodus. He had "eaten to the limits of the possible," as the popular expression went, and yet he was not generous enough, at least in the view of the afflicted. The nobles grumbled that they were slipping into a vassalage under his kingship and soon began intriguing with the heirs of the spiritual leader Karamoko Alfa. Often away on campaigns, Sori was being undercut by those whom he put in key posts at home. Not only were his appointees unpopular, some were corrupt and rapacious. They underreported tax revenues and were guilty of hoarding. These abuses undermined Sori's popularity and doomed his efforts to establish the equality of believers promised in the constitution of the confederation.

The catalyst of rebellion against Sori was Karamoko Alfa's son Saalihu, who had grown to a handsome maturity in the eleven years since his father's death. This tall, courtly Pullo, backed by his family's immense fortune and by support from all parts of the population, threatened a *coup d'etat* in 1759. The nobility supported his bid for power, as did the elders of Futa, eager to replace the warrior *almaami*. In polling his army and followers, Sori was startled to find dissatisfaction even there. Resistance, he concluded, was impossible. His pride wounded, Sori denounced his thankless fellow citizens, quit Timbo, and, taking his family and herds, retired to Mount Helaya.

It was a curious exile. A mountain top was a small stage for a giant to brood upon. And, since Mount Helaya overlooked Timbo, scene of happier days, it should have been all the worse. But Sori may have liked the spot. The mountain blocked the morning light from the city. The sun would have to labor up its summit, and when its light fell on Timbo at last, it would have seemed to be coming from his own mountain. The town could look up and see the sun and think of another eminence that loomed there. Sori would have enjoyed the metaphor. Out of power, "the beloved of God" did not intend to be out of mind or even out of sight.

There was one happy moment, when Abd al-Rahman Ibrahima was born in 1762. The name, by traditional naming practices, suggests Ibrahima was born on a Monday or a Friday. Although Ibrahima would later claim to be Sori's principal son, it seems that he was not. Ibrahima was simply one of a large number of male children the old king fathered, though clearly he was a favorite. Nothing is known of Ibrahima's mother, one of Sori's four wives, except that she was supposed to be a woman of rank and blood. History is equally mute as to the prayers and celebrations commemorating Ibrahima's birth. There must have been some, perhaps the customary parade of women around the house, carrying the newborn child and the instruments of war that would be his as an adult.

But history gives somber colors to these years. Sori was deeply troubled. The father had had a dream whose meaning no one could interpret. He had seen the long-dead Karamoko Alfa, a man whom everyone regarded as saintly, standing with a great wound on one arm.

Ibrahima, son of the mountain years, had been born into a world falling to pieces.

The new *almaami,* Saalihu, was weak. He seemed unable to take control of the country. Feudalism grew in the absence of Sori's strong hand, as Saalihu struggled continually with those who usurped his authority. He also had to contend with Sori's partisans, who worked to undermine him when possible. The result of this dissidence was an erosion of order, and, for the first time in decades, an increase in lawlessness in the country. But it was failure on the battlefield, where Saalihu hoped to become indispensable, that brought disaster to him and to everyone else. In 1762, the year of Ibrahima's birth, a Fulbe army attacked the kingdom of Wasulu, east of Futa. That country was populated by non-Muslim peoples called collectively the Wasulunke, "the people of Wasulu." In the past Sori had gone there with such success that a difficult campaign was not expected. True to form, Konde Birama, who commanded the Wasulunke, was beaten wherever he appeared. But the rains set in early that year, and the Fulbe withdrew before the Wasulunke were broken. Incredibly, Konde Birama came across the wet savannas after them. Now harassing, now ambushing, now feinting, this habitual victim showed an activity and skill that shocked the Fulbe. Twice they turned about and forced battle, only to be routed both times.

The Fulbe were staggered, but fate had not finished with them. The Solima, their allies to the south, tired of them and seeing the opportunity to throw them off at last, did not send assistance to the front. In retaliation, Saalihu executed some Solima chiefs. This, in turn, brought a Solima declaration of war, the last thing the Fulbe needed, for Konde Birama was preparing an invasion of his own. Murders on both sides followed, with travelers and even students at the schools fleeing for their lives. Finally, a great army of Solima and Wasulunke moved toward Futa, driving wild animals from the woods before it. Deer are said to have appeared in the streets of villages where they had never been seen before. Advancing on the plateau, the enemy coalition seized Timbo in 1763 and razed it totally. Homes, storehouses, and crops were destroyed, along with the old mosque, where the constitution of the state and other historic papers were burned. The remnants of the Fulbe army could do little now except watch at home a performance they had often given abroad. For two months the foreigners raged throughout the countryside. Slaves and goods disappeared. Cattle unable to be moved were slaughtered. Mass executions took place. Then, to the horror of the Muslims, Konde Birama disinterred the body of Karamoko Alfa and cut an arm off the corpse. With this indignity he retired to the east.

The Fulbe returned to Timbo in the spring. Only habit brought them back, for there was little city left to see. The scene was desolate. In the underbrush were found the remains of Karamoko Alfa.

"Here is that which my dream foretold," said Sori, as he viewed the corpse of the one he had often called "my great brother."

At the insistence of the people, Saalihu was deposed and Sori brought back to head a common war council. Who else could save the state? Although the old warrior was awarded a less important title than *almaami* by the jealous elders, the crisis of the moment put him in no mood to argue with them. There would be no preferments or federation to give them if Konde Birama and his allies could not be stopped. At Timbo, Sori hastily erected a stone and clay bank thirty to fifty feet high and one hundred and twenty feet square, "elevated by the labors of half the country," and on top of it he put a square tower hemmed in by sixteen-foot-high walls. Constructed under the direction of a man in Timbo who had spent time in England, this fortress gave the city the security it had lacked the year before. Here, and in similar fortifications in the north, loopholes were cut in the palisades for the defenders to fire through.

The Solima arrived in Futa that year (1764) after murdering all the Fulbe they found in their own country. Literally burning a trail through the south, they seemed intent on murdering all they found there, too. But Sori soon demonstrated how little he had forgotten in retirement. The Solima were beaten and for one season, at least, the Fulbe caught their breath. The coalition returned, however, in annual campaigns in the late 1760s and early 1770s. It orchestrated its attacks and employed its numbers in ways that Sori found impossible to resist. His country became a cache to which the enemy came each year and picked out whatever it wanted. Konde Birama even established personal control over a large area of the plateaus. A tradition states that, as an act of submission, he required each Pullo to bring a rock to a site near Fugumba. He erected a stronghold there with them and from it governed the area of his conquests. Konde Birama's throttle was so tight that many Fulbe, powerless to oppose him, became his subjects.

"Now I am the master, I am the law," he said, "and if the Fulbe do not work their fields and work them well, I will cut their throats."

No one doubted he would. To eject this infidel it was clear that a long and bloody war of liberation would be required.

It is a comment on their love of learning that the Muslims managed to keep the schools at Timbo open during this time. Ibrahima, Sori's son, began his studies there when he was seven, in 1769. His education was traditional; first he learned to read, then to write, passages from the Qur'an. Community schools in Egypt and Morocco taught the same way. These were the first lessons of young Muslims everywhere, learned by rote and endless practice and forgotten only when memory itself was abandoned. Around a fire a *marabout,* or cleric, led the instruction, each student writing verses of the Qur'an on wooden tablets. Such training made Ibrahima literate in Arabic and Pular (the language of the Fulbe), but it did something vastly more important. It put the stamp of his culture upon him, opening to him the Islamic vision and teaching him the omnipotence of God and the importance of the community of believers. This faith was his strongest bond of identity with other people. Its lessons were indelible when fully grasped. To the believer Islam alone transcended the heterogeneity of West Africa and provided a basis for universal brotherhood. Profoundly impressed with its promises, Ibrahima wrote his lessons "forty-eight hours a day."

Seeing this interest, his father decided to send him abroad for further education when he was twelve. Ibrahima had become very familiar with the Qur'an by that age, reading it correctly and fluently, and he was already well on the way to the coveted titles of *tierno* and *alfa,* given, respectively, to those who progressed to make exegesis of the Qur'an in Arabic and Pular and to become masters of Islamic science. Perhaps Sori, head of a large family, intended to tithe this son to the faith. Ibrahima later claimed that the trip was to prepare him to follow his father in office. While Karamoko Alfa is witness to the importance of superior education as a requisite to power, not enough is known of the ages and lives of Ibrahima's brothers to judge this assertion. For one motive or another, however, Ibrahima left Futa in 1774 to study in Macina and at Timbuktu.

The ancestral home of most Fulbe of Futa, Macina lay about one thousand miles to the east, in present-day Mali. The steady Macinan migration to Futa and the flow of teachers and merchants had kept Futa in touch with this kingdom on the middle Niger. Traders often passed between Futa and Macina, selling tobacco, silver, ivory, and slaves from the west. The trip could take months, but it was possible to perform it with relative safety. Picking up a tributary of the Niger in eastern Futa, voyagers simply passed down by the gold country of Bure and onto the Niger itself.

Macina, peopled by rice farmers, herders, and fishermen, was chiefly pastoral and populated by Fulbe. Its principal city was Jenne, a great trading entrepôt of brick and grass buildings on a Niger branch. Here turbaned traders plied the river, their boats poled or rowed along, their salt and cloth and guns covered from the sun by awnings. On small green islands, the Fulbe attended their stock, safe from the lions on the banks. Fishermen drew up their catches in long cotton nets and dumped them in their roomy canoes. The explorer Mungo Park learned twenty years after Ibrahima's visit that more than thirty thousand people lived in Jenne. It took him a day's ride on horseback just to circle it. But the size and prosperity of the place were not Jenne's only fame. There was also its reputation as home for a group of sophisticated Islamic scholars. "God, the Most High, has brought to this fortunate city a number of learned and holy men, strangers to the country, who have come here to live," a seventeenth-century Muslim had written. Such was its attraction to Ibrahima, of whose stay here it is only recorded that he spent it in study. It is easy to imagine, however, the excitement of the Muslim minority in Jenne about his residence, for the *jihaad* in Futa had been an inspiration to the faithful there.

Timbuktu lay beyond Jenne, twelve days' travel by land. Several miles north of the river, it was an imposing city of mosques, markets, schools, and shops. Its population at this time is not known, but, like Jenne, it was much larger than any town in Futa and much busier, too. "Caravans were continually arriving," Ibrahima observed, bringing salt and goods from North Africa. Rising above the two-storied, whitewashed houses of the rich were three ancient centers of worship: Dyingereyber, Sankore, and Sidiyahya. Ibrahima's school, probably connected with one of these, had over two hundred pupils under four masters. "They read the Alcoran, attended to geography, astronomy, calculations, to the Mahomedan religion, and the laws of the country," wrote Thomas H. Gallaudet. Regrettably, the prince gave Gallaudet no bibliography of his texts. The level of his studies might be gauged by them. There are only the statements of two men who met him much later in life. One, whose name is not known, thought him "well versed in Oriental literature," perspicacious, and eloquent. The second, John Frederick Schroeder, an American knowledgeable in Eastern languages, wrote, "He is very familiar with the Koran, many passages of which he read for me with correctness and fluency (according to the usual manner of Oriental scholars)." Ibrahima, he remarked, "read and wrote Arabick for me by the hour."

When Ibrahima was seventeen, he left Timbuktu and returned to Futa to enter the army. His father had made history in his absence. After years of being the fly before the pagan sledge hammer, Sori gained an even hand with the invaders. He regrouped the army and won the allegiance of the bandit chiefs of the west, whose occupation until that time had been attacking caravans to the coast. Small successes followed, and new recruits came forward. Sori turned then against the Solima, as they were less formidable than Konde Birama, pushing them southward and capturing their frontier posts year after year. "At length," wrote Major Gordon Laing, who visited the Solima fifty years after these events and talked with their historians, "the Soolimas, tired of a mode of warfare which yielded no profit, made an arrangement with Konta Brimah to bring a grand armament against the Foulahs, and, if possible, to annihilate them at one blow."

"God has punished Futa," Sori told his sons upon hearing their plans, "and he asks now for an expiation. An angel has informed me that, in exchange for such a sacrifice, God will give us a victory." That sacrifice had to come from Sori's own family. The tradition that reports Sori's remarks also says that each of the thirty-three sons present, even one sick with leprosy, wanted to be that offering. Finally, Mamadu, the eldest son, who had arrived late for the meeting, presented himself. Sori greeted him, the historian Paul Guébhard wrote, as the one "who had come to deliver the country by sacrificing his life, for he alone had the courage of one hundred men."

Mamadu embraced this certain call to death as a duty and rode out with the army to the place where the enemy coalition would approach. Sori had collected all the Fulbe and their allies for this last, great struggle. An appeal to other countries brought in Muslims from distant lands and may even have caused Ibrahima's return from the Niger at this time. At any rate, Sori gathered an army said to number forty thousand (twice the size George Washington was managing in the same year, 1778), and he awaited the coalition on a large plain near a river east of Timbo.

"To you alone comes the honor of this," he told Mamadu when the enemy approached. "Dream of your name living in the memory of all true Foulahs."

Blessed by Sori, Mamadu mounted a horse saddled for him by his brothers and flew into the enemy lines. Tradition says that Konde Birama was killed by him. In the confusion that followed, Sori threw his armies forward. "A most sanguinary battle was the consequence," wrote Major Laing, "long and gallantly contended on both sides." As the fighting became intense, Sori noticed that his troops, attacking from all sides, were actually firing upon each other by mistake. Rising on his horse and holding his arms and face skyward, he pleaded, "God! Help us!" This chilling act inspired those near him to fight madly, and a terrible slaughter ensued. At last the coalition faltered and fell back toward the river, where many drowned. Those who escaped rushed away so fleetly that the Fulbe who followed them lost their trails completely. Mamadu and many others died, but the day had given the Fulbe a second chance.

They would not need a third.

Sori was at the pinnacle of his power. At an extraordinary session of the elders, he was proclaimed *almaami* again and invested with the white turban of office. He was also voted *mawdo,* "the great." Secure in the public regard, he moved the capital from Fugumba to Timbo, followed there by the principal families. When some of the elders subsequently accused him of eating impure meat, a violation of Islamic law for which he could be removed from office, Sori marched to Fugumba, seized his opponents, and executed them. He did not intend to be deposed twice in one lifetime by jealous preachers. With this ruthless step, the *almaami* demonstrated that the fire of 1763 had destroyed not only the text of the constitution but some of its liberties as well. No doubt burdened by his murder of fellow Muslims, Sori sought absolution in building mosques and patronizing *marabouts* with finely flowered robes. But the return of independence had brought honor to him, and that was penitence enough, it appears, to most of his countrymen.

After clearing the remainder of Konde Birama's army away, Sori resumed those wars for the expansion of the faith and the purse which characterized the state. These remarkable campaigns often reached hundreds of miles from Timbo, and it was in these wars that the young Ibrahima first distinguished himself. Sori had assigned him to the cavalry. "Until I was twenty-one," Ibrahima wrote of this, "[I] followed the horsemen." The apprenticeship led at nineteen to an adventure that illuminates the young prince well.

The year was 1781. Ibrahima, under the command of his uncle Sulimina, set out against a Bambara army of five or six thousand. But Sulimina was killed in the first fighting and the inexperienced Ibrahima found himself in charge. Naturally, the army doubted he could lead it into anything happy and prepared to return home with or without him, an inauspicious first command for a son of the *almaami*. Ibrahima persuaded the soldiers at last to remain three days and put him to a test. The Bambara war leader agreed to an armistice of equal length, Ibrahima having convinced him that he wanted to send to his father for the terms on which he might surrender. Ibrahima took the time to move his army back and open a path into a great cane thicket. The road was about one third of a mile long. In the middle of the cane he had a field cleared large enough to contain the Bambara army. The trap was set in seventy-two hours.

To the surprise of the Bambara, the morning of the fourth day found Ibrahima demanding they make an appearance and fight. Angered by his duplicity, they attacked. Ibrahima withdrew by design, reaching the cane and retreating with his men along the narrow road they had cut. The Bambara followed, anticipating an easy victory, but Ibrahima, reaching the center field, led his men onto a second exit that had been built. When the Bambara reached the middle of the thicket, they found Ibrahima blocking one road out and his cavalry following their heels up the other. The cane was so thick it offered no other exits. "Then commenced a terrible destruction," wrote a friend to whom Ibrahima gave this story. "The cane was set on fire. Those who attempted to escape were put to the sword; those who remained were destroyed by the flames. Nearly the entire army was exterminated."

Among the survivors was the dazed Bambara war leader. He was found sitting on the ground, surrounded by a few of his followers. Ibrahima, berating him for attacking the Fulbe frontier, asked what punishment he deserved.

"I must die," said the old warrior, who, looking up and seeing how young Ibrahima was, added, "and I rejoice! I have been defeated by a boy!"

His wish was granted. A broadsword took off his head.

The year of 1781 came to a portentous close. A one-eyed Irishman named John Coates Cox, surgeon of a ship on the coast, went ashore to hunt and became separated from his companions. When he could not be found, they sailed without him. Learning this, Dr. Cox began to wander inland. "Our people saw him," Ibrahima wrote, "and ran and told my father that they saw a white man." Since no such creature had been known before in Futa, Sori ordered him brought to Timbo. Dr. Cox arrived ill and exhausted, one account stating he had been found lying face down on the ground, horribly bitten by insects. One leg was nearly lame from the bite of a poisonous worm.

Future travelers would tell of the intense interest the Fulbe took in them. Brian O'Beirne wrote that they almost got their eyelashes tangled with his in their efforts to examine him. Theodore Canot reported that the press of spectators day and night became a kind of hell. He needed guards just to take a walk. Mungo Park was assured he had been dipped in milk when born, while Fulbe rubbed their eyes in disbelief at Gaspard Mollien and asked if he had a mother at all, speculating he had come from the bottom of the sea. "Being the first white man who had ever been there," Gallaudet wrote, Dr. Cox was "a great curiosity."

"They brought Dr. Cox," Ibrahima continued, "and my father asked him whither he was going. He said he knew not where to go, that the ship had left and that he had a bad sore leg. My father told him he had better go no farther, but stay with him and he would get a woman to cure the leg. My father told him to stay as long as he chose."

Sori proved as kind as his words. He gave the doctor a house and a nurse, and Dr. Cox recovered enough in a few months to go horseback riding. Ibrahima became an intimate, passing time with him and learning a bit of English. Dr. Cox is probably the person whom the traveler Mollien, writing in 1820, mentions as taking a wife and fathering a son at Timbo. According to the historian André Arcin, whose *Histoire de la Guinée Française* (1911) is still a landmark work on Futa in many respects, that wife would have been Ibrahima's sister. The story is credible. Easygoing by nature, Dr. Cox was a warm and impulsive man. A rationalist on religion, he would have thought Islam no worse than Christianity, and in his position as unpaying guest he had considerable incentive to be agreeable. As for the Fulbe, this was the beginning of a long friendship with whites. No traveler was ever to be killed in these plateaus, and, indeed, when another visitor fell sick there fifty years later, one of Ibrahima's brothers was greatly upset, "for, if any accident happened, the character of Timbo might be ruined, and he should never again, he feared, see another white stranger."

Ibrahima recalled that at the end of six months, probably the conclusion of the rains, the doctor had a conversation with his father in which the Irishman expressed a wish to return to his own country.

"What makes you desire to go back?" the *almaami* asked. "You are treated well here."

Dr. Cox replied that he feared his parents would think him dead when his ship returned without him.

"Whenever you wish to go," Sori said, "I will send a guard to accompany you."

Outfitted with clothes and furnished with gold to pay for any passage he might find on the coast, Dr. Cox bid farewell to Sori and Ibrahima (and to his pregnant wife, if one supposes correctly) and quit Futa in company with fifteen warriors sent along for his protection. These men were under orders to leave the doctor if he found a ship, but to bring him back if none was discovered. Sori warned them "not to go on board the ship" themselves, fearing a slaver might take them away. After some waiting, Dr. Cox was so fortunate as to find the same vessel from which he had become separated. Soon he had set sail.

In the years that followed the doctor's departure, Ibrahima married and, in 1786, had a son named al-Husayn. This child, unlike his father, was born in a country at peace. Laws were respected once more, trade was flourishing, herds were thriving. Futa was secure and no longer threatened by its neighbors. Generations would come and go before it knew another invasion of consequence. Sori took pride in the restitution of order, and so it seemed appropriate, at least to him, to build for himself and his family ten fine houses on the summit of the great fortification he had had erected at Timbo after the fire of 1763.

In one of the houses near him lived the favored son, Ibrahima.

2. Across the Broad Casamance

John Ormond of Pisa and of Liverpool came to Africa about 1759 as a cabin boy aboard a slave ship. He liked the lucrative and violent life of the coast, and he stayed, first as an assistant in a slave factory on the Sierra Leone River and later as an independent trader to the north on the Rio Pongas. Trading shrewdly in human cargoes, Ormond built himself a little empire of wives, land, and slaves. He was illiterate, superstitious, and afraid of curses, but he knew his business and became so expert at it that the value of his principal establishment grew to thirty thousand pounds. He was exceptionally notorious for his cruelty, and he thought little of taking human life. A Scottish minister who stopped at his factory several years after his death wrote, "I felt an involuntary horror at landing at a place which had witnessed such cruelties as Ormond was in almost the daily practice of perpetrating." The trader was what the age termed "a gentleman of the coast," with credit in Europe, a child in an English school, and a good reputation among ship captains from the Senegal down to Cape Palmas.

He was well known in Futa, too, for the principal branch of the Rio Pongas rose in the western part of the plateau, and nature and convenience had conspired to make it a highway to the coast. "Riopongas . . . is one of the principal rivers for trade in this part of Africa," wrote Lieutenant John Matthews in 1788, "and has many large, extensive branches, where European and native traders are settled." The Susu near the mouth of the river had given Portuguese traders the right to settle many years back.

20

The Fulbe sent their caravans down from the mountains accordingly and dealt with the *Portoobe* at the marshy end of the river. Ormond had followed the Portuguese, attracted by an estuary that permitted slave ships with drafts of up to sixteen feet. He used the river route to supply the Fulbe with guns, manufactured goods, and even a red silk flag. He took hides, ivory, gold, and slaves in exchange. One imagines the Muslims felt a private contempt for such a drinker, illiterate, and believer in witchcraft. But the Fulbe dealt with Ormond and his kind, or they did not get European goods.

It was disturbing news, then, when several ships on the coast were pillaged in 1787. For years Sori had fought the riverine Susu in an effort to secure the route to the sea. The campaigns were costly and inconclusive. More recently, he had tried diplomacy, giving the Susu king at Tia a turban of authority in return for tribute and obeisance. But conditions on the river were exacerbated soon again by a widespread war between the Susu and their neighbors, making the route dangerous for commerce. Sori determined to take retribution. A raiding party prepared to depart for the coast as soon as the clouds spent their rain for the season.

In 1788, around January, when Fulbe trading parties set out for the Rio Pongas in peaceful times, a Fulbe army of two thousand, including three hundred and fifty horsemen, left the plateaus. Ibrahima was in command. "I was made captain when I was twenty-one," he wrote later. "After they put me to that and found I had a very good head, at twenty-four they made me a colonel. At the age of twenty-six, they sent me to fight the Hebohs because they destroyed the vessels that came to the coast and prevented our trade." The "Hebohs" have not been identified, but they were a non-Muslim people evidently hostile to the Fulbe.* Enough refugees from Futa lived in the basin of the Rio Pongas for one to wonder if Heboh is simply a corrupted form of the Pular word *habe,* by which the Fulbe designated strangers, slaves, or pagans in general.

Advancing into their country, Ibrahima attacked and burned several towns. It was a surprisingly easy campaign, for the Hebohs refused to challenge him and scattered before his num-

* They should not be confused with the Ibo of Nigeria, who lived more than one thousand miles to the east.

bers. His father avenged, Ibrahima withdrew, sending the infantry home and bringing up the rear himself with three hundred horse soldiers. But Ibrahima had underestimated his adversaries. They had fled to fight in a spot more to their liking. By moving rapidly along back trails, they managed to find hiding places in a narrow pass through which he would have to go.

"We could not see them," Ibrahima wrote, "and did not expect there was any enemy." The cavalry arrived at the pass, dismounted, and led their horses up the mountainside. Halfway to the top a devastating fire opened up on the horsemen. "We saw the smoke, we heard the guns, we saw the people drop down," he wrote. A withering blast of bullets ran up and down the slope. "Men dropping like rain" was the image that the scene brought to his mind. The air was filled with the shrieks of the wounded and the panic of the horses on the path. It was chaos.

Ibrahima would never forget these minutes. "I told everyone to run until we reached the top of the hill, then to wait for each other until all came there, and we would fight them." Remounting, Ibrahima bolted to the summit, where he saw how bad the situation had become. Only he and his guard had reached the spot, and the Hebohs pursued, firing at them. "They followed us and we ran and fought. I saw this would not do. I told everyone to run who wished to do so." Some fled, while others clustered around Ibrahima for a last resistance. The Hebohs quickly surrounded them.

"I will not run from a [Heboh]," Ibrahima said. He jumped off his horse and sat down on the ground, holding his charger's bridle in one hand and a sword concealed beneath him in the other. An arrow hit him in the back, but it glanced away, wounding him only slightly. A Heboh soldier appeared before him, leveling a musket at him at point-blank range. Seeing Ibrahima's clothes and ornaments, however, and realizing his rank, the man reversed his weapon and others did likewise, a signal to each other, and perhaps to Ibrahima, too, that his life would be spared.

"I had a sword, but they did not see it. The first one that came, I sprang forward and killed." It was the last act of his life as a warrior. A gun barrel cracked against the back of his head, the world spun, and Ibrahima fell unconscious in the dirt.

The next thing he remembered was his being dragged from a

pond. The Hebohs had thrown him in to revive him. When he recovered enough to look around, he saw that almost his entire army had fallen prisoner. His clothes were stripped, his sandals taken, and his hands tied, probably with the stout ropes and bamboo hoops of the country. Then he returned to the embrace of a country he had just desolated. "They made me go barefoot one hundred miles," Ibrahima wrote, "and led my horse before me."

Sori's reaction was swift. The old war horse, feeling the effects of age, had led no campaigns personally since 1784, but when stragglers from the disaster arrived at Timbo with the news of Ibrahima's defeat, he raised an army and set out immediately. Within a week his pursuit was forcing the Hebohs to move. The presence of Mandinka *slatees* was propitious for them. These black merchants traveled great distances in the interior to buy prisoners of war and other goods to sell to Europeans. They were Muslims generally, people of influence and often of great wealth. These *slatees* from the Gambia River were those who would set in motion the irremediable slide to a distant port, sale to a slaver, shipment beyond the sea, and bondage or worse in a land from which no one returned.

Ibrahima knew it, and he proposed great, then exorbitant ransoms for himself, including—he would later claim—one hundred cattle, as many sheep as a man could drive, and as much gold as a man could carry. But the war had kindled feelings that were not to be quenched so easily. An English slave trader who dealt with these *slatees* wrote on such subjects, "If they are captured that have been particularly active in wars—a King, Prince, or their sons—no price can purchase them." It was also true that the Hebohs "refused to exchange him [because they] feared his vengeance." At length he was sold to the *slatees,* along with most of his army. By his own account, Ibrahima was exchanged for two flasks of powder, a few trade muskets, eight hands of tobacco, and two bottles of rum.

"My father came and burnt the country," Ibrahima wrote, but the *slatees* had already begun moving their new property north. They crossed the rolling coastal hills and went down into N'Gaaba, "the land of the hippopotamus," where pagan Mandinka lived in the area the Fulbe termed the *daarul-harb,* the land of war, of those who refuse the faith. Ibrahima called it "the wilderness." The sluggish, marsh-lined Casamance lay to the north. In one generation N'Gaaba would ring like a belfry under the blows of the *almaami* of Timbo, while near the Casamance a Fulbe state would be erected with the help of Ibrahima's nephews and cousins. But in 1788 it was world's end. And Ibrahima was going across it.

The Gambia has its source in Futa, running north, then west in its seven-hundred-mile trip to the Atlantic. The most navigable waterway in West Africa, it had been a highway for slave ships since long before Shakespeare's time. Even at low tide there were always twenty-five feet of water on its bar; once past that, seagoing vessels could travel easily 150 miles upstream. The river was close to Europe, and the voyage from it to the West Indies was a comparatively short one. Although the commerce in slaves had been greatly reduced during the wars of the American Revolution, by the late 1780s the volume of trade was increasing. About twelve hundred Africans left the Gambia factories in an average year, compared to ten thousand from the Gold Coast and twice that number from the Calabars and the Cameroons. Only eight to ten ships a year might be seen. Still, the English conserved the Gambian trade for themselves as much as possible. Their tenacity was rewarded in 1783 when the Gambia was consigned to them by the Peace of Versailles. A mud-walled barrack near the river's mouth was the only French presence of consequence on the Gambia, and it was watched suspiciously, for the French indulged in the habit of paying higher prices for slaves than did their national rivals. On the north and south banks near it, and much farther upstream in the Mandinka kingdoms, English traders lived.

Robert Heatley was a coaster equally at home in London and at Niani-Maru in the Mandinka kingdom of Lower Niani. Fluent in Mandinka, Heatley had been in the Gambia trade for twenty-five years by 1788, and had lived on the river seven. He was intimate enough with the Mandinka to have witnessed their trials by ordeal of fire and water for witchcraft, a claim few Europeans could make. Long-settled in the trade, Heatley made seven or eight voyages with Africans from the Gambia to the West Indies and to South Carolina. "I have seen people on the river who had complexions much lighter than the natives and who had the features of Europeans and long hair," he wrote of the Fulbe. "I can't tell whence they came."

Heatley had sailed ships ranging in burden from ninety to 250 tons, but he wished to own the perfect Gambia runner, one he would form, rig, and sail himself. When peace was proclaimed between Great Britain and the United States, he went to London and had a craft built at the Shoreham shipyards in 1784. He christened it the *Africa,* a 110-ton, two-masted brig fitted for a crew of fifteen. It was a clinker-built vessel, whose hull planking overlapped in a lapstreak manner. Sheathed with copper, the *Africa* drew only eleven feet of water fully loaded, and when the wind beat into the leech of its square sails, it ran at a good speed for a brig. "Well-constructed," the slaver termed it.

But Heatley was under the lee of disappointment. He found few Africans to purchase in 1785 when he returned to Niani-Maru, and his trip to Dominica to sell what he could find was profitless. In 1786 he returned to Dominica with twice the number of the year before, only to learn that three giant slave ships from Liverpool had put eleven hundred Africans ashore in the previous week, ruining the market. He island-hopped to unload his cargo for whatever he could and returned to London with more pence than pounds in his pockets.

Under these circumstances the *Africa* passed to Barnes & Company, 23 St. Mary Axe, London. John Barnes was an educated Englishman with a genius for accounts who had spent thirteen years at posts and factories from the Senegal to the Windward Coast. In 1763, when Ibrahima was one year old and the Wasulunke and their allies were destroying Timbo, Barnes had been appointed governor of Senegal for the Company of Merchants trading to Africa. The formal duties of this office were to give order and assure free trade in slaves and goods in the region. In effect they amounted to commanding "a set of the most mutinous, drunken, abandoned fellows I ever met with," Barnes wrote the company in 1764. He was so disgusted with the avarice of the traders and the recriminations they joined together to heap upon him that he wrote London, "Every trader should bring out his own Governor." Begging a passage home, Barnes left Africa in 1766, never to return. He settled as a wine merchant in London, selling firearms and liquor to the company's forts and representing on the company's governing committee the great Liverpool traders who did more business in slaves than did traders from all the other English ports combined. His experience made him one of Whitehall's authorities on Africa. He was at the arm of Lord Sydney and had the ear of the Council of Trade. If Heatley was a cut above Ormond, Barnes lay higher still, near the top of the trading hierarchy.

Barnes had visited Niani-Maru in 1753 and felt the natives of the region were "the best-disposed people in the world; strict and fair in their dealings." Upon his return to England he had imported twelve tons of ebony from the Gambia, but he found the quality poor and sold it at a considerable loss. He had tried mahogany, but it was coarse and cost more to bring to London than mahogany from elsewhere. Barnes had no hope of importing rice or cotton from the river because he did not think the Africans could be induced to grow either in quantity. In fact, Barnes was of the opinion that Africans were too indolent, their governments too loose and imperfect for them to cultivate for export anything other than their own sons and daughters. Most of those sold, he felt, were criminals, condemned in fair trials, and the remainder were prisoners of war. Although he had never purchased a slave personally, he had no qualms about the humanity of the business at all.

Or about its profitability. Captain Heatley, recruited for a voyage in 1787, did for Barnes what he had been unable to do for himself. Sailing the *Africa* to the Gambia, he found slaves abundant and cheap, as a war on the Senegal had diverted numerous *slatees* south. He slipped his cargo past the posts on the lower river, where a dispute had led to the seizure of three English vessels, and arrived in Dominica with 165 Africans well ahead of the Liverpool traders. He returned to London on August 7, 1787, in ballast and success.

By January, 1788, the *Africa* was ready for a fourth voyage around the great triangle. The rains had stopped over the coast, a crew of sixteen had been drawn together, the ship provisioned and insured by Lloyd's of London. Heatley gave way to John Nevin, a competent sailor and a friend of Barnes's. Thomas Clarkson, the antislavery crusader, was told once by a veteran seaman that "he knew but one captain in the trade who did not deserve long ago to be hanged." Nevin was not that captain, but neither was Nevin the dregs of the trade. He was a rough man who, when interviewing Africans, brimmed with pistols. "I have never ventured a boat upriver without its being well armed," he once said, "for the crew would be murdered." Captain Nevin knew the Gambia well—he had almost been buried there. When he spent half a year at Niani-Maru waiting to buy slaves in 1784, one third of his crew died. "I was ill myself," Nevin stated, "and think my life was preserved by Bitters and Bark." The captain felt himself respectable, little fouled by his line of business, and his appearance before a Parliamentary committee in these years inclines one to think many others felt the same way.

On January 30, 1788, Captain Nevin set sail on the *Africa* for the Gambia. The mouth of the river was usually reached in less than thirty days. After paying a customary toll at Juffure, it took another week to ride the tides upriver to Niani-Maru. The *Africa* reached this place about the first week in March.

Niani-Maru was a Mandinka village of several hundred houses on the Gambia's north bank. A map of the period contains this inscription from Harry Gandy of Bristol: "Yanimaroo is a delightful country abounding with provisions . . . [and] inhabited with honest, hospitable people; their houses are provided with various kinds of household furniture, etc." This place had become wealthy through the taxing of caravans and the slave trading that had thrived since the 1600s. Mandinka cultivators and traders had resided here for centuries. They were a tall and slender people, black, active, and warlike. The *mansa,* or king, of Lower Niani, of which Niani-Maru was the chief town, lived in a nearby town. With his permission Heatley and two other Europeans maintained establishments dealing in slaves, ivory, wax, and a little gold.

To Heatley's eyes, Ibrahima and the remnants of his war party, appearing from the hot lowlands south of Niani-Maru, would have looked similar to groups he had seen many times before. "They come down in large bodies, tied together by the neck," he wrote, "perhaps loaded and whipped along the same as a horse." With fifty of his command Ibrahima was soon purchased by Captain Nevin. "The nature of the slave service in the West Indies, being chiefly field labor," Barnes wrote at this time, "requires for the immediate interest of the planter a greater number of males." Nevin shopped accordingly. Ibrahima could see that for every four men brought on the *Africa,* there were only two women and one child. The men were clamped in irons immediately ("We should think it very dangerous otherwise," Heatley noted) and taken below. Bulkheads separated them from the boys abast the mainmast and pumps. Several dozen women were put aftward between the boys and the ship's square stern. In the bow to Ibrahima's front was the "hospital," an isolation room for anyone developing fever. Precise figures are lacking, but it appears about 165 or 170 Africans were crowded below deck. Captain Nevin also stowed in 456 pounds of beeswax and twenty-three ivory tusks.

Heatley said it was quite common for incoming captives not to understand each other and not to know the full extent of what was taking place. Ibrahima, who was fluent in Mandinka, knew precisely what was going on. While it did not lessen his alarm at his fate, it meant he knew what the fate was. The time passed with Dr. Cox had made him familiar with whites, and he was no doubt less afraid of them than were many other people in the interior. But of help, there was none. Although there were Muslims in Lower Niani who might have been expected to save Ibrahima, political and cultural considerations bade otherwise. And the Fulbe here, divided by dialect, caste, and religion, showed little intergroup feeling as well. Reserve—even hostility—between them was common. There was nothing at Niani-Maru for Ibrahima but the tow that pulled him on.

After a rapid loading, the *Africa* began downstream in mid-March. The bamboo and swamps of Niani were soon succeeded by mangrove thickets so inpenetrable that the banks were hidden from view. Salt water was encountered a hundred miles up the river at Elephant Island, and the country became flatter and more monotonous each mile. Villages of cane huts alone appeared. At last, the ship came to the level lower river, where all the winding was rewarded. The *Africa* slipped past Barra Point and spread its sails to the northeast trade winds. Its prow pointed for the Windward Islands, more than three thousand miles to the west.

Ibrahima was sixty-six when he told Gallaudet about the voyage. For two reasons it seemed best at that time to suppress an account of it. Slave ships were so familiar to people in 1828 that the biographer could say of Ibrahima's trip, "It would be useless to describe its horrors," and everyone would know what he meant. In this way it was asserted that Ibrahima underwent a passage as ordinary and as abominable as had 75,000 other Africans in 1788. Also, his biographer did not wish to arouse ill will toward slaveholders, and this was another reason to let the matter pass. And so no full account of these weeks was ever published. What is left, rather disconcertingly, is a few facts, a few hints, and a tradition. They are not what one wants, but they do give an idea of the passage.

For one thing the *Africa* was very crowded. One hundred and seventy people aboard a 110-ton brig meant there was less than a one-ton burden for each slave. Two tons were considered minimal by English reformers. If the average height of five feet in the tweendecks applied, no one could stand up in the men's quarter, and those on the side platforms could not sit up from where they lay. One can imagine what this meant for the Fulbe, who were tall people. Ibrahima, himself six feet tall, was chained by the ankle to another passenger. His confinement was broken only for meals, and those were customarily served twice a day. It was also customary for the slaves to sing their country songs and dance about for exercise, males on the main deck and females up on the quarter-deck with the captain. As the Fulbe, who were Muslims, did not dance, perhaps Nevin's quirt was employed to get them moving. At any rate, Ibrahima was more impressed with Nevin's habit of having tea served at a table in the late afternoon. He could not have seen this unless he was situated near a grated hatch, which tells something important about the voyage. There was no first class in the tweendecks, just levels of hell such as Dante provides, but if Ibrahima was at a hatch, he had a good position for fresh air and sea breezes and a better chance of surviving. It meant being the first out and the last in during musters.

But the hours below are the measure of the voyage. Despite the ports and gratings that Heatley had given the *Africa,* ventilation was poor, with partitions shutting the hold into breathless compartments that were hot during the day, cold at night. Human excrement raised a stench that was fetid and noxious and killed appetites more effectively than seasickness. Nausea, weakness, and debility followed. From dysentery and guinea worms, a mortality of at least five per cent was expected. Ibrahima's impression of the trip was that it seemed to go on and on and on. "Tedious" was the adjective Gallaudet used, tedious in the nineteenth-century sense of "overlong" and "wearisome." Inevitable physical and mental deterioration resulted. "The horrors he felt so deeply" was the expression used to characterize the trip many years later. "[The] Prince's sufferings were very great."

Captain Nevin thought the trip went well. Behind him on the Gambia the *L'Aimable Louise*'s cargo had revolted and taken over the ship. Barnes would receive no letter to that effect, nor would he read in the newspapers that the *Africa* had floundered like the *Minerva* or exploded like the *Tartar.* However protracted the voyage seemed to Ibrahima, the *Africa* had really been scudding the swells as if it were being chased. A quick passage was made. When the Windwards buoyed near, there appear to have been no deaths in the crew, and, miraculously, just a handful in the hold. Of the 164 Africans alive when port would be reached, all but seven would be judged "prime Negroes" in adequate health for sale.

Dominica is the tallest, most northerly island in the Windward chain. It was the landing place of Columbus on his second voyage. He described it by crumbling a sheet of paper in his hands to give a notion of its jagged, compressed appearance from the sea. Behind a rocky and forbidding coastline lay its heavily wooded shoulders "of mists and torrents and rainbows." Three hundred inches of rain might fall in one year, moisture that gave Dominica a green luxury that seemed otherworldly to anyone quitting a black and scurvy-ridden tweendeck. The cinnamon-colored Carib Indians, native to the island, had been pushed to the interior in the centuries after Columbus to make room for French and English planters who cultivated sugar, coffee, and cotton. Lately the island had been a haven for Loyalist fugitives from the American

Revolution. Twelve hundred whites and fifteen thousand blacks lived in this frontier colony, one of Britain's least populated West Indian possessions. In a generation it had shown little advance and looked as unsettled in 1788 as it had thirty years before.

Though Dominica was French in culture, Britain had gained it in the same agreement at Versailles in which the Gambia was acquired. The island was valued as a *point d'appui* should war with France occur. Consequently, it had been well fortified and the captain of a man-of-war, John Orde, was made its governor. The island endured Orde with a surliness appropriate to civilians, but had been thankful he was on hand six months before the *Africa's* arrival, when an invasion by the French appeared imminent. "We are all here in the utmost consternation by orders which [the governor] has received to prepare and defend against immediate attack," the merchant Christopher Robert had written to a relative in New York. Orde rolled out his twenty-four-pounders, ready for the worst, but most English residents were less determined. With the French island of Martinique so close to the south that it could be seen across the straits, and Gaudaloupe not much farther to the north, Robert and his peers were secretly resigned to learning French. The island was reprieved, however, for the alarm proved baseless.

Dominca was, in any case, in a better position to trade than to fight. In the preceding September it had become one of four English islands enjoying a coveted "free-port" designation. The free-port act was designed to further exports of British manufactured goods to foreign islands, but the sale of Africans was a mainspring in the machine. Dominica had the privilege of exporting slaves landed at Roseau without paying a custom on them. "Do not give your assent to any act imposing duties on Negroes imported into Dominica," Governor Orde had been instructed in his commission from King George III. "Acts passed in some of our plantations lay duties on the importation and exportation of Negroes to the great discouragement of merchants trading thither from the coast of Africa." This policy, and the British dominance of the slave trade, had turned Dominica into a great debouche of Africa in America, an anchorage where traders of every blood gathered to see what the Captain Heatleys of the world had found. In 1785, 6,254 Africans arrived here aboard twenty-five ships, 8,407 came aboard twenty-nine ships in 1786, and 5,709 aboard twenty-five ships in 1787. Two thirds had left the island within a month. Most were purchased by planters or merchants from the nearby French sugar islands, but Spanish ships and even Dutch and Danish vessels called for "guiney-birds," too. The Spanish had a reputation for paying large sums to secure the prime males from incoming cargoes.

Not surprisingly, the Spanish seized the opportunity of legal trade with the island. In January the schooner *Governor Miró,* captained by Daniel Clark of New Orleans, sailed into port. It was the first vessel from the Spanish Province of Louisiana to be seen at Dominica in a long time. Merchant, slave factor, and landowner on the Mississippi River, Clark was perhaps accompanied on the trip by Jupiter Dawda, the Hausa slave who served him. Clark purchased 121 Africans from the cargo of the *Madam Pokata* of Liverpool and returned with them to New Orleans. It might be expected the merchant would have gone to Jamaica, which was much closer to New Orleans, or to New Providence in the Bahamas, which had been opened specifically to lure the Mississippi River trade. But the selection of slaves was best at Roseau, there were fewer local buyers to compete with, and the list of goods besides slaves that could be traded was longer than elsewhere. News of Clark's coup soon rang in New Orleans's trading community.

On Monday, April 21, 1788, the *Africa* entered the azure blue road of Roseau, on the leeward side of the island. Ibrahima and his companions were the first arrivals from Africa in three weeks; anchored six hundred feet from the beach, the Africans shared the harbor only with schooners trading in French molasses and cocoa. The number of African vessels was down somewhat due to war scare and hurricane damage. Captain Nevin reported his cargo at the customhouse, contacted his agent, Samuel Chollet and Company, and made certain that announcements of his arrival were sent to Martinique and Guadaloupe. Meanwhile, Ibrahima and the rest of the hold were mustered up into the sunshine of a brilliant Dominican spring. The weather was delightful that year, the island's sugar and cotton crops thriving. Cool and green, the island provided a contrast with the previous weeks that must have been startling to Ibrahima. It was customary at this time in their passage to "refresh" slaves with provisions from shore. Before they were shown to prospective buyers, it would be necessary to close their wounds with mercurical ointments, wash them, and rub their skins with oil to give them healthy appearances.

Notice of the *Africa*'s arrival sent to the French islands paid an immediate dividend. Within twenty-four hours a sail of Spanish flag was seen hieing in from the south. It was the schooner *Navarro* of New Orleans from Martinique, at the helm the Irish-born Thomas Irwin, a dealer in slaves and West Indian produce. Irwin knew these waters well, having traded in the Windwards often. This time he had come to the West Indies to collect a note due him in Cuba. Little did he expect, when he left Philadelphia, "the unforeseen disappointments and misfortunes" that awaited him, as he wrote a friend, "the greatest of which was a man breaking in my debt at Havana to the amount of 9,000 dollars, which has disturbed me very much." To recoup Irwin had leased the *Navarro* from a New Orleans businessman, and, accompanied by a crew of nine, voyaged to the Windwards in a trip that probably took as long as had that of the *Africa*.

Irwin was a middle-aged man, well connected in Philadelphia, where the extensive loans he had made to revolutionary agents had helped finance the War for Independence. During that struggle he owned all or part of two dozen well-equipped privateers whose ravages had built him a quick fortune. "No person's vessels delivered more English prisoners to the American commissary," he boasted once in a letter to George Washington, "either in the American or the French ports than mine did." Toward the end of the war, however, fortune proved unkind. Irwin had more than a dozen of his ships captured by the British. Even the Moroccans got into the act, plucking one of his brigs, crew and all, from the Mediterranean. Formerly wealthy, he was much reduced by 1788. A Pennsylvania friend termed his state "rather unfortunate." As a consequence, Irwin, who had traded to New Orleans since at least 1782, had immigrated there to take advantage of the generous Spanish land-grant policy and to profit by the growing trade between that city and Philadelphia.

Governor William Patterson of New Jersey, who knew him well, thought him "honest, industrious, attentive to business and well-versed in accounts." The extant business records that bear his name are not so flattering. They show he was an aggressive and venal merchant. On one occasion he attempted to sell a sick slave, on another to negotiate a bond without being particular as to its terms. Even his presence at Roseau was against Spanish law. New Orleans merchants had been free to import slaves from the French islands for twelve years, and a *cédula* of 1782 from King Charles III had liberalized their trading privileges further. But the English islands were off limits. Consequently, Irwin would get a permit for Martinique, set sail, and if he happened to find himself in Nassau harbor or Montego Bay, who was to say it was not God's will? The demand for labor was so great that Spanish officials winked at the business.

On May 1, Irwin purchased Ibrahima and fifty-six others, about one third of the *Africa*'s cargo. He gave Chollet and Company his note for $4,090 "in hard Mexican-minted dollars" for the amount. Records indicating the sex of those purchased show three fourths of them were men. A good number of the Fulbe soldiers were among them, as well as some of the women and children added at Niani-Maru. It is not clear if the Africans ever set foot on the island itself. Although it is probable they did, their transfer could have taken place in the road. Others from Ibrahima's army were bought by Jerome Fuiget, captain of the brig *Catalán* of New Orleans, which arrived later in the month. Fuiget took one hundred on board. As the Africans changed ships, Nevin filled their places in the tweendecks with casks of indigo and barrels of sugar for the London market.

After two weeks at Roseau, Ibrahima left for New Orleans on May 2 on the sixty-five-ton *Navarro*. His route was west sixteen hundred miles across the Caribbean Sea to the Yucatán Channel, then northwest seven hundred miles more to the Mississippi River. This voyage and others like it rivaled the Atlantic crossing in horror, yet many historians have failed to mention them. The schooners, sloops, and one-deck vessels of the intercolonial slave trade were not adapted to carry people, as Sir William Young would point out in his *West-India Common-Place Book* (1807). They could never stow goods, or people, equal to their measurements, not even in the limited, brutal manner of ships like the *Africa*. "Foreigners only purchase the healthy and merchantable Negroes," wrote John Robinson, Dominica's Collector of Customs, in 1788, for "others would not bear the voyage to their settlements." Captains like Irwin hoped to hedge against poor conditions and problems of health by fast sailing, but debilities acquired during the middle passage generally became worse when the slaves were returned to their "apartments," and maladies not previously apparent broke out with virulence. Judicial records at New Orleans tell how red boils and other diseases manifested themselves for the first time on the trip from the islands to the city, causing great numbers of deaths. It appears Ibrahima escaped such a personal disaster, for when he landed his dollar value as a slave was normal. But he was very lucky in that regard. Something terrible happened on the *Navarro,* something no account describes but that a simple statistic brings well to mind. The number of slaves Irwin would land was short of the number he shipped by fourteen human beings.

When Daniel Clark had brought his *Governor Miró* into the river's crescent at New Orleans in March, he must have received an enormous shock. Shortly before his arrival, Don Vincente José Nunez, the military treasurer, had lighted fifty or sixty wax tapers in the private chapel of his home on Chartres Street on Good Friday, March 21. While he was at lunch, the candles set fire to the ceiling of the room. Soon his entire house was ablaze. Fanned by a wind from the south, the fire spread to the nearby cathedral. In an hour it was rushing through the structures of the city as if they were mere kindling. With no fire engines at hand, no buckets, no hooks-and-ladders, every effort to stop it was wasted. It progressed so rapidly that little could be saved. "The whole town was reduced to ashes except about two hundred houses in the outskirts," Clark wrote to a Philadelphian. Eight hundred and fifty-six buildings were destroyed, including all the business houses, the residences of the aristocracy, the church, and the convent of the Capuchins. Residents fled onto open fields nearby to watch the city burn.

"The darkness of the night effaced for a time the picture," Estaban Miró, the provincial governor, reported to his superior, "but with the dawn the scene appeared more horrible and pitiful; seeing so many families who a few hours before enjoyed large fortunes and more than the average comforts of life, spread all over the fields, crying and filled with consternation. Their tears and sobs and the ghastliness of their faces were clear demonstrations of the fatality befallen this city, which, in less than five hours, had been transformed into an arid and horrible desert—a city which was the product of seventy years' labor."

The fire had been the last of a string of hardships equal to any people's spirit. Two hurricanes had hit the Province within a year, and an unusually hard winter succeeded them, killing one quarter of the livestock. The bad weather ruined the indigo crop, which was foreknown to be poor. Epidemic fevers followed the decline of public health after March 21, with almost continual burials by the advent of summer. One hundred and forty million pesos in buildings had been the cost of Don Vincente's experience at home worship. Slave merchants shared in the loss. Alexander Baldwin, who had not paid the crew of his *Felix* since 1786, would find them shoving him through the door of bankruptcy by 1789. Joseph Connand of New Orleans, owner of the *Navarro,* retrenched by preparing to sell the schooner when it returned.

Sailing with the Caribbean trades, the *Navarro* voyaged to the Mississippi in four weeks. The river was easily found, for it spread a three-mile apron of muddy water into the gulf. With spring freshets over, the Mississippi had settled down by the first of June to "a total rising of the river," as a New Orleans priest phrased it. The schooner reached the Balize and made its way up the one hundred miles from the mouth of the river to the city. Its gulfside approach to New Orleans passed marshy flatlands. The cypress swamps and willow thickets found here were so impervious they reminded some travelers of the mangroves' arrogance in West Africa. Only just below the city did homes and farms appear along the banks.

Ibrahima arrived in New Orleans about June 9, 1788. It could not have been an impressive introduction to North America. The population of the city was only 5,300, two thirds the size of Timbo, and there was little of it to see. The fire had spared only the buildings on the riverfront, and the forts, where the scarlet and saffron of Spain floated, at both ends of the city. The *cédula* of 1782, intended to build up the Province's population by the immigration of Africans, among other means, did not require Don Tomás Irwin to pay an import duty on Ibrahima. Officials wanted slaves, not itineraries, and they paid little attention to where the slaves had come from. If the importation of Africans from their native continent were to be left solely in Spanish hands, Intendant Martin Navarro, namesake of Irwin's schooner, had written the preceding December, "this colony, which promises to become one of the most considerable in America, [will] soon . . . be the poorest and most miserable."

Ibrahima spent a month there. Why the stop occurred is speculative. Irwin could have been having difficulty in finding provisions, or doubts about the swollen river. He did take the opportunity to sell seventeen people from the schooner, in a series of sales lasting through June 26. A single sale of thirteen to Juan Dartigaux of Natchitoches more than paid for the entire number purchased at Roseau. While Irwin bargained, the stop gave Ibrahima and the rest of the cargo a chance to recover their health. The prince had been traveling for six consecutive months, continually under constraint, seldom exercised, poorly fed. Since Irwin did not intend to sell him there, a rest probably seemed advisable. Whatever Irwin's reason, Ibrahima no doubt welcomed it, as did Samba, a member of his command who had been with him since their capture. "Sambo," to which this name became corrupted in English, would be offensive to some blacks by the time of the Civil War, connoting a shuffling, obsequious slave. In Pular, the name meant simply "second son," and, ironically enough in view of its American usage, it was the name given in the legends of Futa to any bold and reckless warrior.

In July their travels resumed, the number of captives now reduced to some twenty-five or thirty of the original passengers of the *Africa*. Irwin intended to take them three hundred miles upstream to Natchez. If the *Navarro* had not been needed at New Orleans, it could have been sailed or pulled up the Mississippi. The trip might have taken as long as a voyage from New York to Liverpool and killed a quarter of the slaves by overwork, but seagoing vessels, even brigs, attempted the passage from time to time. Irwin could have settled for a barge with sail and oars. Short passage by such means was fifteen to nineteen days, a long trip twenty-seven. With the delay at New Orleans, Irwin had already lost time to his competitors. When he arrived in Baton Rouge, for example, a group of Africans purchased in Dominica three weeks after the *Navarro* left Roseau had been sold there already. Their nationality is not given in their Spanish bills of sale, but the previous year had seen Chamba, Fulbe, Wolof, and even Bantu offered for sale, as well as mulattoes from New Orleans and American blacks from Kentucky and New York.

The land was flat for most of the 175 miles between Baton Rouge and Natchez, the midsummer river brown and treacherous. An occasional scow of tobacco or a small settlement was the only sign of human life in this immense wilderness which no European called home a century before. Then the countryside began to roll. At last there appeared on one bluff a prominent earth-and-wood fort with a three-mile view of the river. Fort Panmure de Natchez was an old structure, somewhat run down in recent years, with large wooden towers at its corners. The center of Spanish administration for the Natchez District, it served as courtroom, archive, arsenal, and jail. A road ran down into a gorge below it leading to about twenty wooden houses under the bluff. This was Natchez proper, where merchants and tavern owners lived, while planters and slaves, the bulk of the population, lived on creeks inland. Under the eye of guards, boats stopped at the landing to load or unload tobacco and manufactured goods, or for the passengers to show their passports. The commerce was light enough that five boats, arriving one day in 1790, looked like an invasion flotilla. The drummer at the fort beat to arms at the sight of them.

Ibrahima's journey of six thousand miles ended at these muddy, willow-lined banks in the backcountry of Mississippi. He was led from the barge, his long, unkept hair falling in ringlets below his shoulders, his skin copper-colored in the summer's sun. Even at his worst, there was something impressive about him. "The prince," wrote a man who knew him, "is one who, having been once seen, would not be readily forgotten."

His sharpness of expression must have caught the attention of a young white man who had come to the landing. He was a tobacco farmer, a person of simplicity and reserve, tall, dark-haired, serious in aspect. He was twenty-six, the same age as Ibrahima. There was a plainness about him that seemed to say little money, little humor, little style.

For the rest of Ibrahima's life there would scarcely be a day when this man did not loom in his thoughts.

3. "A Common Slave"

When the American Revolution came to the South Carolina backcountry in 1780, times grew so chaotic they seared themselves into the memory of anyone who lived through them. In the Ninety-Sixth District, said to be the home of the earliest Fosters of Natchez, there were a major battle, an occupation, pillaging, and extensive partisan activities. Though the Fosters were revolutionary in sentiment, the upheaval settled their minds on emigration. They departed South Carolina during the closing days of the war and by 1783 were living near Natchez. The family included Mary Foster, a widow in her sixties, and her sons John, James, William, and Thomas. The youngest of the brothers, Thomas was also the most retiring.

The Fosters serve as a typical representative of the many immigrant families who came to the Natchez area at this time. Spain had taken control of the region from Great Britain during the Anglo-Spanish War of 1779–83. The residents, principally of English stock, were alarmed at the change in government, but they had little to fear. The Spanish regime would be popular. Liberal immigration laws, religious toleration, and land grants drew in hundreds of settlers from the United States. Although the site was an isolated one, the population grew enormously.

Like most of these immigrants, the Fosters were yeoman stock. Upon their arrival, they began to develop a 574-acre tract that Mary was warranted by the government, six miles northeast of the fort at Natchez. It is thought the family lived together in an old blockhouse whose thick log walls were chinked with moss and

39

mud. They grew tobacco and tended cattle. Their debts were few, their deals honest, and their reputations good. The simplicity of their affairs is indicated by a family petition to the commandant of the fort in 1784 concerning "a mare and a one-year-old chicken" that had been promised them, but not delivered. Could the defaulting party be forced to furnish the animals? Such concerns explain why *don,* the Spanish title of gentleman, seldom appears before the name of Foster in the records of the time. The family would have to write its name large in other ways.

In 1788 the brothers began buying lands of their own or securing grants near their mother on unclaimed lands of the Crown. In February of that year, James bought a farm of two hundred acres and moved into a tobacco-curing barn atop a burial mound of the long-vanished Natchez Indians. John and William angled for even larger tracts. Thomas alone stayed behind with his mother, though not out of any nostalgia for the blockhouse. He had charge of Mary's farm. By working her crop on shares, he had a place to live, was free of mortgages, and could put his earnings into slaves, anticipating the day when she would sell him the farmstead.

Soon after he had come to Natchez, Thomas and his brothers John and James had married three daughters of Zachariah Smith, a neighboring farmer. Sarah Smith, Thomas's wife, was a woman of rare courage. When she had been living in the East during the Revolution, British troops entered her home and demanded she show them the hiding place of certain valuables. When she refused, she was hung up by the neck. Although choking and almost unconscious, Sarah had no more to say dangling above the floor than she had had standing on it. The soldiers left in disgust. "Grandmother Smith was a woman of very sterling character," a great-grandson would recall, "with much will and a strong personality in every way." Two daughters had followed their marriage, and in the summer of 1788 Sarah was pregnant with a third.

Thomas rejoiced in his rising brood. A believer in the Bible-based integrity of family life, he viewed himself as an Old Testament patriarch. It was a happy outlook to hold, since Sarah, who was pregnant more often than not, seemed certain to give him a progeny of legend. But more children meant more responsibility, a need for more money, more land, more patrimony—in effect, more work. In March, as Ibrahima lay coffled in the *Africa,* the widow received formal title to the land warranted her earlier by the Spanish government. The deed was a compliment to the family's industry, as it would not have been made unless they had improved their holdings substantially. About the same time, the farm was expanded considerably with the purchase of a nearby parcel of 425 acres.

But purchase and grant lands, amounting to one thousand acres, lay in a wilderness of forest and canebrakes. A lifetime of labor would be required to clear fields and roads and put up fences, jobs enough even if one did not have to make a living at the same time. The departure of the older brothers had reduced the farm's labor force considerably. Thomas owned only one male worker, fifteen-year-old Jesse, an American-born black purchased the previous year out of a group of young people brought down from Kentucky.

Word of Thomas Irwin's arrival was timely, then. On about Saturday, August 16, Thomas rode into town with his brother-in-law William Gilbert, a small-time merchant who knew Irwin and had bought Africans before. Thomas was a regular at every sale in Natchez. Prices for manufactured goods were so high in this backwater that he sought out every bargain he could, such as the fine set of crockery he bought for eighteen dollars from the estate of a local tradesman. Here, too, he indulged his limited social life, hearing the news, posting a letter, and ambling over to the quarter-mile horsetrack on the batture. A Spanish officer had written three years earlier that the settlers loved to come to the landing on weekends. Saturday was court day, and "every time that an inhabitant comes to present his complaint, he passes the entire day in the town . . . where it is the custom, particularly of the common people, to deliver themselves up to drink with the greatest excess." Much business was done in Natchez, and boats usually left for New Orleans on that day. The dirt streets thronged with farmers, flatboatmen, visiting Choctaw Indians, and slaves on a pass or on the sly from the country.

The predictable crowd had gathered to see Irwin's cargo. No lot of new Africans had been offered for two months, and with the tobacco harvest near, strong backs were at a premium, despite the heavy African immigration into the District in the last year.

Seeing the "yellow-looking" Fulbe, the knot of farmers was probably pleased that Irwin had not brought them "savage and intractable" Iboes, the least popular Africans at Natchez. They were thought poor workers, inclined to despondency and suicide. While the planters disliked them by name, they made few fine distinctions between Africans based on their ethnic groupings. Most were sorted into great clumps like "Gold Coast" and "Congo." Muslims were termed "Mandingoes," the Fulbe being considered a Mandinka "tribe." They were admired for their intelligence, but believed less capable of sustained labor than "Guiney Negroes" from under the West African bulge.

Thomas Foster joined a group of four men who pressed forward on Ibrahima and the others. These prospective buyers were an inauspicious bunch. One of them, Jeptha Hidgon, could not write his own name. Another, the equally illiterate George McKnight, was a dirt farmer who had never owned a slave before. The third, William Calvit, was an inebriate so penurious and cruel he would not give clothes to his own wife. Calvit's father, Frederick, was also present. All four had received grants of land within the last twelve months and now were in search of labor, although between them they could not put a *réal* into Irwin's pocket. Only Thomas had money with him. The rest were talking, as usual, of two-year notes on their future crops of tobacco. As long as the Spanish government persisted in buying the tobacco harvest, "tobacco-notes" sounded sweet enough to Irwin.

On Monday, August 18, Thomas purchased Ibrahima and Samba in an agreement signed at the fort in the presence of Don Carlos de Grand-Pré, civil and military commandant of the District. The Fulbe, not identified by name, nationality, or even sex, were simply *"dos negros brutos,"* two freshly imported Africans, sold as captives of war subject to service for life. *"Bruto"* customarily meant newly arrived and untrained or uncivilized. The deed of sale, a copy of which was filed at the fort, was standard in form and made no special guarantee of health. Thomas paid $930 for the two. As this was seven per cent below what other pairs from the barge were fetching, their vigor must have seemed diminished. In any case, the farmer was satisfied. He paid Don Tomás $150 in silver, giving his bond for $250 more in January, 1789, and the balance of $530 in January, 1790. Gilbert stood as surety for the debt.

Led along behind Thomas's horse, Ibrahima trudged the ancient Indian road onto a bluff north of Natchez, then turned eastward toward the area called Pine Ridge. The yellow-green hue of ripe tobacco lay on the country. The land was rolling, much cut up by ravines, and the open spaces were filled with the waist-high hogweed of summer. Moss dipped from the limbs and bows of trees "like a Dunker's beard." At last the Foster settlement appeared. There were probably no more than five acres in fence and a few simple buildings, surrounded by piles of brush, stumps, and the muddy sod of newly cleared land. The old blockhouse, if it did date back to the French occupation of the District, as tradition holds, would have been a half century old. It was little more than a "hut," according to one of Thomas's granddaughters. Unclaimed, unsettled lands stretched out from it in trackless distances of forest.

Arriving at Thomas's farm, Ibrahima identified himself and offered his owner a ransom. It is possible his remarks were translated by a Mandinka intermediary, for several lived in Pine Ridge and a teen-age Mandinka boy resided on the neighboring grant. Picture that extraordinary conversation: a scorned Muslim endeavoring to explain to an incredulous and little-schooled farmer about a kingly father whose generosity would pour gold if his son was returned. Thomas could have been no more surprised if Ibrahima had expressed a desire to enter Harvard College and study for the ministry. Had he been the most humane, best-disposed citizen in Natchez, it is problematic what he could have done. Futa appeared on few maps of the period, and references to it were limited to specialized books on travel. There is no reason to think these works were in Thomas's library (if he had a library) or on the best bookshelves in Natchez, even if he had felt an inclination to check the claims of this stern-faced African. As it was, he looked about uninterestedly while the plea went on, a bit apprehensive about the quality of his new hand. Whites were suspicious of pretentions to royal birth. They caused dissension in the quarters and were an annoying source of extra-institutional authority.

Ibrahima's effort was wasted, of course. "His story was not credited," Gallaudet wrote, Thomas paying "no attention to his royal blood." The prince had followed a natural impulse, playing a card that had to be dropped, but it drew attention to him and opened the prospect that he might be ridiculed. The speech gained only a backhanded concession to Ibrahima's identity, though that was an important one. Thomas decided that his slave name should be "Prince." People later thought this "a kind of mock courtesy," but Thomas may not have intended it that way. The self-assured African acted the role to which he had been born, even after the hell of the last eight months. The name struck Thomas as a clever and a fitting thing, and the matter was settled. As for ransom, Ibrahima need worry only about paying off the one that had just been promised to Don Tomás.

With that business closed, Thomas moved to more pressing concerns, such as some homespun trousers and a haircut for Ibrahima. The story of the countryside is that Ibrahima did not understand that his locks would be cut at first, but, when he did, a wild and resolute look swept his face. He "would part with [his tresses] in his own country only with his life," wrote a friend to whom he told the story in later years. As the shears were brought forward, he struggled violently to avoid them. He was knocked down and roped to a tree. Off came the plaits, marks of great beauty in Futa. Though concerned with lice acquired after months in unsanitary confinement, Thomas was no doubt smart enough to know that he could initiate as well as disinfect with this rite, cut off the ornaments of the past and with them a little of the past itself, perhaps. But he never knew how truly devastating his ploy had been. The cutting was more than a humiliation. He had given the son of the *almaami* something very close to the haircut of a Pullo child.

An account of Ibrahima's life states that he was confined for three days following this incident to get himself oriented. Then he was brought out. He was needed to help gather the tobacco, which at last was thick enough and of the proper color. A newly imported African like Ibrahima was seldom given the strong sharp knife with which the ripe plants were cut. Not only was there the possibility that the edge might be put to something other than tobacco, but also even a person cutting on the right object had to cut on it judiciously. An experienced hand always sliced the leaves, while a *negro bruto* followed behind and carried away the harvest on his arms and shoulders.

The prospect of this work, however, was as mortifying to Ibrahima as being scalped. Even as Ibrahima's people had become sedentary, their low opinion of farming had not improved. The pastoral Fulbe were, according to a twentieth-century authority, "full of horror and disdain at manual labor" and considered agriculture "contemptible." James Watt, who was to spend some time with Ibrahima's brother six years hence, wrote, moreover, that the Fulbe aristocracy "seldom, if ever, put their hand to work of any kind." The labor Thomas expected him to do had always been performed by the Jalunke. It was antithetical to his concept of himself and infinitely below his caste. Ibrahima's feelings flared. He refused to work and would not go to the field. Attempts to coerce him met with "repeated resistance." Defiance, in turn, brought the whip, which availed Thomas nothing and deepened Ibrahima's resentment. "The bonds of servitude lay heavy upon him," wrote Major Steve Power in *The Memento* (1897). "He was restive against all authority and impatient under restraint, and soon [he] became a most undesirable element in the plantation life."

But a single avenue led out of the maddening cycle into which master and slave had fallen, and Ibrahima took it resolutely. He slipped away from his bed one night and crossed to the woods beyond the field. Another minute, and he was racing away through the darkened forest.

"Fugitives from labor" were nothing new to Natchez, and the standard steps were taken. Since there were no newspapers in which to advertise, announcements of his flight were posted at the fort, at taverns, and at the other public places. Boatmen were alerted, and searches were made along St. Catherine's Creek and in Pine Ridge. But the patrols ferreted nothing out of the woods except the ordinary number of bear and Southern panther. No sign or track of the African was found. Days stretched into weeks, "all efforts to ascertain his whereabout proved unavailing," Major Power wrote, "and after a while . . . inquiry was abandoned." The interest shifted to post-mortem, the taprooms filled with theories

on what had happened to him. Had he crossed paths with some
unfriendly Indians? Fallen into a bayou and been torn to shreds
by an alligator? If he had made it to the Mississippi and trusted
himself to a homemade craft, surely he had drowned. Or, lost in
great, uncut forest, "he could have miserably perished from fatigue and hunger." Each sounded plausible. The country was too
raw for anyone so uninitiated and ill-equipped to survive where
woodsmen went only armed and in party. Ibrahima was given up
for lost.

In the forest, meanwhile, a private drama was reaching its
climax. Ibrahima had no place to go. He realized this and appears
to have stayed near the farm, although his actual whereabouts are
conjectural. The thought of fleeing to the North would not have
occurred to him. Slavery had been outlawed in the Northwest
Territory of the United States the previous year, but that fact
would be important only to a person who understood American
geography and politics. It was the thought of an acculturated,
traveled slave, not a newly arrived African. Flight had no meaning
for Ibrahima unless it resulted in a return to Futa, something
he knew was impossible. Occasionally, a runaway African would
be found standing on the shore of the Gulf of Mexico, looking out
to sea. Ibrahima was not that naïve.

Chilled by the autumn nights and half starved, he hit the nadir
of his existence. To be taken from his family and his father's
court and thrust into a meaningless foreign bondage was cruelly
unfair. He was no slave in Africa, swapping a black master for a
white one. He fell from freedom, a stunning and agonizing experience made all the worse because he was a prince, a man "brought
up in luxury and Eastern splendour, now compelled to taste the
bitter cup of poverty." A primitive future stretched before him at
a labor he could not imagine himself performing. Nor was it less
loathsome, for a Muslim, to become the slave of a Christian.
Where the two religions came in contact in Africa, as at Tripoli,
Islamic law expressly forbade such a thing.

Suicide must have suggested itself, an old remedy liberally used
by Africans of all classes who found themselves in his situation.
Surely the aggregate of his humiliations warranted it, and "humiliation," says Thierno Diallo, foremost historian of Ibrahima's
people, "was an intolerable burden to the Fulbe aristocracy." Yet,

when hunger and exposure forced him at length to decide what he was going to do, he chose against it. It was not the fear of death; as a solider he had learned to ignore that fear as much as he could. More possibly, Ibrahima strove to accommodate the will of God as he understood it. Each Muslim must give an account of his life. The Qur'an makes clear that the gates of Paradise are shut to those who murder themselves. However unfair his fate seemed, Ibrahima felt his misfortune came from God. No affliction befalls a person without divine permission. This knowledge, this "fatalism," was sustaining.

For Ibrahima it may well have been the reason why he chose to live.

One morning, after "many weeks" in the woods, Ibrahima returned to the farm. He walked up to the old blockhouse, opened the door, and stepped forward on the eave. Sarah Foster, who was sitting alone in the room sewing, looked at him in shock. "The recreant Prince stood before," Major Power wrote. "He was a man of powerful frame, well proportioned. . . . His tattered garments hung from him, and his fierce eye was riveted upon her." From the tortured expression on his face, Sarah thought he intended to kill her. "Death seemed imminent," as Major Power phrased it. With marvelous presence of mind, given her belief, she rose, smiled at him, and held out her hand. It was a disarming thing to do.

The meeting was Ibrahima's, however, and after touching her hand, he did something Natchez would long remember. He laid himself prostrate upon the floor. Taking one of her feet in his hand, he lifted it up and put it down upon his neck. The gesture was a special one to a West African soldier like himself. A conquerer's foot on a Pullo neck often preceded a spear thrust into the heart. Ibrahima meant by it something his ignorance of English did not let him say. He was placing his life in the hands of the Fosters. If they wanted him back, here he was; if they wanted to kill him, they could do that, too.

Sarah, not an easy person to impress, was absolutely astonished. She understood Ibrahima had returned, though not why, apparently. Indeed, she felt flattered by his action, by his "absolute surrender to the power of [her] smile and [her] touch." It was a happy misunderstanding, since she may have befriended him because of it. Her husband, informed Ibrahima was back, was so pleased, moreover, that no punishment of the prince was forthcoming. Subsequent events suggest not, at any rate, and Major Power, who presents the story that has just been related as a paean to Southern womanhood, would not have one think so. "From that day," the Major concluded, "Prince was a faithful, loyal servant, and I may add, trusted and beloved."

"He sank into a common slave," wrote someone who knew the situation more intimately. His return to the farm closed a full year of war, confinement, and deprivation. Ibrahima was exhausted. Though a tall person, he was not stocky or exceptionally muscular: he lacked a physical as well as a social aptitude for agriculture. All he had was the stamina characteristic of his people, who could walk fifty miles a day. Stoically and without expression, he went to do whatever labor Thomas assigned, working long hours in the fields through all types of weather. He would describe the work as severest toil. Natchez was not as temperate as Futa, and the summer months could be hotter. Still, "he submitted to his fate without a murmur." His countenance was equanimious, his conduct unobjectionable. The rich and guttural chatter of his Pular soon sounded in the fields. Wooden plates replaced the calabashes of his former life, and the harsh ring of an anvil replaced as reveille the muezzin's call to morning prayer.

Quickly immersed in the world of slavery, Ibrahima was appalled by the absolute nature of his predicament. Natchez society lacked the variety of semifree and slave classes found in Futa. A large proportion of the slaves at Timbo, descendants of those Jalunke defeated during the *jihaad,* had traditional rights, especially in regard to their labor and to being sold and removed from the country. They lived in their own country, moreover. "Serf" might be a more meaningful name for this group. The *nangaabe,* prisoners of war who became Fulbe slaves when captured in the campaigns of his father, fared worse; chains and whips were as well known in Futa as at Natchez. But Ibrahima now enjoyed the liabilities of this class and none of its assets. As Fulbe "slaves of the field," the *nangaabe* worked a limited number of days. They ate better than Natchez slaves, as they produced crops principally for consumption, not export. They kept their own customs and even selected on occasion the person they wished as village superintendent. In time their grandchildren might assimilate with the free population as they were Islamized. Being stationary, these Jalunke developed a sense of community, often working the crops of their sick friends, and they showed a cooperative attitude that did not exist among the disparate Africans, Americans, and West Indians at Natchez. The latter had nothing in common except their color, while there was no racial basis to slavery in Futa despite some differences in skin tone. Even co-religionists enslaved each other at Natchez, and all fell under the heel of a leveling that was devastating to Ibrahima's sense of Pullo superiority.

He was asked in later years, when he had learned to speak English, if slavery at Natchez and at Timbo weren't really the same.

"No, no," he replied earnestly, "I tell you, [a] man own slaves [at Timbo]—he join the religion—he very good. He make he slaves work till noon, go to church, then till he sun go down, they work for themselves. They raise cotton, sheep, cattle, plenty, plenty."

Unprepared for fieldwork, Ibrahima was familiar nevertheless with many crops grown at Natchez. He recognized tobacco, cotton, and rice immediately. He was surprised to see the pains taken to grow coffee, which flourished wild at home and was largely neglected. Several types of indigo grew abundantly in Futa, and Ibrahima thought they produced richer blues than the plants at Natchez. At Timbo indigo leaves were gathered and crushed into a paste that was rolled, dried, and later diluted in a solution into which fabrics were placed. At Natchez the plant, left to steep in great vats, became a filthy and unhealthy thing to be near, a labor in "putrid weed and hordes of flies," according to B. L. C. Wailes, an antebellum geologist. The languor and debility of indigo workers testified to the destructive nature of this commerce. "It killed every Negro employed in its culture in the short space of five years," wrote a visitor to Natchez. Fortunately, Thomas eschewed this crop, possibly due to its expense. The vats and other necessary fixtures could cost well over one thousand dollars.

Ibrahima was strongly impressed by the advance in technology

he saw. "The most ordinary mechanical arts are in a very imperfect state [in Futa]," wrote a friend with whom he held long
conversations on the differences between the two places, "not that
the people [there] are destitute of the facilities for acquiring them,
but they are totally averse to all innovations." The use of plows
and draft animals, for example, was unknown at home, where a
small hoe and sickle were the basic farm utensils. Ibrahima felt it
was sinful for mankind to plow the earth with horses, since those
animals had been given by God for other purposes, but he could
not deny the utility of the sacrilege. Certain other things, such as
glass windows, he viewed as luxuries proscribed by the faith,
although his people did use locks and keys on their doors. Most
items he simply marveled over, much as Peter the Great had marveled at mechanical objects on his trip through western Europe a
century earlier. When James Watt visited Timbo in 1794,
watches, compasses, and even canteens attracted attention. Each
time some new device was shown from his pack, Watt related, a
chorus of *Allah ackbar* ("God be praised!") rang forth from his
hosts. "There was no satisfying their curiosity," he wrote.

Tobacco, the staple crop of the District, was well known to
Ibrahima, although he had never seen it cultivated on such a
scale. The acreage devoted to it represented a great change from
the cereal orientation of agriculture at home. Tobacco at Timbo,
smaller than the Natchez variety, was grown near the houses,
where only enough was tended for personal use. At Natchez the
crop was grown for export, via New Orleans and Veracruz, to the
widely known tobacco factory in Seville. "The tobacco was of a
good quality," wrote Wailes, "and esteemed for smoking and for
making snuff." The rich soil of the District could yield up to two
thousand pounds per acre. Ordinarily, the harvest was fashioned
into weighty carrot shapes, which were wrapped in ropes made of
lime-tree bark. The twisting involved in making these carrots,
however, damaged the product and mixed mature and immature
leaves together. The planters had decided, accordingly, that the
1789 crop would be pressed into huge oak casks called hogsheads.

Encouraged by the Crown's munificent offer the previous year
of ten silver dollars for each one hundred pounds of tobacco,
Thomas planted the crop heavily in 1789. The laborers were

Ibrahima, Samba, and Jesse. Thomas himself probably worked alongside them as crop master. By March the agricultural year was well under way. Much time was spent on the knees, transplanting the seedlings from plantbeds to mounds. Farmers preferred this work done in the rain when possible. Hoeing around the plants followed, with subsequent topping to reduce the leaves to the number that would be left to broaden. The last steps were cutting and curing. The labor was tedious and routine, much of it done under a blazing Mississippi sun. It was especially tiring at harvest time, when Ibrahima handled much more tobacco per acre than his counterparts in the Chesapeake Bay area or in North Carolina. The result of their efforts was a respectable harvest of eight thousand pounds, more than twice Thomas's harvest of the previous year. The 263 farmers in the District reported a grand total of 1,402,725 pounds for the year, a figure that may include the weight of a few wooden blocks and cypress knees added in by avaricious planters. When all was packed, scows filled with the crop descended the Mississippi to the royal warehouse in New Orleans. There the tobacco was graded and sold. Occasionally, the tobacco commissioner discarded someone's leaves, but a purse of *escalins* was said to have a most formidable influence on his thinking.

The price that the government paid for Natchez tobacco was artificially high. It encouraged overexpansion and credit buying. A thirst for land raged in 1787 and 1788, while reckless speculations in human beings were indulged. Such was the chief reason for the importation of Africans like Ibrahima from the West Indies. But an economic crisis was resulting from a shift in imperial policy. Mexican markets were glutted with tobacco and the treasury at Madrid harassed by the premium price paid to the farmers. This situation came to a head shortly after Ibrahima's arrival, the very moment when Governor Miró wished to win friends in American Kentucky and spread his influence there. Consequently, a decision was made to purchase a diminished amount of the Natchez crop for His Majesty's account, while giving favored treatment to Kentucky tobacco. The result was that the government, instead of paying ten pesos for the 1789 crop, paid only eight. Much worse, it was announced that from the entire Province of Louisiana only forty thousand pounds of the

1790 crop would be purchased, an amount one of Natchez's largest planters alone could provide. Although the figure was raised somewhat later, the death knell of tobacco culture had been rung in the District, leaving Thomas heavily indebted and forced to find a new crop that could lift him out of this vortex.

In 1790, along with his brothers and practically every other person who could hold a pen, Thomas signed a petition to Governor Miró that begged him to save them from their creditors. The document complained of exorbitant prices and usurious rates of interest charged on unpaid accounts. Thomas had not been able to pay Irwin the first installment of money due on Ibrahima in 1789, and he missed the second payment in 1790, too. The other purchasers were in even worse shape. Irwin, set upon in the interim by Oliver Pollock, a prominent merchant who was one of his creditors, received permission from Miró in the spring of 1790 to have the Natchez commandant call Thomas and the other laggards to the fort and demand the money from them. By November of that year, Thomas paid off at last the $780 remaining for the Fulbe, tobacco money made by their own labor. Quite a few other purchasers of the prisoners of war brought to Natchez with Ibrahima had not paid their notes even by 1797, and one slave had to be taken back by the merchant.

Encouraged in 1791 by a conditional debt moratorium, Natchez planters turned to finding alternate cash crops. Some switched to indigo, despite what a contemporary described as the "monstrous and murderous" propensities of the culture. Thomas, who had planted decreasing amounts of tobacco in 1790 and 1791, experimented with cotton. By the latter year Ibrahima had helped produce sixteen thousand pounds of the fiber, which, together with the amount grown by Thomas's brother William, made the Fosters one of the leading cotton families on the creek. Thomas's financial situation had improved enough by the close of 1791 for him to swap the last tobacco he would grow for another slave. This was Dublan, a twenty-five-year-old man from the slave marts of New Orleans.

Numerous objections could be made to cotton as a staple, but the choice was wise. In 1792 an insect plague ravaged the indigo in the District. Thereafter, the culture slipped quickly from prominence. Tobacco fell so precipitately that by 1796 Natchez, like

Timbo, produced only enough for its own needs. The future of the District, and, indeed, of much of the lower Mississippi Valley, would be found in following the spoor that Thomas and Ibrahima were busily laying.

Robert Stark arrived in Natchez during the winter of 1790–91, after a two-thousand-mile trek through the wilderness from Tennessee at the head of a party of traders and travelers that included Rachel Robards and Andrew Jackson. A fifty-one-year-old resident of South Carolina, Stark had served as a colonel during the Revolution and had even spent time in a British prison, "loaded with chains." When the war concluded, he had moved west. The District appealed to him, and he sent for his wife, four children, and "a large number of slaves." Soon he petitioned the government for land. Manuel Gayoso de Lemos, the governor of the Natchez District, learning he was "a man of consideration in his own country," authorized the issuance of a warrant of survey for two thousand acres about forty miles south of the fort. Stark, his overseer, family, and hands moved there and farmed in 1792 and 1793, but soon the veteran grew tired of the arrangement. Although he had not yet received formal title to the land, he asked Gayoso for permission to sell it, saying he intended to return to the United States. The governor, who by this time had developed a personal dislike for this "discontented old man," not only refused his request but turned the land over to another person, who seized Stark's farm tools and corn crop and forcibly ousted him from the tract.

Early 1794, when these events took place, found Stark in no position to recriminate. He was in the stockade, arrested for making "disloyal expressions." Secret letters were allegedly circulating among the planters about an imminent invasion of the District to be led by the American George Rogers Clark. Stark, no longer enthusiastic for the Spanish regime, had talked freely of the project, even with the militia officers of the Crown. He felt, an associate explained, "that if the [American] enemy did come . . . such of the inhabitants of this District as took up arms against them would be roughly treated." Subsequent investigation revealed there were no letters. The entire affair was only flatboat gossip, grown wilder with each retelling. Still, Stark had been

indiscreet enough to show his colors, and he fell with new speed
from official favor.

Released on a two-month parole in March, 1794, Stark found
himself in a deplorable condition. He was landless now, yet he
still had to watch after and feed his slaves. As he could make no
plans until a key witness in his case returned to Natchez to testify,
Stark decided to dispose of seven of the people brought from the
East. A private sale was accordingly held. On April 23, 1794, Dr.
Samuel Flower, who counted a Mandinka among his chattels,
purchased three of the seven for eight hundred dollars. The remaining four, three children and a twenty-five-year-old woman
named Isabella, were bought by Thomas. He paid seven hundred
dollars in cash and nine hundred pounds of cotton.

It was cotton that had interested him in the four. The Natchez
fiber, grown with seeds from Georgia and Jamaica, was beautifully white and fine, but each large black seed seemed to cling to
the lint with a hundred desperate hands. As there were no cotton
gins in the District before 1795, the crops that Ibrahima helped
raise in 1792–94 had to be cleaned in a more mundane way. The
lint was picked free of the seeds either by hand or by a primitive
"rolling gin" not dissimilar to a device used by the ancient Egyp-
tians. Both processes were time-consuming and monotonous, and
it was costly to put Ibrahima to picking seed when he could be
clearing fields and building fences.

This, most probably, was Thomas's motivation for buying Isabella and the children, who were Jacob, age ten; Anaky, five; and
Limerick, two. The deed of sale does not say if Isabella was the
mother of the three, but clearly she was the mother of Limerick
and possibly of the other two, as well. Isabella, born about 1769,
was "a Negro native of the United States." It seems likely she had
lived for a number of years in Edgefield District, South Carolina,
where the Stark plantation was located. She would be described
later as "an interesting, fine-looking . . . woman," quite affectionate and easygoing. A strong Christian, she had an interest in medicine.

Isabella brightened slave life on the farm immediately. The first
or, at most, the second black woman there, she helped end the
barrackslike character of the place's early years. She was an

encouraging presence in another way, too. Although the population of the District had tripled in the last ten years, the proportion
of black males to black females had increased dramatically. In
1784 there were more than three women to every four men. By
1794, however, the ratio had dropped to a little over two to every
four. White males, who outnumbered white females considerably,
cut further into the number of the unattached. The Natchez District, then, had become a difficult place for male fieldhands like
Ibrahima, many stuck off in areas remote from town, to find
mates.

Not long after her arrival, Isabella was married to Ibrahima.
One writer, reporting local tradition, states that the ceremony was
performed on Christmas Day, 1794, by Thomas, who read passages from the Bible and blessed their union. A wedding feast of
roast and brandy followed, the writer continues. While the details
of this account are of dubious value, there are facts from the historical record that the story itself contains. In late 1794 or early
1795, Ibrahima and Isabella were *married*. The term "wedlock"
was later used to describe their status. Formal marriages of slaves
were not customary in the English areas of Louisiana, so the ceremony shows a side of Thomas's personality. Of course, he wanted
his slaves to have children, but they did not have to be married
for that. The formal service suited his religious sensibilities, and
perhaps Isabella's, too.

For Ibrahima the event was no ordinary milestone. It marked a
coming to grips with the terrible life in which he was trapped. His
wife at Timbo had probably remarried; his son, just two years old
when he left, would not even remember him. Isabella was here
and now, a calm and positive influence on him. Conversant in
English and quick-witted, she eased his immersion into American
life whenever possible. The early arrival of a child brought a still
deeper involvement in his new world. Simon, his eldest American
son, was born not long after the marriage. A boy named Prince
and another son whose name is not known were born to the
couple before the end of the decade. Each occasion tied a
heartstring between Ibrahima and the land of his enslavement.

There were other currents for accommodation, too. General
religious tolerance was common in the District—the Catholic

empire tolerated the Natchez Protestants, for example. Governor Miró had blocked efforts to establish the Inquisition in the Province in 1790, and Governor Gayoso of Natchez even owned books that were on the *Indice último* of the Church. Two centuries earlier the Spanish had prohibited the introduction of African Muslims into the Western Hemisphere, but that policy had been long forgotten. Each slaveholder was pretty well free to do what he wished about Islamic practice on his plantation. It could be an important decision. The annual fast, the dietary rules, and the work lost due to the frequent prayers of a practicing Muslim required forbearance from an owner. Ayuba Sulayman, a Pullo who was a slave on Kent Island in the Chesapeake Bay in 1730, was mocked and had dirt thrown in his face when he prayed. Just as common, however, were examples of indulgence. The Muslims were to Western eyes, certainly, the most intelligent of the Africans brought to North America. "The active and intellectual principles of the Africans have never been completely unfolded, except perhaps in the case of the Foolahs . . . , a great part of the Mandingoes, and one or two other tribes," wrote Carl Wadstrom, who visited the Gambia in 1788. True or not, the planters agreed, for they turned to the Muslims for drivers, overseers, and confidential servants with a frequency their numbers did not justify. It is not surprising that George Proffitt, a major New Orleans slave trader who had a wide variety of Africans from which to pick, had "Big Jack, a Mandingo, 30 years old," as his overseer and thought him a very good one. Sober, self-disciplined, and generally honest, a Muslim could be so useful that a planter might give him berth solely for financial advantage.

Thomas was no fool. He recognized Ibrahima's personal qualities, the "fundamentalism" and the ethical system like his own in many ways. These similarities were not superficial. Part of the inscription on Thomas's tombstone reads, "He lived in the discharge of all the duties of social order and exemplified through life the character of the doer of good." Compare the import of that with the insight into Ibrahima that the main themes in the writing of his contemporary, the Pullo poet Mohammadou Samba Mombéyâ, can afford: the militant faith, resignation to the will of God, support of the order of society. "Mr. Foster . . . well knew," wrote a Louisiana newsman years later, "the Negro [Ibrahima] to have an education superior to most white people." Nor could he deny Ibrahima's usefulness or how his age and habits were making him a second authority on the farm. There should be no question why Thomas, given these views, allowed him freedom of worship. Two letters written in the 1820s are evidence of this tolerance, and they also give proof of Ibrahima's steadfastness in the faith. Caroline Thayer, a Mississippi poetess and teacher, wrote in 1827 that the prince was "a Mahometan, and has adhered strictly to the forms of his religion" through the years. The second letter, written a few months later by Mississippi printing pioneer Andrew Marschalk, also used the phrase "adhered strictly" in describing Ibrahima's religious devotion in slavery.

For his own part, Ibrahima had numerous incentives to tolerate Christianity. The Muslims of Futa were not bigots. It was in the years during and just after their seizure of power that Islam was most intolerant. Then, even the Quranic punishment of mutilation for theft had been executed. By Ibrahima's lifetime, however, Islam was passing from revolution to institution, the animists little troubled for their religious opinions. In fact, Islam in Futa and in Macina was much influenced by the ideals of the *qadiriya* brotherhood, which stressed personal piety and tolerance. Ibrahima had always lived with non-Muslims and gotten along with people of diverse religious views, though he obviously had never seen the faithful with so clearly the lower hand.

Tolerance of the faith or no, Ibrahima's intellectual circumstances were undeniably restricted and severe. The Greek poet Homer wrote once that when Jupiter condemned a person to slavery, he took from that person half his mind. It was taken from Ibrahima in a slow intellectual strangulation. If the Americans and Europeans at Natchez felt isolated, one can imagine how the African felt, and how he fared. The exhaustion of the field did not encourage literary pursuits as the political and religious excitements at home had done. Anyway, Ibrahima had no access to pen and paper. He had no Qur'an. Years became decades, and he did not see a single Islamic text or piece of Arabic writing. To retain his own literacy he took to tracing Arabic characters in the sand when Thomas would call a rest during work. His entry into

American life, whatever the compensations it might have contained, was erratic and incomplete. He learned to speak in halting phrases, omitting conjunctions, and saying "he" or "de" for "the." And never was there an effort made to teach him to read and write. Thomas often did business with illiterates, and neither his wife nor his mother could write her own name. The secret superiority that Ibrahima might have felt on this subject rang hollow in the rude atmosphere of the farm. In fact, the environment itself sapped the mind. The Frenchman Saugnier, a seminarian who was taken slave by North Africans when his ship wrecked in 1784, was a captive only a few months when he felt his own culture eroding inside himself. "We naturally assume the manners of the people among whom we live, however savage they may be," he wrote, "especially if there be no blows in the bargain."

Thomas Foster's dream of affluence surged ahead. In 1795 he began to accumulate real estate. First he bought five-hundred acres of land on St. Catherine's Creek from Dr. Flower and the Calvit family for $1,250. Two years later, when his mother reached the age of seventy, he bought her plantation for a pittance. Mary gave as a gift to Thomas's first-born son, Levi, then still a minor, 170 additional acres. To this Thomas added eighty-five acres from his brother William, whose land adjoined his own to the north. In addition, a grant of some 650 acres on distant Buffalo Creek was made to him by the Spanish. In 1799 Thomas purchased four lots in the town of Natchez, which was being developed on the bluff above the river. For these quarter blocks, two of them on the main street (and one of those with a house on it), Thomas paid $1,800. In no case was it necessary for Thomas to sign a note for the balance of his purchases. Every cent was paid immediately.

Cotton explains his ample purse. The establishment of Whitney gins after 1795 meant a new age for Natchez, since that gin could clean tenfold as much cotton as the roller method could. The crop quickly eclipsed all others, as planters produced one thousand, two thousand, even twenty-five hundred pounds per acre. Though the boom was reminiscent of tobacco days, this prosperity was firmly based. The cotton was of good quality and, after the government burned one planter's harvest because he had wet it to increase its weight,* it improved even more. In 1800 cotton sold for a quarter dollar a pound cleaned. Single bales at New Orleans fetched twenty to thirty dollars.

Since women worked in the cotton fields along with men, Thomas mustered about ten hands by 1798. Each produced five to eight hundred pounds of clean cotton apiece. They faced a crop less challenging than tobacco. The routine was basically plowing, planting, hoeing, harvesting, and clearing the fields of old stalks. Exact jobs varied with the season of the year, and time had to be made for raising corn, tending livestock, fencing, and so forth. As the Fosters made the clothes that were worn on the plantation, some cotton would be kept. Most of it, however, was put in bags and sent to nearby gins, where it would be cleaned, the ginners keeping one fifth to one eighth for their trouble. In time it would find its way to an English textile mill. *Hottohoh,* as cotton was called in Futa, was well known to Ibrahima. It grew wild, but was also cultivated near the houses of the Jalunke in land enriched by the wastes of the village. At Timbo the cotton would be carded and spun by the free and slave women and sent to a caste of weavers who transformed it into cloth. Of course, this cotton was not grown for export, but there was a more important difference to Ibrahima. Cotton cultivation at home was the labor of women.

Other tasks on the plantation were more to his liking, such as working with the cattle, a natural employment for any Pullo who happened into slavery. According to the Spanish census of 1792, Thomas Foster owned twenty-five head of cattle. Over the years, as the plantation grew, this number did, too, until by the 1820s he owned 140 head. Thomas is credited with twenty hogs in the Spanish census, a number that also swelled in time. Ibrahima would have been loath to touch one at home, but this is a point his biographers pass over in silence. Did he escape the common pork diet of the District? Precedents are at hand, such as "Nero," a Muslim slave in South Carolina who drew his meat ration in beef, not pork, according to entries in the farmbook of his owner.

* "A false balance is abomination to the Lord, but a just weight is His delight."—Proverbs 11:1.

Natchez diets could also be supplemented with venison and other game. Still, there is no information on Ibrahima's diet. Obviously, though, his enslavement put an end to regular meals of mutton, the dish most popular with the aristocracy of Futa.

Horses provided another link between the old and the new that did not seem as bizarre as the upside-down world of farming. Thomas owned both work and riding horses. The number was about ten to fifteen, rather constant over the years. Every now and then a stray was taken up on the plantation. When that happened, it would have to be brought to the barn, where appraisals of the animal were made. Thomas brought oxen to the plantation in later years, and he also kept a number of mules. All livestock received a brand of *T* over *F,* with an underbit in the left ear as an extra precaution of ownership.

Horse racing was a serious business in the District. Its purpose, ostensibly, was to improve the blood of Natchez stock, but "like the fabled Upas tree of Java," a minister wrote, "it poisoned the moral atmosphere in all the region round about." A track operated during the 1790s on the creek several miles below the plantation. Thomas, fond of this sport, was often on hand for the races. One story makes Ibrahima his groom at the turf, a claim that is credible since he was extremely familiar with horses and racing. On a particular day, the account continues, Thomas raced and won against the lanky and uncouth Andrew Jackson of Tennessee. But Jackson was more interested in Thomas's groom than in his horse, and he even offered to buy Ibrahima. The planter refused. This tale, like that of Ibrahima's brandy-laced wedding feast, is probably just a piece of local pride by which the "heiristocracy" has distinguished itself over the years. Andrew Jackson did run a trading post in a log cabin north of Natchez during the winter of 1789–90. In 1791 he was married in Natchez, and in late 1811 he was back in the region slave trading. But this story, completely unsubstantiated as it is, must be viewed skeptically. If it has any value at all, it does not concern racing, or Jackson, but Thomas Foster, who knew how wisely the money for Ibrahima had been spent.

Thomas allowed Ibrahima and Isabella the small privileges, such as working a garden for themselves. With a pass in his pocket, Ibrahima would take any surplus produce into town to

sell. He also sold Spanish moss, which was dried and fashioned
into a cool "moss mattress" much preferred for summer sleeping.
These activities brought Ibrahima humbly onto the fringe of
Natchez's cash economy, an economy not widespread in Futa.
More important, perhaps, it allowed him to mingle with the
slave population in Natchez on Saturdays and Sundays, a time
equivalent for religious and social activity to Fridays in Futa.
Hardly any language other than Ibrahima's own could have given
him conversational ability with Africans on such a wide scale. A
herder of Baguirmi, or a Tokolor warrior, despite differences in
the manner of speaking, could understand him without great
difficulty. These occasions were his only chance to pick up news
from Africa. Tidbits were provided by newly arriving Africans
from Futa or neighboring states. Little is known of this international slave-trade grapevine, but it did exist, as Ibrahima discovered. Some years after he had been at Natchez, he met a
person from home.

"Abduhl Rahahman [Ibrahima]!" the man cried at seeing
him, dropping his face to the earth.

It was a tribute of respect to Ibrahima, done out of habit,
though then wildly out of place. The person is identified only as
"a Negro from [Ibrahima's] father's dominions." Possibly he was
a Jalunke who had been sold or stolen from the country.

People such as this could bring Ibrahima news from home. It
was sketchy and distorted reporting, but it was news of his family
and country, the only news he was likely to get. Ibrahima learned,
for example, that his father had died shortly after his capture. The
event occurred in northern Futa while Sori was preparing for
a *jihaad* in N'Gaaba. Ibrahima's brother Saadu took their father's
turban and had himself crowned the fourth *almaami*. He was a
"pious, learned, and ascetic" king, according to traditional history, who "never imparted a false oath, never took a person's
goods, never touched the wife of his neighbor." If morality had
been the sole requisite for holding power, the brother would have
grown gray at the job. But a son of Karamoko Alfa wished power
himself. With the help of the elders, the son arranged a coup
about 1795 in which the *almaami* was knifed to death. Many of
Saadu's followers died, too, and one suspects even Ibrahima
might have perished as well, had he been present.

How much the prince knew of the details of these events is not clear, but he did find out the succession of monarchs and something of their fates. He lived at Natchez under the impression that his father had died in a civil war. Actually, and rather ironically, the old warrior had gone peacefully in his bed. Ibrahima thought Saadu had ruled briefly, just a matter of days. In fact, his brother ruled about seven years, those terrible first years of Ibrahima's own life in Natchez. He was correct to believe, however, that Saadu had been murdered. Though his informants rearranged some details and compressed the span of years in their reporting, it is apparent that Ibrahima received at least the headlines, as it were, of the news from home.

Timbo was not the only place where the government was changing hands. Natchez and the remainder of the east bank of the Mississippi River above the thirty-first parallel were ceded to the United States by Spain in 1795. When the Spanish delayed evacuation, Thomas and his brothers, part of what has been termed "the religious element on Pine Ridge," proved restless, disaffected subjects. Tense days passed, but at length the Spanish gave up, departing in March, 1798. The Natchez District became the Mississippi Territory.

Natchez above the bluff took shape in this decade. Regular lots were marked off and sold. A two-story Church of San Salvador was built. Ironworks, brick kilns, and cordage yards sprang up. Numerous merchants left the landing for the bluff, and the slave mart was moved to "Forks of the Road," where the Natchez Trace entered the town. A graceful common was reserved to separate Natchez from its cliff, and a public market was put there later. By 1798 there were eighty or ninety houses scattered over the "upper town." The great planters were already beginning to build their ostentatious mansions in and near Natchez. Fine furniture, billiard tables, and four-wheeled carriages appeared. A consignment of goods arriving from Bordeaux at the time included almonds, linens, white silk stockings, kid gloves, and playing cards. In August, 1798, the Territory received its first American governor, the Massachusetts Federalist Winthrop Sargent. Daniel Clark wrote to the surveyor Andrew Ellicott that President John

Adams, in appointing the man, "conceived that a General is too high a rank for us and therefore sent a Sergeant to govern us" instead. For his part, Sargent felt Natchez, "from the perverseness of some of the people, and the inebriety of Negroes and Indians on Sundays . . . a most abominable place."

"Slavery, though disagreeable to us northern people," Ellicott wrote in the fall of 1797, "it would certainly be expedient to let continue in this district." It made the whites licentious and idle, "as is generally the case where slavery is tolerated," but it was in the fabric of society. The Natchez Permanent Committee, in a petition to Congress signed by Clark, begged leave "to represent that a great part of the labor in this country is performed by slaves . . . without which, in their present situation, the farms in this district would be but of little more value to the present occupiers than equal quantity of waste land." Expediency had its day, for the law organizing the Territory allowed the system to continue. Still, some of the planters were aware of the iniquity of their property in people. "That we deprive the [slaves] of the sacred boon of liberty is a crime they can never forgive," Sargent told a gathering of militia officers in 1801. "Mild and humane treatment may for a time continue them quiet, but can never fully reconcile them to their situation."

In Natchez the Fosters were part of a group constantly wanting to tighten the policing of the slaves. John, an *alguacil* (constable) during Spanish rule, damned Governor Sargent for tolerating the blacks' drinking, profanation of Sundays, and weekend games of dice and chuck-penny. Fresh from an encounter with two of his own runaways, Thomas condemned the territorial slave law in 1805 "because it does not provide for taking such runaway slaves as go armed and make resistance when pursued." The brothers' worst fears were never realized, however. Though the District simmered at times, it never boiled over. No insurrection occurred to equal that at Pointe Coupée, Louisiana, in 1795, or even that at Timbo during Saadu's reign, when thirty revolutionaries were executed. There were proportionately more blacks at Pointe Coupée, it is true, and the Anglo-American was severer in his police than the Spaniard or the Frenchman. But more subtle considerations must be added.

Ibrahima was a professional soldier, an officer and a strategist. Who better to lead a vengeful slaughter across Pine Ridge? The fact is that he inclined strongly the other way. There were never enough Muslims at Natchez to develop New World Islamic communities comparable to those in South America or to organize revolts like those in Bahia, Brazil, in the 1820s and 1830s, which were really cisatlantic holy wars, directed not only against whites but against pagan and Christian blacks as well. Lacking the fellowship of numbers, beset with language and identity problems, Ibrahima felt a strong temptation to do his own time, what a frontier preacher termed "the Negro's eleventh commandment— every man mind his own business." Important, too, were his own beliefs and prejudices. Torn from the nexus of his social and personal relationships, he fell back on what was transcendant, his faith and a pride in his culture.

It took him years to recover from the shock of what had happened to him, to escape the despondency and self-neglect that engulfed each new arrival. Later still, his language, customs, and incomplete entry into American life made him seem bizarre, not only to whites but to American-born blacks, too. With a hauteur befitting a Pullo prince, Ibrahima, in turn, did not feel the non-Muslim Africans and Americans were his equals, despite the way whites lumped all of them together. The plantation was his reality now, as much as it was Thomas's, and the tug was powerful to identify his interests with those of his owner, not against them. Sarah's "smile and touch," Thomas's "uncommon benevolence" aside, the seeds of his accommodation had been sewn at Timbo.

Ibrahima's tall form became a familiar sight over the years at the market in Natchez, but his bearing became less than noble. From the day his hair had been cut, he had neglected it entirely. It became coarse and mazy, and he left it short, an ornament that no longer concerned him. His skin, much battered by the sun, grew weathered and dry. He lost interest in how he looked and had little time for cleanliness. Even the great Fulbe regard for one's hands was impossible to maintain when they became the calloused companions of froes and weeding hoes and oxcarts. "The privations incident to the lower order of community," as a friend termed it, ate into his health, spirit, and self-respect.

He remained a model of probity, hard-working and dependable

at whatever he gave his attention. He never drank, he never cursed, he was never caught in a falsehood or dishonest act. He meant to survive, and he did, but the personal price was staggering. A man who knew him intimately for two decades said that—despite the passage of the years, despite the love of his wife, the cheer of his family, despite the respect of his owner—in all the time he had known Ibrahima, he had never seen him smile.

4. *Annus Mirabilis* and After

The Natchez country was pre-eminently a land of rumor. Isolated from the United States to the east and north by wilderness, its residents were always suspicious of what went on beyond the territorial borders. The planters had seen the District's fate change time and again at the behest of those who lived thousands of miles away. Consequently, they not only wanted the news, they had a thirst and a passion for it. Each traveler from the settled area was assured of a welcome if he would but say what Congress did about the land law, how Napoleon fared at Austerlitz, or if the mail rider had been seen. Neighbor to the Indian and Spaniard, the District also listened for rustlings closer to home, rustlings that could have immense military and economic consequences. A bit of information, once secured, traveled around the countryside so quickly that those who did not know what was happening within a day or two can only be labeled the willingly ignorant. Natchez's newspapers, far from dispelling the anxieties, were so partisan in their reporting that they added to the confusion at times.

It was alarming, then, when word circulated early in 1807 that Colonel Aaron Burr, the former Vice-President of the United States with designs of some type on the West, was descending upon the region with an armed flotilla. What Burr wanted is no clearer now than then—there was even gossip he would free the slaves—but the administration of the Territory sensed a menace to it and called out the militia. In January, 1807, when Burr docked upriver from the city, he was arrested, despite the fact that his "corps of invasion," far from awesome, would have done poorly at a local bear hunt, since less than half of his men had long rifles. Burr was released on a ten-thousand-dollar bond, free to squire a local heiress, while a jury was empaneled to hear the charges against him. On February 2, the case of *The United States v. Burr.* commenced at Washington, a village of thirty houses not far from the Foster plantation, which by the combined efforts of politicians and real-estate speculators, had been made the capital of the Mississippi Territory. Judges in the case were Thomas Rodney, an old-fashioned liberal and member of the Continental Congress, and Peter Bryan Bruin, an alcoholic who "sometimes took a nap on the Bench." The crowd in attendance was so large that the trial, tradition maintains, was held outside under two great oaks that still stand in the village. The proceedings were immediately anticlimactic. The United States attorney stated at the outset that he felt a territorial court lacked sufficient jurisdiction to prosecute the defendant. Even more embarrassing to the Territory was its initially heavy-handed use of the military in reacting to Burr's presence on the river. When the arguments were concluded, the jury refused to indict Burr, instead criticizing the Territory for its role in the affair.

Burr was soon swept away to an appropriately larger stage in the East, but he had played in the county long enough to sow great ill will. Robert Williams, the Territorial governor at the time and a person remembered as "a rough customer, a plain, blunt man who did not possess the art of making friends," fired those subordinates who had bungled the proceedings. The controversy resulting from their dismissal raised acrimony to heights for which even Mississippi was unprepared. "It seems the smaller the society," Thomas Jefferson wrote of the haggling, "the bitterer the dissensions into which it breaks." There was little to compete with it for the public attention, however, except the burning of William Dunbar's cotton gin, mill, and outbuildings, valued at sixteen to twenty thousand dollars. The season had been healthy, and the winter one of the coldest in memory, but spring did come. By March, onions, lettuce, and "spinnage" were on the tables; by May, corn, cucumbers, and plums. August brought the usual fevers and, for the further inconvenience of the residents, a first-class drought.

One day during this summer of 1807 Ibrahima walked into
Washington, a large basket balanced on his head. Samba was with
him. It was a trip they had made a hundred times, along a dirt
road that ran from Pine Ridge to the village. Washington was
less than an hour's walk. Ibrahima had some sweet potatoes he
intended to sell; the money he received would be his own.
Thomas was more liberal in this regard than some of the other
planters were, and although Ibrahima never had a significant
amount of money, he was able in time to buy decent clothes for
everyone in his family.

Ibrahima looked for customers along the main street. There
were always slaves and Indians in town trying to sell pumpkins,
turkey, moss, brooms, even hand-carved trays on occasion.
Among the passers-by that day was a middle-aged white man. He
rode so peculiarly that he caught Ibrahima's attention. There was
not only something peculiar about him—there was something
familiar, too.

"Go see that man," he told Samba. "If he [has] but one eye,
I've seen him before."

That was the case, and when Samba told him so, Ibrahima
rushed into the street as the man rode past. Not wishing to stop
him without a reason, Ibrahima held out his basket and said,
"Master, you want to buy some potatoes?"

"What potatoes have you?" replied the man, pulling up.

"While he looked at the potatoes," Ibrahima said later, "I
observed him carefully, and knew him, but he did not know me."

The rider studied the Pullo in the face. His eyebrows came
together and his mouth pursed. "Boy, where did you come
from?" he said.

"From [Mr.] Foster's."

"And were you raised in this country?"

"No," Ibrahima said, "I came from Africa."

"You came from Timbo?"

"Yes, sir."

"Is your name Abduhl Rahahman?"

"Yes, that is my name."

"Do you know me?" the rider asked.

"Yes," Ibrahima replied, "I know you very well. You be Dr.
Cox."

"By this singular [act of] Providence," a contemporary wrote, *"Dr. Cox was brought to recognize in the person of this slave, the son of a king who had treated him with so much hospitality in Africa."*

When the doctor said his name, Ibrahima felt as if he had been hit by something. His body could not handle its emotions. Some say he bowed to the doctor, others that he danced or jumped or threw a watermelon high into the air. One thing was for certain. He was smiling now. The one white man in the world who owed him a great favor was there in the street before him. It was wildly improbable, it was fanciful, it was insane, but it also was happening.

Springing from his horse, Cox seized Ibrahima and embraced him violently. What was he doing here? How had he come to this country? The questions poured forth, for Cox was no less shocked than Ibrahima. "Such a meeting," Gallaudet wrote, "can more easily be conceived than described."

"Dash down your potatoes and come to my house," the doctor said. The joy of even this minute, however, could not efface nineteen years of poverty. Ibrahima could not let his potatoes go. Cox mounted, rode quickly away, and returned with a woman to watch them for him.

Soon at the doctor's lodging, Ibrahima laid out the tale of his woes—the war, the capture, the bondage. A little later, Governor Williams appeared. The doctor, whom the governor had known for years, had sent a note on impulse to the little plantation at Washington where Williams resided, asking for his presence. "I have been to this boy's father's house," Cox said to the governor, "and they treated me as kindly as my own parents." Cox told Williams, Ibrahima stated later, "if any amount of money would purchase me, he would buy me, and send me home."

The good doctor, it developed, had suffered troublesome years since he had last seen Ibrahima. Shipwrecked twice since leaving Futa, he had bade the sea farewell in 1786, and, after marrying a fifteen-year-old girl from County Antrim, he immigrated with her to the United States. A daughter was born to them in New York in 1787. By 1790 Cox had moved to Rockingham County, North Carolina, a farming area in the north-central part of the state, bought a small farm on the Haw River, and begun practicing medicine among his neighbors, many of whom were fellow Irish. Two more daughters and two sons were born in the 1790s. In 1799 Cox settled in nearby Leaksville, where he bought numerous lots and began to dabble in land speculation. It was the wrong thing to do, for he lacked the mercenary spirit. He became indebted to many people, including John Lenox, a local high priest of Mammon who owned a spring "of curative properties." Early in 1806, Lenox secured a crushing judgment against him in the county's Court of Pleas and Quarter Sessions. It could be satisfied only by selling the land on which he lived. This Cox was forced to do. The appointment of Williams, a North Carolina congressman from the county, to the governorship of the Mississippi Territory, turned his now desperate attention there. After seventeen years in North Carolina, he emigrated in the spring of 1807, little richer for his time there but in experience.

The morning after their meeting, Cox rode out to the Foster plantation. With Ibrahima beside him, he told Thomas of his African adventure. "In the fullness of his gratitude" for Sori's humanity, the doctor stated, he wished "to intercede for [his son's] liberty." "He inquired how much would purchase me," Ibrahima said, but "my master was unwilling to sell." Cox began to name figures of his own, each a little higher than the previous one. Each was refused. Finally, he offered one thousand dollars —money he may not have had—and nearly twice the going rate at Forks of the Road. Again the planter said no. The doctor "made every possible exertion to obtain the liberation, but Prince's master would not part with him for any price."

Years later Ibrahima's friends professed themselves unable to understand why. "Exertions were made on the part of Dr. C[ox] to emancipate him, and enable him to return to his native country," Cyrus Griffin wrote, but "from causes altogether inexplicable to me, it was never effected." The reasons were simple enough. Thomas thought it idle to speak of returning home. How, then, would Ibrahima fare beyond Pine Ridge, an indigent African without skills or means of a livelihood? "His master doubted whether his freedom would increase his happiness," wrote Gallaudet. Added a Connecticut editor who would meet Ibrahima subsequently, "[Thomas knew of] no other place in which he thought the Prince would be more comfortable than on his estate." The truth was that Thomas depended on Ibrahima. The African was his steadiest worker, a faithful two hands at every task. And there was his moral example. "He was so valuable as a slave, and so serviceable to Foster by the salutary influence which he exerted over all the slaves on his plantation, that he could not consent to part with him." Simply stated, Ibrahima had made himself invaluable.

"If you cannot part with him," Cox said at length, "use him well."

The twenty-four hours had been astonishing to Cox and to Thomas, but they had been racking to Ibrahima. Flung skyward, he came crashing to earth amid fresh evidence that his life was not his own. How bizarre that ethical and inoffensive ways condemned him to further slavery. How much better if he had been malingering and insolent. Still, there is no evidence that he changed in any way after the meeting. He was bitter and disappointed, yes, but he did not suddenly turn bad, just as he had not suddenly turned good. He had not been assuming a personality for his owner. He was what he was, a product of the *marabout* and the mosque. His conduct was not a strategy. It grew out of a vision of life. That vision had cushioned some high falls before. It could cushion one more.

Of course, the doctor would be nearby. Cox liked Washington and decided to stay. During the following fall and winter he bought a house and eighteen acres in the village near the governor, and his door was open to Ibrahima. The Pullo had gained a small notoriety for his conduct and religious practices previously, and his voluntary return to the plantation after so complete a disappearance had made him a part of the local folk history. The meeting with Cox, while not changing things dramatically, did effect him in positive ways. The doctor's tale became known to almost everyone. Like most stories, it grew to epic size with retelling, until the aimlessly wandering surgeon who had been brought to Futa "as a curiosity" was presenting himself as the heroic lone survivor of "a party of exploration from England . . . to Timbuktu, every individual of the party [dying] except Dr. Cox who, on his return, was taken sick at Timbo" and so on. There was no mention of an African honeymoon along the way, either, and Ibrahima was discreet enough not to bring it up. But the real kindnesses of his family to the doctor were creditable enough, and, as Cox confirmed his claims to royal blood, the affair made Ibrahima a celebrity. Though Cox was unable to buy him, the doctor's mere presence, Ibrahima's first relationship of significance with whites beyond the Foster family, broadened his vistas remarkably. Cox's patronage, his genial willingness to do Ibrahima little favors meant more to the isolated African than a twentieth-century mind can easily imagine. It made Adams County a more humane place, the world a little less toilsome.

A mild winter brought the year of 1807 to an end. Historians would remember it as a mediocre season for cotton. It was the year of the Burr business, those fleeting moments beneath the oaks that put Washington village in the nation's newspapers. Most other memories are gone or sadly distorted, including a truthful one of what the doctor and the prince were all about. Time passed, and the great-grandchildren of the Foster brothers even forgot who owned Ibrahima. He was passed around in memory among Thomas and James and William according to the exigencies of genealogy. The descendants of the doctor forgot, too. One of them said Ibrahima had captured the doctor while he was exploring in Africa and held him there for years against his will. Another, that Ibrahima was "a cannibal chief" who could barely be persuaded not to eat his guest.

All the while it was Ibrahima who was being devoured.

"Fancy that you see a tall, gaunt, long-armed personage with eyes like two balls of fire set in a face of iron, with long teeth like the tusks of an alligator, and you will have some idea of Prince Abduhl Rahhahman," a Louisianan wrote. Ibrahima's expression was leaden again. The most lasting aftertaste of the meeting had been to deepen his sense of fatalistic accommodation. There appeared no prospect that he would ever leave Natchez. If he couldn't escape with Cox's help, he was not going to get away. The entire affair had the effect of turning his mind further from Futa, concentrating his attention more completely than before on his wife, his children, the plantation—on the one and only world that was his.

No one raised in Sori's court, especially a principal son like Ibrahima, could escape the desire for power. The habit of com-

mand was too engrained and it coincided too perfectly in an aris-
tocrat like himself with cultural prejudices that also beckoned him
forward. Mungo Park, writing of the Fulbe of Bundu, observed
"they evidently consider all the [African] Negro natives as their
inferiors, and when talking of the different nations, always rank
themselves among the white people." This is precisely what Ibrahima meant when he told Cyrus Griffin "explicitly, and with an
air of pride, that not a drop of Negro blood runs in his veins."
While this was not true of his people biologically, the statement
was an accurate representation of their social feelings in regard to
their neighbors. No doubt this aspect of Ibrahima's personality
manifested itself early. Thomas observed it and exploited it as
best he could in the years before the Cox meeting and afterward.
For Ibrahima, the opportunity to move up in the plantation
hierarchy was irresistible, so starved was he for distinction. He
became the farm's driver and probably something more. Traditional history relates that Thomas "employed him somewhat in
the capacity of overseer, on account of his unusual abilities." The
job brought favors, lightened labor, and increased rations; in
return it meant watching the plantation, keeping the other slaves
at work, detecting and reporting their transgressions. Though
Thomas was the legal source of his power, Ibrahima exercised
what was really a threefold authority—proprietal, through Thomas;
familial, through his own growing family, the largest unit of
laborers on the place; and cultural, through his African identity
and influence.

It would be claimed later in his lifetime that Ibrahima, in his
position as driver or overseer, was barbaric to his comrades.
There were some despotic African nobility in the Old South, and
so, knowing the Fulbe sense of superiority, one is impelled to
examine this charge carefully, a charge made by an anonymous
writer of 1828 in the New Orleans newspaper the *Louisiana
Advertiser*. The article at issue is so jaundiced and violently political that the temptation is strong to ignore the accusation as
simple propaganda. Still, whoever wrote the piece should be
heard, since he either knew Ibrahima or had talked with someone
who did, for the article contains original anecdotes about him.
They are the least sympathetic memoranda of his life. "Mr.
Foster," the writer stated, "actually made him manager of his

plantation. [He] had continually to keep an eye upon him and to curb his sanguinary temper to prevent him from exercising cruelty on his fellow servants. . . . Foster's Negroes lived in more awe of him than [of] their master. . . . His blood-thirsty disposition caused him to be viewed by the Negroes in the neighborhood as a *bug bear* or *Negro devil,* whose very name would terrify the unruly into obedience." The context of these imputations, the presidential election of 1828, will be presented fully subsequently, and the conditions under which they appeared may be best appreciated there. For the present, suffice it to say that the anonymous writer painted Ibrahima "a blood-thirsty, tyrannical Mahometan Negro, the most cruel and vindictive wretch that ever existed."

Was it true? A dozen statements from other sources contradict it. Gallaudet remarked on Ibrahima's "most exemplary character for kindness. . . ." "His kind and pacific temper gained the good-will . . . of all who knew him in his state of bondage," wrote another. Still another said, "The humanity of the Mohammedan is proverbial." A Natchezian, "from an intimate knowledge of twenty years standing," said specifically that he had never seen Ibrahima angry. That does not sound like a despot.

A survey of the extant issues of every newspaper published at Natchez and Washington from 1800 to 1828 reveals but one instance of slaves fleeing the plantation. In the fall of 1805 Peter and Vincent, two twenty-one-year-old blacks from Kentucky whom Thomas had purchased in 1801, ran away. The fact that Thomas advertised for them only once suggests, among other things, that they may have returned themselves, or that they should be considered truants rather than fugitives. This could have happened before as well as during Ibrahima's tenure, since the exact date of his rise to power is uncertain, but a single flight over a period of almost thirty years, and from a force of hands that grew as numerous as Thomas's did, is a very low number. It compares advantageously to his brothers and to the Bislands, Calvits, Graftons, and others on Pine Ridge. The low number may have something to do with Thomas's reputation as a kind master, "a truly amiable and worthy man." Certainly, "Prince uniformly [spoke] of his . . . master with great respect." One deduction may be drawn from the single advertisement, at least. There was no reign of terror on the plantation, as the *Louisiana Advertiser* implies. The several sources of Ibrahima's authority suggest that he had less need than an ordinary driver to use force. A final evidence comes from the person who should know. Thomas himself said in 1827 that he "had never known [Ibrahima] guilty of a mean action."

With the Pullo's help the plantation matured remarkably by 1810. Cotton, which had fetched a high price since Spanish times, still brought twenty-two cents a pound as late as 1807. On the proceeds of his harvests Thomas bought several tracts of land adjoining his own to the south. In 1806 he purchased 179 acres from John Henderson, a Scottish merchant who settled at Natchez the year before Ibrahima. In 1810 he added the 250-acre Gibson place. These acquisitions cost $5,326, all paid immediately. It can be seen, then, that when the War of 1812 turned the cotton market upside down, the plantation, free of any mortgage, had already reached its maximum size, 1,785 acres. It stretched three miles north to south and about one mile east to west. Through it ran 7,260 feet of St. Catherine waterway. The general circumference of the estate was nine miles.

The Natchez lots that Thomas had purchased proved enormously valuable, especially the one on Main Street. It was located ideally, next to the public square, where, in 1812, were found the city cistern, firehouse, and market. Before 1810 Thomas was content to rent the property on five-year leases and squeeze out his return in quarterly installments. When the second flush of cotton prices came in 1815–18, however, he managed nine sales of his Main Street land. The $1,800 investment of 1799 brought in at least $16,270 by 1818 and doubtless more. Some of this income was used to buy choice land in neighboring counties. In 1815, for example, Thomas paid $3,500 for a developed farm on Cole's Creek in Jefferson County.

Thomas's increasing wealth showed itself prominently on the plantation. It was at this time, apparently, that a horse-powered cotton gin was constructed. A grist mill with two sets of stones was erected to grind grain and make cornmeal. The most impressive change was the construction of a new home in 1808. It is not thought that Thomas built an entirely new structure. Evidence is strong that he took the old blockhouse and renovated it extensively. The result was impressive, a two-story "Spanish-style" home with large windows, canted roof, and wide outside stairways. Galleries ran across the front and back of the house, which faced west toward the road from Washington to Pine Ridge. The handsome frame exterior was an excellent camouflage for the four-inch *bousillage* of moss and mud between the walls that belonged to an older, less settled time. The finely crafted interior was mortised and pegged so expertly that a person who saw it remarked that it "looked like a cabinetmaker had built it." The floors were of wide poplar boards, and the rooms were painted blue. There was also a superior brick cellar and cistern. The home, set several hundred feet from the creek on a slight rise, caught the evening breezes that still rustle the live oaks at the site. It was a first-rate country manor, not a mansion, but a fitting seat for a middle-aged gentleman of property and standing.

Thomas Foster never really joined the aristocracy. His name is absent from Colonel Ferdinand L. Claiborne's "List of the Gentlemen Little Nabobs of the Mississippi Territory," circa 1804, and from Judge Rodney's list of similar date. A strong Jeffersonian, committed at the earliest day to Andrew Jackson's prospects, Thomas nonetheless had few political and no social ambitions. He was an erstwhile reader of Gales and Seaton's *National Intelligencer* of Washington, D.C., and of the local Republican newspapers. They satisfied his cultural appetites. He was no planter-classicist, all hogs-and-Homer, pigs-and-Pindar. His favorite volumes were the Bible and the bank book. But that combination, together with a penchant for work, won him a respect that some of the aristocracy never knew. In 1801 he was well enough regarded to serve as a tax assessor for St. Catherine's township. He was the sort of person to whom John Bisland would turn to evaluate a house, or Judge Rodney to divide a contested tract of land, or James Smith, his violent brother-in-law, to provide bail. They knew he was honest and efficient. In 1803 he was chosen one of three "Inspectors of Cotton" for Natchez. He was to certify the quality of cotton deposited in a warehouse at the landing in an effort to protect the reputation of the Territory's export. In the land of cotton the appointment was an honor and, for the unambitious Thomas, it was the capstone of his public life.

His civic involvement was limited less by his interests than by the demands of his burgeoning family. Thirteen children, nine girls and four boys, grew to adulthood on the plantation. Their number left Thomas with little time for anything unconnected with home. Foremost among the children was Levi, the eldest son, "a thrifty and energetic [person] of some education and intelligence." He worked the estate with his father in 1811, but moved for some reason to Bayou Teche in Louisiana's Attakapas region by 1813. Levi's place in Thomas's confidence was taken by Ephraim Foster, who married daughter Cassandra in January, 1807. Ephraim, a robust commoner and a man of many practical skills, may have been a country cousin, but records do not say. Other advantageous marriages included that of daughter Ellen to a Pine Ridge ginwright and of daughter Barbara to a wealthy militia colonel. With his own family, with his in-laws, with mother Mary (still alive and nearing ninety in 1815), and with other relatives and acquaintances who, in that day, came to stay not for the weekend but for the winter, twenty people might sit down to eat dinner at his house on an average day.

The black community was numerous, too. Thomas's plantation contained more land than his older brothers' holdings combined. Since half of his holdings was first-class cotton acreage, there was always a need for labor. Unfortunately, there are no records of Thomas's slave purchases after 1801, but an idea of the increase in the slave population can be gained from territorial tax records and from censuses. The plantation grew from a nucleus of four, with Ibrahima and Samba's arrival in 1788, to six in 1792, and to about twenty in 1800. In 1805, of about 305 slaveholders in the county, Thomas, with twenty-one people, was twenty-third in prominence. The number of slaves went to forty by 1810, almost seventy by 1818. In 1819 it broke one hundred. Purchases and inheritance account for some of the increase, but there was as well a high birth rate in the quarters, which carried the population forward in disregard of the price of cotton.

Ibrahima's family numbered five sons and four daughters. Only three, all sons, are known by name. Simon and Prince have already been mentioned. The third was the youngest son, Levi or Lee, named after Thomas's child. He was born in 1806, when Ibrahima was forty-four, the year before the meeting with Dr. Cox. Samba, who married a woman named Celia, had at least three sons himself, including Sulimina (called "Solomon") and Samba ("Little Sambo"). In an arrangement reminiscent of home, where the Jalunke lived in villages separate from the Fulbe, Ibrahima and his fellow slaves did not live near Thomas. Their settlement was several hundred feet away, where the Washington–Pine Ridge road crossed the creek at a gravel ford. Here, on a little bluff on the north bank, were the plantation quarters. The best homes were "box houses" made of foot-wide cypress boards; the worst were "shacks." The site was close enough to the creek for washing and fishing, when time permitted, and a black cemetery was located nearby.

Thomas had caught sight of the scriptural truths at an early age, but brother William so distinguished himself in this regard that he is better remembered. William and his wife Rachel first attended Methodist services at a schoolhouse in Washington in 1799. Riding home from one "love-feast," William remarked that Tobias Gibson, the minister, "prayed like he was right close up to God. How different," he said to Rachel, "from the mumbling we sometimes [heard] from the priests of Natchez." William joined the church that year, becoming a patron of Methodism and of the Mississippi Bible Society. He was widely read in religious literature and in 1806 was selling hymn books, concordances, and theological titles from his home. The most spiritually minded brother, William was opposed "not only to the African slave trade," wrote the Reverend John G. Jones, "but also to the perpetuity of African slavery." His slaves were, too. Despite what must have been a comparatively tolerable regime, several fled his plantation in 1805 and 1821.

The traditional Presbyterianism of the Fosters was Thomas's choice. His interest in it is evidenced by a letter he received in December, 1800, from six Natchez Presbyterians urging him to join them in "establashing [sic] a settled ministry of the Gospel throughout this Territory." True progress, however, had to wait the arrival of missionaries from the Carolinas several years later. In the spring and early summer of 1807 a log building named Salem Church was erected by slaves a little distance west of the plantation. This first Presbyterian church in Mississippi had as one of its maxims never to admit to its pulpit "new and strange teachings, [but] strictly retain the order and simplicity of primitive Apostolic worship." The Reverend James Smylie was its pastor, a man who would gain fame in later years with his scriptural defenses of slavery. Brother James Foster was one of Salem Church's original subscribers, and William, escorting mother Mary, was broadminded enough to be a communicant occasionally. Thomas alone is not listed in the church records, a curiosity since he is known to have had strong religious feelings. Perhaps some peculiar theological belief kept him from a formal affiliation. At any rate the tradition that he attended Salem Church persists.

On these alleged visits, Thomas brought his slaves with him, Ibrahima included. The African was not forced to attend. It is more likely that he looked forward to Sunday as an opportunity to escape the routine, and he must have enjoyed the social aspects of the day. Ibrahima and his family went to Baptist services, too. Isabella was a Baptist and had been since 1797, a date that makes her a Founding Mother of the Baptist church in Mississippi. Ibrahima may also have gone to Methodist meetings, for it was long a popular belief of Natchez Methodists, though an incorrect one, that Ibrahima and his wife were the two slaves of unknown name who joined that church with William Foster in 1799.

These references to Ibrahima's interest in the principal Protestant denominations are important. Religious services were more than a diversion for him. As he came to understand English, he was avid to have the Christian beliefs explicated. One who understood Islam and the Qur'an was on the way to understanding the Fulbe of Futa Jalon. Could Christianity be equally instructive about Natchez? His study of Islamic literature is assurance that he already knew the people and events of some Christian preaching, particularly the Old Testament favorites of Natchez. Adam and Eve, Abraham and Jacob, Moses and David, and many details about Jesus were known to him before he left Africa. To learn the rest became his ambition. Unable to read the Bible, he listened to it read and heard sermons on its teachings.

Mississippi Presbyterians certainly did not want slaves like Ibrahima as fellow members. In 1816 blacks could be seen hanging uncertainly around the doors of the church in Natchez, anxious to enter, yet afraid to do so as no place had been assigned to them. Wealthy and conservative Salem allowed no slave members. The Methodists were more receptive, and so were the Baptists, and it was these two faiths, particularly the latter, that appealed to Ibrahima. Among the early injunctions of the Mississippi Baptist Association had been for its white members to "deal with [the slaves] in brotherly love, according to the rules of the Gospel." From 1818 onward Ibrahima attended their services consistently, though maintaining his Islamic practices at the same time. He was impressed with what he heard, impressed enough to consider in time a profession of Christian belief. Conversion held out the hope of a closer relationship with his owner, one of the few steps he could take on his own in that direction. Doubtlessly, it would make him less outlandish to the community and even to his own family. Not only had Ibrahima been largely unable to pass on with effect his own beliefs to his children, his son Simon, who also attended the Baptist services, had become an extemporaneous speaker on Christian themes. Beyond these social attractions of conversion lay the spiritual ones, well raised in the emotional messages of born-again ministers who promised a better world for the worthy. The effect of it all was great on "a man of genuine piety." It opened a struggle between the African and the American inside him, a war for his ultimate allegiance.

The outcome may never have been in doubt. It is difficult to imagine the nephew of Karamoko Alfa queuing up for a communion wafer, and one need not try. "The Mahomedan priests fix a bias on the minds and form the character of their young disciples," wrote Mungo Park in 1799, "which no accidents of life can ever afterwards remove or alter." Ibrahima gives breath to that statement, for his conviction of the superiority of Islam was not destroyed, though he was violently pulled by currents of accommodation in other areas. There is no reason to present him as a distinguished *marabout,* weighing the points of metaphysical controversy between the faiths. He lacked the time and the knowledge for that. Well educated as he was, he was the full possessor of his people's superstitions and fears. He believed firmly in ghosts and in spirits, like the ones that, he claimed, prevented anyone from coming within twenty-five miles of the source of the Niger River.

But Ibrahima had definite objections on Quranic authority to several Christian claims, and a succession of Christian ministers and laymen, some counseling personally with him, were unable to overcome his deference to the sacred book of Islam. Ibrahima was prepared to give full credence to Jesus's miraculous birth, his divine mission, his miracles, and even his offering himself up as a sacrifice for the sins of the world. But he could not accept Jesus as the Son of God or agree that his place in Heaven was higher than Mohammad's. It followed from these beliefs, then, that the doctrine of the Trinity was unacceptable to him, too.

Ibrahima's statements on Christianity show his particular disappointment at the social consequences of conversion. It has already been stated that the Fulbe had scruples about enslaving their fellow Muslims. The conversion of slaves to the religion of their owners in Futa may not have brought automatic emancipation to all, but it did to many and it opened the door to the rest. The "curse of Ham," the color basis of slavery, had been laid aside in West Africa by the arguments of Ahmad Baba, a seventeenth-century scholar of Timbuktu, and by others. The practice of one Christian enslaving another at Natchez bothered only the minority of conscientious whites like William Foster. As early as 1820 even Methodist ministers in the county, heirs to the antislavery legacy of John Wesley, would be offering theological justifications for bondage. At Natchez the slave Christians prayed and attended church regularly, but this elevated them little in the regard of whites. Color and their degraded position made a state of true brotherhood unachievable.

Ibrahima's opinions remained firm, though he was not antagonistic in discussing them. "Prince speaks of the Christian religion with strong evidence of mature reflection," Griffin wrote about 1827. "I have conversed with him much upon the subject, and find him friendly disposed" toward Christianity. "[He] admires its [moral] precepts. His principal objections are, that *Christians do not follow them.* . . . He points out very forcibly the incongruities in the conduct of those who profess to be the disciples of the immaculate Son of God."

"I tell you," Ibrahima said to him, "the [New] Testament very good law; you [Christians] no follow it; you no pray often

enough; you greedy after money. [If] you good man, you join
the religion. [But] you want more land, more neegurs; you make
neegur work hard, make more cotton.

"Where you find dat in your law?"

Dr. Cox was—well, another case. He attended no churches, for
he admired independent thinkers like Rousseau, after whom one
of his sons was named, and he much preferred the classics to the
Bible. The doctor has been described as "a man of some eccentricity" by John F. H. Claiborne in his *Life and Times of Gen.
Sam Dale* (1860). The attribution lives on, though its meaning is
gone. Claiborne did not elaborate his characterization, and no one
now living knows what the idiosyncrasies were. The writer must
have had more in mind than Cox's religious views or the peculiar
riding habits that Ibrahima observed. Most likely it was a reference to the doctor's reckless self-confidence, to an unconvention-
ality produced by world travel, to a clever and uninhibited
manner. "D[ea]r Sir," he once wrote John Bisland (in one of his
few letters to survive), "I am like the Sons of Abraham, in want
of corn, and am obliged to send unto you (a second Egypt) for
30 or 40 bushels . . ." It was a waggish note for an infidel to send
to an old Presbyterian Scot, very much the thing a "village character" might do, but it got the corn. Adams County liked the
doctor, and, more important, it trusted him. "He was a respectable man," said Colonel Israel Trask, a neighbor, "and his word
might be relied upon."

Cox's professional reputation, quickly established at Washington, was extremely high. He was not what was termed "a regular-
bred physician," that is, one educated at a medical college. His
training had been done aboard British ships, apparently during
the war with France and the United States. To be precise, then,
he was just a "surgeon," though that designation, inferior to a
"physician," was little used on the frontier, where either was
called a "doctor." Cox was very good at his work. His specialty
was fevers, and he was generally the first doctor called in such
cases. The historian Claiborne described him as a man "of very
decided talents and great eminence in his profession. As a surgoen
and physician, he never had his superior in the South." Joseph D.
Shields, a contemporary of the doctor, who wrote a history of

Adams County, called him "the most distinguished physician near here." Both may exaggerate, but there is no doubting that Cox was one of the best of the eight doctors practicing at Natchez in 1812.

Irish by birth, Cox was second to none in feelings of pride in his adopted country. At a dinner honoring Judge Rodney, held following the British attack on the U.S.S. *Chesapeake* in 1807, he offered the toast, "The exports of the U.S.—May their enemies be the first!" Three years later, at another public entertainment (he missed few), he toasted, "The produce of the Mississippi Territory—May those who don't like cotton, have plenty of hemp!" Small wonder he found his way to a justice of the peaceship by 1811. When word of the declaration of war with Britain reached the Territory in the summer of 1812, he enlisted immediately as surgeon in the territorial brigade, and he served with the troops during the winter of 1812–13 at Baton Rouge.

It was at this time that his son William Rousseau enlivened things with his appearance. William, born in Rockingham County in 1793, had moved with his parents to Washington, but returned to North Carolina in 1810 to enter the University at Chapel Hill. By 1813 he was back in the state as surgeon's mate in the First Regiment of Mississippi Volunteers. Hostilities with the Creek Indians in the eastern part of the Territory began that summer. Early in September he made a breakneck ride that brought the first news to the territorial capital of the massacre at Fort Mims. In early 1815, when the wounded and ailing from the Battle of New Orleans arrived at Washington in six oxcarts, "Doctor" Cox the younger was hired as physician and surgeon for the convalescents. "Doctr. William R. Cox was employed . . . at a time when his services were much wanted," an officer wrote, and he performed "to every satisfaction." Among the notes given William in payment was a twenty-five-dollar draft on General Andrew Jackson.

The Coxes saw Ibrahima often in these years. One account states that the elder Cox bought him a pen and some paper for his own use. It would have been a precious gift if he did. But the same source goes willy-nilly on to say that he arranged for Mary Foster to teach him to write English. That would have been challenging work for mother Mary, since she never learned to write herself. One does wonder, however, if Cox, so convenient to the plantation, was the family doctor. There is no direct information on the question, but he was sometime-physician to the Bislands, Thomas's neighbors, and to reach that farm he had to take a road that passed within a few yards of Ibrahima's cabin. He never forgot who lived there. *"Le protecteur du Prince"* was the title a newsman gave the doctor. It implies an active, friendly agency in his behalf. As for anything more substantial, "Dr. Cox often renewed his application [to buy Ibrahima]," Gallaudet wrote, "but [always] in vain."

"He offered large sums for me," Ibrahima said, "but they were refused."

Their long friendship closed in December, 1816. The doctor fell ill with an unknown sickness that month and went rapidly down. He had recently found time for the latest Waverley novel and for Chateaubriand's *Travels,* but, true to form, he had not bothered to make out a will. Governor Williams, at his home on Sunday, the fifteenth, heard his oral testament.

"I wish my wife to have one half of all my estate, the other half for the use of my children and their education," the doctor told him.

Thirty minutes later he was dead.

The *Washington Republican and Natchez Intelligencer* printed his obituary on December 18.

COMMUNICATED

Died, on the 15th instant, at his residence in the town of Washington, Doctor JOHN C. COX, after an illness of four days. He died in his senses, with uncommon ease and composure of mind, not losing his vivacity of disposition.

The eminent rank he held in the science of his profession; and his planthropy [*sic*] and character in private life; and [his reputation as] a gentleman, together with his [widespread] general acquaintance, render any obituary remarks unnecessary.

Happiness, too, is inevitable.
—Albert Camus

5. "Unbroken in Body and Mind"

"Thirty years I labored hard," Ibrahima said in 1828. "The last ten years I have been indulged a good deal." The prince referred to his superannuation from the field in 1818. He was fifty-six then, and, although he had lost most of his teeth, his general health was still good and he showed promise of surviving for some time to come. He had long had the confidence of his owner. Now it meant a new level of plantation responsibility that a future acquaintance, Edward Everett, termed "employment in confidential trusts." With it came a precious amount of unsupervised time. "The Negro [Ibrahima] was not kept under much subjection as it respects his personal liberty" from that year, stated the *Louisiana Advertiser,* "and he frequently came to Natchez."

One of his new duties was to sell the plantation's vegetables at the market house, a brick-and-frame building located next to one of Thomas's lots. Here Ibrahima met hundreds of people, for most of Natchez passed the market stalls during the course of a morning. So many acquaintances were made by 1828 that Captain James Cook, editor of the Natchez *Ariel,* wrote in that year that Ibrahima had become well-known to the citizens of Natchez.

William Cox, who had opened a "Drug and Chemical Store" nearby, was one of his frequent visitors. There was a charming innocence about the young doctor, a Byronic man with ruddy cheeks and dark, bushy hair. In money matters he was heir to the family misfortune, spending twice what he made, and he went for years without entering a charge against any patient in his books.

85

Indifference to such a subject, the *raison d'être* of his peers, left him free to be himself. "His courtesies were never bartered for wealth or distinction," wrote a friend. A historian, reviewing the list of slaves, wharf rats, and urban detritus whose death certificates bear Cox's signature, is forced to agree it was not money that got him up each day.

Like his father, William was interested in Ibrahima and did not abandon the idea of purchasing him. Like his father, he could not have gotten the money to do so from his own pocket. William's attempt to settle his father's estate was so unsuccessful that a court ordered everything, from the house and the land to the kitchen furniture, sold from under his mother. Only the intervention of a solvent brother-in-law, Dr. Joseph Lyons, prevented that embarrassment. It was Lyons who lent William one thousand dollars in 1820 and took for it a mortgage on Caroline and Albert, the two slave children William owned. The doctor needed the money to establish his practice. Not able to repay it, he lost the children. Later that same year he misplaced a packet of papers while on a professional visit. Contents, four to five hundred dollars. Nor did things improve. A random dip into the circuit-court executions for the May, 1824, term turned up three suits against him, all for small amounts. He was lucky that spring that his bay horse, saddle, and bridle were not confiscated. And it is not surprising to learn that he figures in a volume of records from the local bank titled "Notes for Collection in the hands of the Bank Attorney."

"After [the elder] Dr. Cox died, his son offered a great price for me," Ibrahima said. Imagine the confusion if Thomas had suddenly said yes.

Luckily Ibrahima's future did not rest solely with him. A new and remarkable person named Andrew Marschalk had entered his life. Marschalk, son of a baker, was born of Dutch ancestry in New York State in 1767. The runaway apprentice of a New York printer, he served subsequently as an infantry officer during the Indian wars in Ohio in the early 1790s, and he came to Mississippi with the army at the time of the Spanish evacuation in 1798. He brought with him the first printing press in the Territory, a small mahogany unit with a thirty-pound font of type. In 1802 he settled permanently in Adams County, establishing the *Mississippi*

Herald, first in a line of free-hitting newspapers. In addition to holding the contracts for government printing at times, Marschalk sold books, quires of paper, and, in his early days, even a little "patent medicine, cheap." He published the *Washington Republican* at the territorial capital during the War of 1812 years, but afterward returned to Natchez, a more prosperous place. In 1819 he was editing the *Mississippi State Gazette* there.

With triple chin and button-popping maw, Colonel Marschalk is said to have resembled Benjamin Franklin. His hair was black, his eyes brown, and his fair complexion pitted with smallpox scars. He was a gregarious man, sunny in his disposition and quite friendly. "A communicative temper" was his main affliction, a love of talking to anyone who was willing to listen and to anyone who was not. In 1807 "a very, very secret" mission to Bayou Pierre was given to him by Governor Williams, and, "strange to tell," wrote a rival, "not more than one-third of the citizens of Natchez and [but] one-half of those whom he met on the way were told anything about it at all! Wonderful change!" Marschalk's prose was easy and self-confident, intelligent enough though not learned. For the right cause it was passionate, sarcastic, even vitriolic. The principal recipient of his bile was George Poindexter, Mississippi's first congressman and second governor. Marschalk accused Poindexter of sitting out the battle of New Orleans in 1815 by cuddling behind a wall in the lap of a manservant. The congressman, subsequently seeing him standing at the door of his home in Washington, picked up a brick and chased him inside, yelling, "You damned old son-of-a-bitch!" Marschalk would be beaten, fined, and jailed during the course of his career. For most of his life, however, "the Col. was satisfied," as Captain Cook wrote, "to move along with his 'Old Wheel Barrow,' as he called it, without troubling himself much about either affairs of church or state, or such as were of a literary character. He published the laws for the government and printed the advertisements for the people, he got paid for them, and that, very properly, was the extent of his ambition."

"The Galley Slave," the first imprint in Mississippi, was an appropriate piece for Marschalk to have issued, for he had had an experience with slavery of sorts himself. While visiting England as a young man, he had been seized by a press gang looking for crewmen for a frigate. Having no intention of swinging a hammock with the hands in the forecastle, he contrived to escape and return home, but the experience was a formative one that made him hate despotic power. The colonel owned one or two slaves, who cooked and kept house for his family. Though he expended vast efforts, he accumulated little, and he was always a plebeian compared to Thomas Foster and the other planters. When they expected it, he gave them chest-thumping defenses of the South's institutions that might have flowed more logically from the press of someone distended with acreage and fieldhands. However, when he might express himself without reserve, different sentiments surfaced. In a letter to a friend in Rhode Island, written after thirty years in Adams County, he referred to slavery as "a cruel and savage practice, the curse of our land."

It may have been as early as 1803 that Ibrahima met him, but the opportunity for a close acquaintanceship did not come until the African began frequenting the market. Marschalk's first wife had died in the interval, and, though he had remarried, his brick-and-stucco home at North Wall and Franklin Streets was a lonely place at times, in need of company the colonel found diverting. "Prince is really a most extraordinary man," he wrote a lady friend, "born to a kingdom—well-educated, for he now writes Arabic in a most elegant style—brought a slave into a foreign country. He has been faithful, honest, humble, and industrious." "I did not look upon Prince, or Ibrahim, as a mere biped slave," he wrote elsewhere, "but as a dignified captive, a man born to command, unjustly deprived of his liberty. . . ." The colonel, to use his own words, "was much in the habit of conversing with him on the customs and manners of his country, in which he is very intelligent." "The narrative of the captivity of this man previous to his leaving his native country—his rank and station there," he related, "is no doubt critically correct—it is the story he has uniformly told, and the general tenor of his conduct for many years, during which even the *suspicion* of an *untruth* never attached to him, his information respecting the history and geography of his country, taken in connection with recent circumstances, all go towards establishing its verity."

One day in 1820 or 1821 Ibrahima was in the colonel's printing office, next door to his house, looking longingly at the volumes on his bookshelf. "I produced to him a printer's grammar," Marschalk recalled, "containing, among other specimens of type from a type foundry, one in Arabic." Ibrahima was immensely interested when he saw the script and remarked "it was the first of his country writing he had seen since he left home." He requested permission to copy it, "which he did in a very neat and handsome style, producing a facsimile; he also rendered it in English."

Ibrahima's next remark was as momentous as any in his life, although it did not seem so at the time. "He expressed a wish to write a letter to his own country," Marschalk continued, "if he knew how to send it." Seldom short of answers, the colonel knew exactly how. Thomas D. Anderson, a friend of his from Pennsylvania, was then a United States consul in North Africa. Anderson could forward it from there. "I . . . assured Prince I would send his letter for him," Marschalk stated.

Ibrahima's reaction was unexpected. He refused to write anything. "Although repeatedly urged by me," the colonel said, "he did not write the letter." The year passed; 1822 came, 1823, 1824, 1825 and still no letter, though the colonel suggested it often. Ibrahima had forgotten so much grammar by his fourth decade in slavery that only sections of the Qur'an came to him effortlessly; he could not have written a proper letter home. But rusty calligraphy alone cannot explain his reluctance.

Did it come from a misunderstanding of where "his own country" was? Marschalk believed he was a Moor, and, in fact, "belong[ed] to the royal family of Morocco." Ibrahima himself said so, the colonel wrote. In the closing years of the century French imperialists in Futa would claim that deception was a principal trait of Ibrahima's people. It was at least a national problem, for in proverbs and maxims long antedating the French, condemnation of treachery and imposture are abundant. "The lie comes quickly to a ripe age," "he who digs a hole will be the first to fall into it," "if day-light came suddenly one night, we would find that hyneas aren't the only evil creatures on the loose," and so on. Could Ibrahima, famished for attention, have observed the colonel mistake Futa for Morocco, found the error convenient, and adopted the place? The conjecture has a virtue. It explains why no letter was written that day or could ever be written. Ibrahima was no better known in Morocco than Marschalk. A reply would embarrass and discredit him.

This interpretation of motives is flawed, however. Ibrahima was soon to have an interview with Cyrus Griffin, a man who knew something Marschalk did not, the difference between a Moor and a Pullo. Since Griffin learned from him precisely what his country was, Ibrahima must not have been rusing. Morocco, it appears, was the colonel's own notion, Ibrahima supplying, and truthfully, the fact of his royal family. Hampered by the prince's imperfect English, Marschalk let Islamic beliefs and literacy in Arabic mislead him. It may have been a fortunate mistake if it enhanced the colonel's interest, but it was not a purposeful misrepresentation. So Ibrahima, conscious of no deception, did not delay writing—in this case to the wrong country—for fear of exposure.

Why he did delay is speculative. Could it have been the fear of offending Thomas, of seeming restless or unappreciative of the scraps of distinction thrown his way? Could it have been that he considered the gesture futile? Isabella did, the colonel said. She was "unwilling to believe that there was a reality in his project of being liberated" by writing home. Would such a letter even be delivered, or be answered, and what might the answer be after so many years and so many turns in fortune, not only in Natchez, but in Futa, too? Was it worth awakening the old hopes, resurrecting the old hurts, or was it better to forget it? Was it better instead to draw the blanket tightly on up over his head and just die?

Thomas was wealthy now and enjoying it. "He had accumulated quite a fortune," wrote a granddaughter, and his plantation "became famous for the great number of acres under cultivation and the number of Negro slaves which he owned." A generation of African muscle had hacked the forested grant lands of 1788 so clear by the 1820s that the farm came to be called "Foster Fields." Mahogany and rosewood furniture from New Orleans, clocks and decorative tiles from Europe graced the house. Expensive carriages and coach horses stood await. For the children of Thomas's old age, there was a complete indulgence in money,

servants, and opportunity—everything he had lacked. "Old
Thomas Foster gave his children good advantages," a family historian wrote—an education at the Elizabeth Academy in Washington, steamboat cruises, trips to fashionable spas in Virginia
and Alabama. When his youngest daughter, Caroline, married in
November, 1824, Thomas gave her a set of house servants as a
wedding present.

"As far back as I can recollect," wrote James Pennington, a
slave for many years in Maryland, "it was a remark among slaves
that every generation of slaveholders are [sic] more and more
inferior." His statement has relation to the Fulbe saying, "The
dog carried on the shoulder does not take to the chase." A few of
Thomas's children turned out to be shrewd like him or strong-
willed like their mother. Levi, who had moved to Louisiana,
became a successful planter and militia officer and in 1823 began
seven years in the state legislature. The smartest thing he may
have done, however, was to leave home. Those who stayed behind got caught in some sort of mire.

Take Ephraim and Cassandra, for example. Ephraim Foster
was an awkward, talented man whose tall frame was topped by a
beaver hat and silver spectacles. Generous and easygoing by
nature, he would not punish his most truculent slaves. In 1807 he
wed Thomas's daughter Cassandra. Unhappily for Ephraim she
was absolutely devoted to her father, "whose parental kindness &
pecuniary bounty were alike ample," she wrote of herself, "and so
enjoyed by her previous to sd. marriage as to render her situation
comfortable & happy." Nevertheless she was married and was, so
she claimed, "a kind, affectionate, and dutiful wife." Ephraim, for
his part, attempted to earn the family's regard by ferrying Thomas
into town, collecting his rents, even fetching his other daughters'
marriage licenses for him.

The son-in-law showed an independent streak when the couple
moved to Wilkinson County before the War of 1812, but, failing
there, they soon returned to Foster Fields. In January, 1821,
Thomas gave them two Coles' Creek farms, "a very considerable
estate." Ambitious for a future of his own, Ephraim sold them
and instead entered nine bonds totaling five figures to buy a beautifully developed plantation with livestock, tools, orchard, and resident slave population. The place was at the creek about a mile

from Washington on the Natchez road. The deal meant mortgaging everything he owned and much he did not, for he promised to deliver at the landing 140,000 pounds of clean, merchantable cotton each March for the next nine years for the account of his lien-holder.

By the summer of 1823 the ambition lay in ruins. The responsibility of fulfilling his bonds was too great and the pressures to duplicate the success of his father-in-law unbearable. Hit by poor harvests and a chaotic domestic situation, his personality began to change. "Ephraim contracted those habits of excessive intemperance and debauchery," wrote Cassandra, who went on to refer to herself in the third person, "which rendered [her] life most unhappy and miserable—that instead of treating her as a wife, she then became the object of his most wanton and cruel abuse. . . . Her unremitting exertions to reclaim him by an increased devotion & kindness . . . seemed to encourage and aggravate *the mad career* which Ephraim was running. . . . He was guilty of the most extreme cruelty towards her, so that her personal safety and even her life was much endangered. . . . He was repeatedly guilty of the crime of adultery—in cohabitating for many days at a time with lewd & dissolute women." About February, 1824, she came home to her father, for which Ephraim posted her in the local newspapers as a runaway. When he came to the plantation to claim the horse she had ridden away, Thomas rushed out of the house and assaulted him. The planter appears to have gotten the best of the fight, as Ephraim promptly sued him for damages.

Thomas hired Governor Poindexter's law firm to obtain a divorce, but none was necessary. In 1824 Ephraim's health declined. No longer having a place to live, he had taken lodgings in Natchez. A seasonal fever hit him, and the usual doses of quinine were ineffective. As winter came, he burned firewood bought on credit and rode around Natchez in a rented gig. By Christmas he was too ill to write his own name. Strangers and their servants saw him slip away in January, 1825. He did not die, however, before disinheriting Cassandra, his last known act. She may not have minded, for she remarried within the month. The family had no objections whatever to her new husband, except the matter of his allegedly having one wife already.

There were other troubles, too, like the violent death of Thomas's son-in-law David McIntosh. He was an affectionate and high-tempered man, fond of hunting and an expert shot. Allowing his children a dip of snuff in order to watch them sneeze was great sport for him. "He was a bottle man and proud of the fact." One evening David attempted to ride his horse across the creek when it was full and carrying everything which stood on its banks. He did not make it to the other side. "That was a dreadful night," a descendant wrote. "All night long watchfires were kept burning up and down the creek and search parties patrolled its banks." The next morning David's body was found wedged between some logs. His skull was crushed. A slave woman, name unknown, who held a grudge against him, was questioned in regard to his death. It seems that she had thrown a board in the water toward him as he gestured for help. Was it a handhold to stop him from sinking or a cudgel to crack open his head? The Fosters could never decide.

Son James had been born on the plantation about 1804, a stout and athletically built man, six feet tall, with black hair and a full, round face. A stammer was sometimes detectable in his speech. He was "one of the finest looking men in the country," an acquaintance wrote, "a member of a wealthy and respectable family." It must have been while living with Levi in St. Mary Parish that he met Susan Alfhari, who was to be his wife. At least she was a native of Attakapas, fifteen years old, and very beautiful. They were married in June, 1833, and came back to the plantation at year's end.

One day the following March, James asked her to take a walk with him. As they passed down to a bayou below the mill, he began whipping Susan on her back and thighs. In a moment he beat and kicked her to death. "Her neck and shoulders . . . from one point to the other as far as [I] could see," stated William Foster, who viewed her body, "[were] all black and blue [and] some streaks of blood [were] flowing slowly or oozing out of her left nostril." F. L. Claiborne found her left arm broken and "every part of her body [with] blisters . . . produced by the whip." James said that he had "switched" her to gain confession of an infidelity he suspected, that she fell into a fit and died. He carried her to the cabin of Ibrahima's son Prince, then to the house. Bridget, Prince's wife, assisted in dressing her body. The slaves buried her the next day in the family cemetery.

Suspicions were aroused, however. James was arrested and charged with her murder, but the indictment against him was quashed due to a flaw it contained. The son was told by the court he was free to go. When he left the courthouse in Natchez, a mob of two or three hundred was waiting. It seized him and conducted him to a field on the outskirts of the city, "where," according to a newspaper writer, "Judge Lynch usually presides and where no flaws in an indictment are suffered to interfere with the administration of justice." There he was stripped, beaten, lashed, partially scalped, and tarred and feathered. "The mob believed he was a monster at heart, and were determined that his external appearance should correspond with the inner man." Then he was marched to the beat of a drum through the streets of the city. Some wanted to brand him on each cheek and on the forehead, others shouted, "Hang him, hang him," or "To the river, to the river," "but," the newspaper account continued, "owing to the lateness of the hour, this was dispensed with." James was just alive enough to flee. He did, and never returned to Foster Fields.

Thomas Foster, Jr., while still in his early twenties, owned plantations in two counties and assisted his father in the management of the homestead. He admired his brother Levi and was devoted to him, but he was little like him in character. Less often was he found at work than at the grocery near the bridge, "his usual haunt," where he got drunk and stayed drunk for days. Intemperance did not help his gambling, either, for he lost his carriage and the better part of a valuable slave at the tables there. Such a scion was not prime matrimonial material, but he was wealthy and not without other charms, so, in 1820, he wedded Susan Carson, thirteen- or fourteen-year-old daughter of the Reverend James Carson of Natchez. The Carsons were new to Mississippi, having recently arrived from New York.

Thomas the younger was fascinated with Susan and that was his problem—not Susan, his wife, but Susan, or Susy, his slave. His marriage had seemed normal until December, 1823, when Susan Foster went to stay at her father's in Natchez during a confinement for pregnancy. She was surprised when Thomas seemed less affectionate to her on his visits, if he visited at all. Returning to the plantation, she discovered why. She found Thomas and Susy at the quarters in Susy's cabin and in Susy's bed. "Dumb-struck and almost motionless," she confronted him nevertheless. "He expressed the deepest and most heartfull repentance for his conduct," but, rather than bedding with her as before, he took to sleeping on the gallery of the house, pretending the weather was too warm for them to sleep together. Some time later Susan saw Susy dart out of her cabin. She went inside and found Thomas scrambling into the loft to conceal himself. He left the plantation, found his courage at the grocery, and came home to pull a sword on Susan and chase her from the house, swearing he would kill her.

Their marriage was failing fast in the spring of 1824, the same time Ephraim and Cassandra hit the shoals. By the summer following, "his intimacies with this base wretch," wrote Susan in a petition, were "undisguised and open." He slept with Susy at the quarters and did not care who knew it. Sarah, his mother, "expostulated with him and asked him if he were not ashamed." He replied only, "so she is . . . so she is." Thomas senior manifested "evident displeasure," but with no results. His son would promise to reform and forget Susy, his eyes glistening in sincerity, yet a week later he would begin anew. He seemed unable and, at last, unwilling to change. He gave Susy his wife's clothes, bought her dresses, and gave her parties. He treated her "with all the kindness and generosity of a wife." Susan called the affair base and degenerate, but Susy meant more to Thomas than she, their children, his family, or the opinion of society. At that price the relationship earns its true characterization. Thomas was in love.

About October, 1826, the pot boiled over. The old planter had advised his daughter-in-law to go to Natchez and stay with her father until the son came to his senses. She did so, and while there got a message from her husband asking her to visit him. Agreeably, she rode out with her father, Reverend Carson, a pillar of Old Zion so devout that when he became deaf in his old age he continued to attend church though not hearing a word spoken there for a decade. They found Thomas napping in the woods. "He appeared to have been drinking pretty freely," Susan wrote, "denied having sent for her . . . told her to shut up and go abou' her business." When she went back to the house to pack some belongings at Sarah's suggestion, he followed her and stopped her from taking her bonnet and bandbox. He thought Susy might want it. An argument with his mother ensued, after which Thomas pushed Susan out of the room, saying she "must be gone, that he wanted nothing more of her—that all he wanted was his children."

"What do you want with them?" Sarah asked.

"To cut their throats," he replied, if he could do no better by them.

A different day, a different man. He got ill and, while confined to his bed, became remorseful. He sent for Susan and agreed to sell Susy if she would come back to him. A bill of sale was executed at his bedside, passing title to his father. Colonel William Barnard and William Collins, two brothers-in-law, witnessed it. Forty-eight hours later, "when he had so far recovered as to be able to walk out and had got over the fears of dying which had before haunted him," he changed his mind again. He tried to retrieve the deed, but Thomas senior refused to let him have it. It was then the son learned that Colonel Barnard intended to put Suzy in irons and carry her out of the county. Thomas became distressed, restless, and irritable. A three-day drunk at the bridge followed. "One morning after a long sleep and restoration from a fit of drunkenness," Susan wrote, "he arose from his bed, pulled a dirk knife from his pocket, and commenced raging and storming about the house about Susy & repeatedly swore that if she was sent away, he would kill two or three of the family." He was finally calmed, but he remained unable to think of anything else. Later he bolted up in bed at night, "under the impulse of strong and violent feelings," and cried, according to his wife, "They have stolen Susy from me!"

Into these tormented lives a final factor needs introduction: the very good possibility that Susy was Ibrahima's daughter. Her paternity cannot be established definitively from extant records, but a case for the idea builds itself. Ibrahima had four daughters. Their names and histories are not known, but they were the same ages as Thomas's children and grew up with them. For a time at least they would have been unattached young women on the plantation. Certainly, Ibrahima's daughters comprised a large percentage of the single females at Foster Fields, and Susy came from a plantation family; at least there is no record of her having been purchased from outside. A naming relationship is relevant, too. Ibrahima's son Simon had his first-born daughter in 1824, a year when Susy was doing well at the farm. He named the girl Susy, particularly appropriate if that was his sister's name. Farm antecedents can be traced in the names of Simon's other children, and there were no other Susans in the quarters or on the plantation except the son's wife, a relative stranger.

And is it coincidental that in October, 1826, the month that Susy headed for a brutal exile, Ibrahima appeared at Colonel Marschalk's office, ready to write that long-delayed letter home? Other things could have influenced him, it is true. That freakishly warm autumn had been unsettling for everyone, as yellow fever took 150 lives in Natchez and reached well out into the countryside plantations. Perhaps the general mortality and Thomas, Sr.'s age and health renewed his fears of the day when his children would be scattered into the hands of the heirs, some of whom clearly were homicidal. Perhaps, too, it was simply that Ibrahima, having been his own master once, was never content being anything else. Given these concerns, an effort at liberation seems inevitable.

Only the timing does not. Why write in 1826 when he was no less concerned for himself and his children in 1820 or 1821? The mind of an African in his situation never got far from those topics in any year. The peculiarity of his sudden resoluteness, of his willingness to step over whatever had previously restrained him emerging at the very time that Susy swapped her bracelets for chains is revealing. It must have been the product of his rage and frustration. Even as a slave he deserved better. Anyone who had served a master in Futa in the positions he had held under Thomas would be an *ndiimaajo,* "a slave of the house." Such a person earned by faithfulness and residence the right for his children never to be ironed and dragged away. A liaison between Thomas and Susy would not only be acceptable at home but respectable, too—an illustration of the assimilation in Fulbe society that rewarded service and brought ability to the top. Sori himself had taken a slave as a wife and reared with her a free and honorable family. Not so at Natchez.

Ibrahima's value at Foster Fields had contributed to his family's security over the years. Except for one son gone to St. Mary Parish, his children had been kept together. He had been able to be more than a biological father to them. His feelings for them were deep-rooted and integral to him. Nothing could have shredded him so much as a parent or a person than what was happening to Susy. Writing a letter may seem ineffectual in such a crisis, but it did make sense. If Thomas's son and namesake couldn't save Susy for all the love and fear he could arouse, Ibrahima could not either. The letter was an outlet for his hostility. And it was something more. It was the most intelligent response he could make, for it looked beyond the bitterness of the moment to what next year and the next and the next might hold.

At the time, Colonel Marschalk was absorbed in an argument with the Natchez selectmen over his refusal to do city printing on Sunday, but he was as ready as ever to help. Ibrahima wrote the only thing he remembered well, the whole of it from the Qur'an. What passage he quoted is not known, as no copy of the manuscript was kept. Taking it, Marschalk wrote a cover letter addressed to Thomas B. Reed, a United States senator from Mississippi then in town. His note reads in full:

> Natchez, 3 Oct. 1826
>
> Dear Sir,
>
> The enclosed letter in Arabic was written in my presence by a venerable old slave named Prince, belonging to Mr. Thomas Foster of this county. I have known him about fifteen years and can bear full testimony to his very correct deportment. He claims to belong to the royal family of Morocco, and the object of his letter, as he states it to me, is to make inquiry after his relations and with the hope of joining them. I have undertaken to endeavor to forward his letter for him and therefore beg leave to commit it to your care, with a request that you will lend your aid to the old man's wishes.
>
> And. Marschalk

Thomas B. Reed had come to Natchez in 1811, a poor immigrant from Kentucky. By 1826 he had climbed high enough to be elected to fill the balance of a term in the Senate caused by a resignation. Delicately built and urbane, Reed was an attorney, "haughty in manner and ostentatious in dress." "He lacked moral courage and promptness of action," an editor wrote, "but none doubted his essential kindness." He would be absent from the state for the better part of a year when he left, and, since the election for a full term would occur in his absence, he wished to do himself every bit of good he could before leaving. A dinner was given on November 2 on the occasion of his departure at the Steam-Boat Hotel, attended by Dr. Cox, among others. There Reed gave a rambling speech on the subject of internal improvements, no doubt made bearable by the thirty-three toasts with which his audience had fortified itself previously. Afterward the Senator left for Washington, D.C., carrying in his portmanteau the letter that he intended to deliver to the State Department.

Susy departed, too, but in unexpected happiness. The son's adamance got her released from her chains. It was not long before she had the run of the plantation again. Thomas, Sr., determined to resolve things, told his son "to settle upon committing to choose one of two alternatives, either to give up this girl Susy and go home with his wife and children . . . or declare his intention to the contrary." With what Susan described as "much serious and apparent determination," he chose the latter. On Christmas Day, 1826, he went looking for Susy and found her at the bridge. Taking her and the rest of his slaves with him, he moved to his plantation in Warren County. There is no record of his ever having seen his wife or children again.

On March 14, 1827, Ibrahima's quotation and Marschalk's letter reached the escritoire of Thomas Mullowny, the United States consul in Tangier, Morocco. Mullowny, a native of Pottsgrove, Pennsylvania, had been appointed to his post in 1820 by James Monroe. He had witnessed the last years of the reign of the great Mulay Suleiman II and the succession of his nephew Abd al-Rahman II. Morocco, as President John Quincy Adams had told him, "was the first to set the example of abandoning the general practice of piratical depredations against the Christian nations." Slavery of Christians had also been abandoned formally by treaty. An important aspect of Mullowny's job was securing the release of any Americans cast away on Moroccan shores. Ibrahima's document was a bizarre twist on the ordinary, then, and certainly an opportunity. It was something to do, as well. The consul had not heard from the Secretary of State since 1825.

On the day he received the communications, Mullowny visited the emperor's *pasha* and laid them before him. "I received through the department of State a letter written in Arabic," he wrote. "The intention of the letter[-writer] appears to me to prove he is a Moor, as [the text] is taken from the Qur'an to excite an exertion for his relief. The documents appear to be clear of deception." No hint of Ibrahima's nationality could have been gained from the letter any more than an excerpt from a Latin Bible would indicate to what country in Europe or America the writer belonged. The text identified Ibrahima only by his faith, then, not his nationality. The large, cursive letters of his hand could have belonged to a subject of the empire. The impression was that they did. Abd al-Rahman II acted with unaccustomed speed. He wanted the writer—possibly a Moroccan, but undeniably a Muslim—free and would even pay for it. "The *pasha* tells me on his arrival here at Tangiers," noted the consul, "all expenses will be immediately reimbursed."

"I submit an opinion to the Honorable Secretary of State," Mullowny wrote to Washington on the subject. "By liberating and sending this man home, it will in the future yield a benefit to unfortunate persons who may fall by accident in the power of subjects belonging to this Empire. . . . I do most earnestly wish this man to be sent here to me, that he may be restored to his King and family. . . . If the Honorable Secretary of State condescends to agree with my opinion, the man can be sent to our Consul at Gibraltar, from thence to me. His liberty would give me an important power, and prove Muslims have more gratitude with other good qualities than they are generally allowed by travellers, who suppress their virtues, which will overbalance their vices." Plaintively, Mullowny added the thought, "The funds I am allowed, I regret to say, will forever check and never produce a generous respect from men in general."

The counsul's letter was dated March 24, 1827. It arrived in Washington on June 5 of the same year. Henry Clay, the Secretary of State, docketed it, "The propriety of a purchase of the slave & of sending him home is respectfully recommended. H.C." The chief clerk of the State Department, Daniel Brent, then took the letter to the White House. It reached President Adams early in July. He wrote in his diary on July 10:

> Mr. Brent came for papers relating to an African, who appears to be a subject of the Emperor of Morocco, but is a slave in Georgia [*sic*]. He procured a letter to be written for him to the Emperor of Morocco, by whom it was communicated to Mr. Mullowny. . . . He has sent a translation of it here, with an earnest recommendation that the Government of the United States should purchase the man and send him home as a complimentary donation to the Emperor. I requested Mr. Brent to write to Georgia and ascertain the price for which he could be purchased, and, if practicable, to carry into effect the wish of Mr. Mullowny.

On July 12 the substance of his concerns was forwarded to Colonel Marschalk in a letter from Brent. "In consequence of the interest which you appear to take in the case," Brent wrote, "[the President] has directed me to request information from you on the following points, viz. 1st. Would Mr. Foster be willing to sell the slave with a view to his return to his native country? 2nd. If so, what price would be demanded for him? On receiving your answers to these interrogatories, the President will be enabled to determine whether he can interpose in any manner tending to promote the object which you desire."

Marschalk received this letter in August, and, as he wrote later, "I took the earliest opportunity of making the necessary inquiries." He found the planter still unwilling to sell. But, Thomas said, he had already told Ibrahima that if he could find someone to take him to Futa, he could go. The possibility of that happening had been nil until now. But, with a chance at hand, he still was agreeable. He had spent too much time with Ibrahima not to admire him, and he felt a certain generosity toward the man who had helped him make it to the court of Croesus. Marschalk reaped the result. "I immediately waited on Mr. Foster," the colonel reported, and "he promptly replied that he had signified to Prince (the slave) some years ago, his willingness to permit him to return to his native country, if it could be affected without any expense to him (Mr. F.) and that he was *at present willing to give him his liberty.*"

There was one condition. Ibrahima should enjoy that liberty only in Africa and not in the United States. Possession of it here, Marschalk continued, "might operate to his (Mr. F.) inconvenience, by an improper influence over his children remaining with him as slaves." Curiously, the planter refused to make a written declaration of his sentiments. "Notoriously a Jackson man," did Thomas loathe the Adams-Clay administration that much, or was he just above condescension to this business? "Mr. Foster declined complying with my request to signify his wishes . . . in writing." There seemed little enough reason why, the colonel merely observing, "he is a planter of very retired habits."

But Marschalk felt odd giving assurances about other people's property. He decided to ask Henry Dangerfield, "a young gentleman of the Bar, of highest respectability," to visit the plantation and get a statement. "Agreeable to your request," Dangerfield wrote Marschalk on August 20, "I yesterday afternoon called upon Mr. Thomas Foster Esq. . . . Mr. F. stated to me . . . that he is now, and has been for some years past willing for Prince to go to his alleged home. That he now is, and during that time has been, ready to resign Prince into the hands of any one who will undertake to return him, or attempt to return him, home; and that he will not demand any price in return. But will give him without any price to any one who will thus undertake to carry him to Africa, upon condition that he should not remain free or at liberty in any part of the United States. That should the attempt to take Prince to Africa be unsuccessful, and he be returned into the United States, he shall in that case be returned to him, and not suffered to remain at large in any place of the United States, but be a slave to Mr. F. again. Mr. F. insists upon this condition because he is persuaded that Prince's present situation under him is a better one than any other he could find in the U.S. and that Prince's being at liberty would make him troublesome, burthensome, and mischievous to others among whom he may be, without contributing to his comfort and happiness.

"I wished Mr. Foster, as you requested me," Dangerfield concluded, "to address a letter to you for the President containing the above. He was, however, indisposed, and thought the statement he made to me and you would suffice—and requested me to say

so to you. I am well acquainted with Mr. Foster and you may
safely rely upon what he has said."

The colonel went ahead. On August 20 he sent Dangerfield's
letter and a lengthy one of his own to Henry Clay. They conveyed adequately the planter's position. Marschalk's letter also
requested a New Testament in Arabic for Ibrahima. "Although
by birth and education a strict Mahometan," the colonel wrote,
"he expresses the most reverential respect for the Christian religion, the moral precepts of which he appears to be well informed
[about] and speaks of having read some of the Christian scrip-
ture of the Old Testament in his own country in the Arabic language. He has very often inquired of me the possibility of procuring a New Testament (or in his own language) 'the history of
Jesus Christ.' " Marschalk closed with heartfelt rhetoric: "Permit
me, sir, to tender through you, to the President, my most respect-
ful acknowledgements for the benevolent interest he has been
pleased to take in the cause of this very interesting old man, who
has been thirty-nine long years deprived of that inestimable bless-
ing which the citizens of our happy country so abundantly enjoy
and who after so long a period of slavery and privation in a distant country, hails with the most pleasing anticipation a return to
the land of his fathers—and invokes blessings in his daily prayers,
on that country whose bounty is about to confer on the remnant
of his days the boon of liberty."

Ibrahima, on whom this storm broke mightily, was yet alive.
He began to show more stir and spring than he had in decades.
"Though sixty-five years of age," wrote someone who saw him
then, "he has the vigor of the meridian of life." He bubbled with
good will and gratitude, as though what was happening was
wiping away every ugly memory of the past. "He will be happy
—he speaks to me upon this subject with a countenance beaming
with joy," an acquaintance wrote, "if he can return to his native
country, live the friend of the white man, and die in the land of his
fathers." "He expressed feelings of the most profound friendship
and respect to all the white men of America, and most particularly those of the State of Mississippi," Marschalk observed. At
Natchez, Ibrahima told him, "all have been his friends, and that
he has by their general kindness to him known slavery only by

name." Even that last barrier began to crack. "He is so transported by gratitude for the efforts of Christians to effect his liberation," said the poetess Caroline Thayer, "that he listens favorably,
and there is a good prospect of his embracing Christianity." "In a
recent conversation with him on this subject," Marschalk
remarked, "I expressed a wish that he would yet become a Christian.

"He promptly replied that 'he thought he would.' "

Summer gave way to fall, and fall to winter, without a reply.
The mail sacks held no letter to Marschalk with the neat frank of
"H. Clay" in its corner. The colonel became anxious. An election
was coming, and he was an antiadministration editor. The very
week he had mailed the letter to the Secretary of State he had also
written in the *Statesman* that "the present administration origi-
nated in corruption." Later he stated that Clay seemed less ani-
mated by good sense and patriotism than by "Pittsburgh porter
and 'old Kaintuck.' " It could not be wise, then, to celebrate before the victory was in hand. One could expect the civility of a
response, however. On December 13, 1827, two more letters for
Ibrahima were written. One was from Marschalk to the Secretary,
inquiring about the letters of August 20. The second was from a
newcomer, Cyrus Griffin.

Griffin was a crippled and friendless young attorney whom the
colonel had introduced to Ibrahima earlier in the year. The prince
had been twelve years in slavery when Cyrus was born in
Andover, Massachusetts, in 1800. A sixth-generation New Eng-
lander, he grew up in the shadow of Old South Church, where his
father, Jonathan, a joiner and tavernkeeper, mended the windows,
set the gravestones, and rang the bell. Zerviah, his mother, was a
seamstress. The death of his father when he was fourteen cut
short Cyrus's formal education, and he was sent to Boston.
During the next few years he worked for a merchant, a printer, a
tailor, a shoemaker, and another merchant, but "unsteady habits,"
plus a "melancholy dejection of mind" gave him but his labor for
his pains. Fleeing a subsequent teaching post in Reading, Pennsylvania, when faced with debt imprisonment, he turned up in
Natchez in 1826, ready to practice law. I. M. Patridge, antebellum historian of the press in Mississippi, called him "a brilliant,

caustic, and satirical writer." Captain Cook, the *Ariel* editor and a good-natured rival, conceded him "intelligent and well read." Still another wrote, "Mr. Griffin was a gentleman of accomplished and well-stored mind, and secured in point of talents and integrity the high respect of all who knew him."

Cyrus was accessible to Ibrahima, having taken an office in September just opposite the market house. He was congenial, too, a man who publicly advocated less punishment of slaves and condemned the shooting of runaways as if they were wild animals. "Born and educated in the North," he wrote, referring to himself in the editorial plural, "it is naturally supposed that we possess the prejudices known to exist there against slavery. —It is true, we believe it to be an evil—a curse entailed upon us. . . ." As for Ibrahima, the young attorney developed what Marschalk termed "a peculiar interest in the welfare of the old man." He was amazed that the African, who was older than his father would have been, were he still living, had been able to remain, as Edward Everett phrased it, "unbroken in body and mind." "We have all seen him bearing up against the sad mutation [of his fortunes] with philosophic fortitude," Cyrus wrote. "We know him to be a man of intelligence, and what is more, a man of integrity. Such a character is sufficient to interest us. We freely acknowledge we have sympathized in his misfortune.

"At my own request, Prince often visits me. He is extremely modest, polite, and intelligent. I have examined him in the geography of his own and contiguous countries—their political condition, forms of government, manners and customs, religion, &c. &c. His knowledge is accurate to the minutest degree, so far as I have compared it with the best authorities." Cyrus took notes on Ibrahima's every remark, from the course of the Niger to the criminal code of the Fulbe and their methods of execution. The prince had talked readily of Africa to Thomas and the colonel over the years. When unleashed, he was just as garrulous as Marschalk, and in Cyrus he found the perfect listener. Never had he met a readier ear and never had he filled it so fully.

Most of what Ibrahima told Griffin was true, if colored by the exaggerations of old age. But he stretched the blanket considerably when he claimed that his grandfather had been king of Timbuktu and then moved his own birthplace there from Timbo.

Timbuktu, unvisited by European explorers in 1827, was an object of mystery to Westerners. Ibrahima assumed a little mystery himself by claiming it. Still, Griffin did not talk with Ibrahima long before he discovered that the prince was no native of Morocco. Marschalk was preparing his August 20 response to the State Department at the time and had wished Ibrahima to meet with the attorney before he put the letter in final form. "[Ibrahima] was sent by Col. M. to my office," Griffin wrote. "I immediately discovered the Col.'s error in relation to the place of Prince's birth—that he was from the interior of Africa, instead of Morocco as stated by the Colonel. I immediately suggested to [Marschalk] the necessity of informing the President of the mistake, as there would be less reason for the interference of the Government (if indeed the Government would interfere at all, of which I had strong doubt) in relation to a personage, however important, from the interior of Africa, than a native of one of the Barbary states, with which it was of the highest importance that we maintain friendly relations." The colonel received his discovery with indifference. Why interfere? he asked Cyrus. If the President was willing to help Ibrahima, let him proceed. Marschalk sent his letter anyway, simply omitting any reference to Morocco. "Receiving no answer," Cyrus continued, "he became ceaseless in his importunities for me to write. For obvious reasons I declined so to do. . . ."

At last the attorney agreed to send a letter to the American Colonization Society, a private organization whose goal was to rid the United States of its black population by sending it to Africa. If the government would not take him overseas, very possibly the Society could. Liberia, its colony, was only three hundred miles from Futa, and Ibrahima knew the country, having traveled there when young. "I address you in behalf of an unfortunate man, a native of Africa, who has been held in slavery in this state for thirty-nine years," he wrote on December 13. "Believing he might be of incalculable importance to the Colony at Liberia, I have no hesitation in offering you the suggestions of my own mind. The person to whom I allude, we familiarly call Prince. His real name is Abduhl Rahhahman." The letter went on to recount Ibrahima's early life, the war with the Hebohs, and the meeting with Dr. Cox. "I have . . . explained to Prince the object of the establishment at Liberia. He speaks with gratitude of the benevolent design; and, taking into view the very short distance between that place and his own country, he feels assured he can be of very great service to that colony. I now commend him to the favourable consideration of your Society. I cannot persuade myself but that you will seize with avidity an instrument that appears so completely adapted to your wants."

There was nothing to do now but wait.

The letter came in February, 1828. It was from Clay and bore the date of January 12.

> Department of State
> Washington, D.C.
>
> Sir,
>
> Your letters, both of the 13th ultimo., and the 20th of August last, have been received. The President is obliged by your attention to the subject of the Moorish slave, now in possession of Mr. Thomas Foster. The object of the President being to restore Prince, the slave mentioned, to his family and country for the purpose of making favorable impressions in behalf of the United States, there is no difficulty in acceding to the conditions presented by Mr. Foster, which I understand to be, that Prince shall not be permitted to enjoy his liberty in this country, but be sent to his own free from expense to Mr. Foster, who is pleased to ask nothing for the manumission of Prince on these conditions.
>
> I have, therefore, to request that you will complete the humane agency which you have so kindly undertaken, by calling upon Mr. Foster, assuring him the above conditions shall be complied with, and receiving the custody of Prince from him. You will please to send Prince to this city, either by the river or by sea, as you may determine to be the most convenient, for the purpose of his being transported to his native country. . . .
>
> I am, with great respect,
>
> Your obedient Serv't,
> H. Clay

On Friday, February 22, Thomas and Ibrahima rode into Natchez. For both of them the trip was a closing of circles, a strange denouement of the day they had ridden out of the city in August, 1788, when youth and uncertainty were before them. Now both were old and worn, and could count what time remained to them in months rather than years. At the printing office Thomas gave the colonel a deed in trust for the prince. "I, Thomas Foster, a citizen of Adams County in the State of Mississippi," the document read, "at present the owner of the slave named Prince, have this day delivered unto Andrew Marschalk of the city of Natchez and state aforesaid, the custody of the said slave Prince, for the sole and only purpose of his being transported to his native country by the government of the United States. . . ." "Moor" was interlined before "slave," probably Marschalk's suggestion. Thomas signed the deed and left the office.

For the first moment since that disastrous day at the mountain pass, Ibrahima was without a master.

"It is impossible for any of us to feel the emotion that must have thrilled in his breast," wrote Gallaudet, "the joy, the ecstasy that he experienced." It was the most magical of all minutes, against which, on the scale of life, a million sorrows weighed nothing. It was the soul's own cutting of anchors and spreading of sails. A slave from North Carolina who had been freed called the sensation "a queer and joyous feeling. . . . I cannot describe it," he said, "only that it seemed as though I was in heaven. I used to lie awake whole nights thinking of it. The strange thoughts that passed through my soul were more to me than sleep. To break the bonds of slavery opens up at once both heaven and earth."

"I immediately . . . set about making arrangements for his departure," Marschalk wrote, "but had scarcely taken the first step, when an unforeseen difficulty presented itself—the wife of Prince . . . exhibited that natural agony of feeling at the idea of separation from her husband, which was creditable to her, and which cast a heavy gloom over the old man's brow." Ibrahima "looked at the old companion of his slavery, the mother of his nine children—he could not agree to part without her. She, too —how could she part with him! She wished to follow him to the end of the earth." Day after day Ibrahima asked the colonel what to do. "Cheering as his [own] situation was, his delight was mingled with the deepest anguish," Gallaudet wrote. "What was personal freedom when such social ties prevented his enjoying it. His

Fac simile of the Moorish Prince's writing

Abdehl Rahhahman

Ibrahima as he appeared in New York in 1828, sketch by Henry Inman, courtesy of the Library of Congress.

Arrival of a caravan at Timbuctu, from *Travels and Discoveries in North and Central Africa* (1857–9), by Heindrich Barth, courtesy of the Library of Congress.

A view of Timbo, at the foot of Mount Helaya, in 1818, with the French traveler Gaspard Mollien in the right foreground, from *Travels in the Interior of Africa, to the Sources of the Senegal and the Gambia* (London, 1820), by Gaspard Mollien, courtesy of the Library of Congress.

The great mosque at Timbo, photographed in the 1930s, from *Moeurs et histoire des Peuls* (Paris, 1937), by Louis Tauxier, courtesy of the Library of Congress.

Street scene in Jenne, a city in present-day Mali, where Ibrahima attended school in the 1770s, from *Tombouctou la Mystérieuse* (Paris, 1899), by Félix Dubois, courtesy of the Library of Congress.

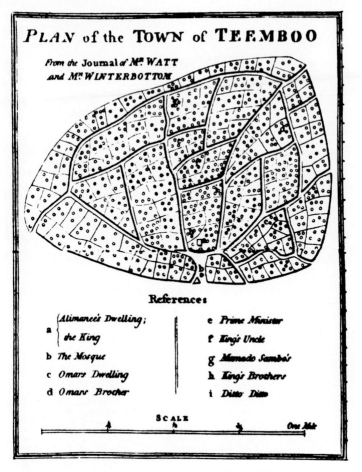

PLAN of the TOWN of TEEMBOO

From the Journal of Mr. WATT
and Mr. WINTERBOTTOM

References

a { Alimancee's Dwelling ; the King

b The Mosque

c Omars Dwelling

d Omars Brother

e Prime Minister

f Kings Uncle

g Mamado Sambo's

h Kings Brothers

i Ditto Ditto

SCALE

One Mile

Plan of Timbo, Ibrahima's home town in Futa Jalon,
West Africa, from *Essay on Colonization* (London, 1795),
by C. Wadstrom, courtesy of the Library of Congress.

Diagram of a slave ship
thought to be the *Africa,*
Document BT 6:10,
appearing by permission
of the Controller of H.M.
Stationery Office, London.

The 1788 deed of sale for Ibrahima, courtesy of the Adams County Chancery Clerk's Office, Natchez, Mississippi, photograph by Danny Richardson. A partial translation from the Spanish follows: "Be it known . . . that I Thomas Irwin do really and effectually sell to Thomas Foster two new negroes [or two black bucks], for the sum of nine hundred and thirty dollars, in specie, payable in manner following, one hundred and fifty dollars which I acknowledge to have received from the purchaser, two hundred and fifty dollars payable in the month of January next, and the remaining five hundred and thirty dollars in all the month of January one thousand seven hundred and ninety. . . ."

Fort Panmure de Natchez, with the town of Natchez "above and below the Hill," as it appeared in 1796, from *A Journey in North America* (Paris, 1826), by Victor Collot, courtesy of the Library of Congress.

Andrew Marschalk, courtesy of the State Historical Museum, Jackson, Mississippi.

William Rousseau Cox, courtesy of Mrs. Albert D. Williams, Lake Forest, Illinois, photograph by Danny Richardson.

Thomas H. Galludet, courtesy of the Library of Congress.

State of Mississippi
Adams County

Be it known, that I Thomas Foster a Citizen of Adams County in the state of Mississippi, at present owner of the slave named Prince, refered to in the annexed letter, have this day delivered unto Andrew Marschalk of the City of Natchez and State aforesaid, the Custody of said slave Prince, for the sole and only purpose of his being transported to his native Country, by the government of the United States agreeably to the stipulations mentioned in said letter, that the said slave, Prince is not to enjoy the privileges of a free man within the United State of America —

In witness whereof I have hereunto set my hand and seal at Natchez, this twenty second day of February in the year of our Lord, one thousand eight hundred and twenty eights

Thomas Foster (Seal)

In presence of
Gabriel B Dunbar —

The 1828 deed of conveyance for Ibrahima from Thomas Foster to
Andrew Marschalk, courtesy of the Adams County Chancery Clerk's Office,
Natchez, Mississippi, photograph by Danny Richardson.

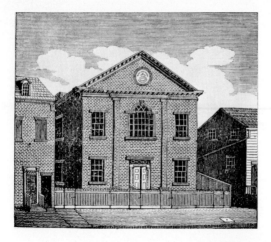

The New York African Free School, which Ibrahima visited in 1828, from *The History of the New York African Free Schools* (New York, 1830) by C. C. Andrews, courtesy of the Library of Congress.

Notice of the loading of the ship *Harriet* in preparation for its departure for Liberia, from the Norfolk and Portsmouth *Herald,* January 2, 1829, courtesy of the Library of Congress.

> Dec 12   t10J
>
> ## For Cape Montserado,
> *(AFRICA.)*
>
> The superior ship HARRI-ET, Capt. Johnson, being chartered by the Colonization Society to carry out Emigrants to Liberia, will sail about the 20th January from this port. The emigrants and others having any bulky freight to put on board, are requested to forward it as soon as possible, as the ship is ready to receive it. The embarkation of the passengers will take place on the 20th, after which the ship will sail with all possible despatch.
>
> JOHN McPHAIL,
> Agent Am. Colo. Society.
>
> Dec 29   tvs

The colony at Monrovia, Liberia, as it appeared in the 1820s, from *African Repository, vol.* 3 (1827), courtesy of the Library of Congress.

very freedom was almost a curse." "What was to be done?" the colonel wondered. "I had no authority to interfere as to her, and I felt almost grieved that I had taken a solitary step in the business, believing that the separation of the old couple would no doubt accelerate the death of both.

"I applied again to Mr. Foster, who is a truly amiable and worthy man," Marschalk continued. Isabella free, Thomas told him, would be an essential loss, for she was the plantation's "obstetrick practitioner and doctress." "Yet he could not bear the idea of parting the old couple." He agreed to sell her for two hundred dollars, "a very small sum compared to the value of Isabella as a servant." Cyrus Griffin prepared a subscription paper, stating the facts of Ibrahima's emancipation (already well known in town) and asking for donations to purchase her. "The kindness of Mr. Foster," the heading on the paper went, "induces him to offer another pecuniary sacrifice to the happiness of these faithful servants." Ibrahima took the paper and immediately plied the market house and stores of Natchez. In twenty-four hours, "so great was the respect for this unfortunate man," Cyrus said, Ibrahima collected $293. One hundred and forty people signed the subscription. "Several gentlemen gave him ten dollars," the colonel noticed, "one gave him fifteen, many gave five and very few less than one dollar." "This fact alone shows in what estimation Prince was held by those who knew him," Gallaudet stated. Isabella, under restrictions similar to her husband, was deeded to the colonel in mid-March.

Voluntarily, several prominent Natchezians came forward with certificates of recommendation for Ibrahima. They included Woodson Wren, the county clerk; Henry Tooley, physician and meteorologist; and John Henderson, merchant and slave dealer. Gallaudet synthesized the contents of their documents: "that they have personally known Prince from 13 to 25 years past, and that he has uniformly sustained the character of a moral, honest man; remarkable for his strict integrity; harmless, faithful, and inoffensive in his conduct; courteous in his behaviour, and friendly to all; and that he has borne his state of servitude with a fortitude and patience more becoming a Christian than a Pagan, being generally respected by a large and respectable circle of acquaintance."

The colonel was beside himself at these developments. He made Ibrahima a guest in his home in the weeks prior to his departure and was so absorbed in the business that he seemed ridiculous to some. "The Colonel absolutely *bored* the President of the United States and the Secretary of State for two or three years with his importunities to get him liberated," wrote Captain Cook, "and when Mr. Clay wrote to him, took his letter to the market-house and made a great parade about it, and *bored* everybody that came in to his office and everybody out of it . . . , boasting and gabbing from day light until breakfast, and up the street and down." To Cyrus's amazement the colonel suggested that they give Ibrahima a public dinner before he left. Here, clearly, was an idea whose time had not come. Afterward, he asked the attorney to draft a document, which he would print on parchment, expressing the esteem in which Ibrahima was held by those who knew him. This was to be attested to by the signatures of numerous individuals and affixed with the great seal of the State. "It is scarcely necessary for me to say," Griffin observed, "that I did not assent to the absurdity of sending home the heir-apparent to the throne of an independent kingdom with *official testimonial* of his industry in the cotton field."

Someone proposed that Ibrahima travel to Washington by way of ship from New Orleans. The colonel objected. He thought it might be beneficial for Ibrahima to pass through the West in order that he might be better able to understand and convey to his countrymen the extent and power of the United States. Accordingly, arrangements were made for Ibrahima and Isabella to take passage on the steamboat *Neptune,* which would call the second week in April for passengers to Cincinnati. Marschalk hoped Ibrahima might later visit the Northeast.

"Perhaps by doing so," he told Cyrus, "he may raise money enough to purchase his family."

The colonel had his way on one other matter. Clay had authorized him to spend two hundred dollars to clothe Ibrahima and send him to Washington. "His master's indulgence had enabled him to possess himself of a very decent and genteel wardrobe. I therefore appropriated a part of the sum placed at my disposal to . . . furnishing him with a handsome Moorish dress appropriate to his rank prior to his captivity." Seventy dollars went to fashioning this finery—a white muslim turban topped with a crescent, a blue cloth coat with yellow buttons, white pantaloons gathered at the ankles, and yellow boots. Even a scimitar was discovered and added to the outfit. "A tawdry dress, to which I most positively objected," Griffin groaned. Those, like him, accustomed to Ibrahima in homespun, thought the clothes' effect on the African was ludicrous. Such was not the colonel's intent. He knew that Ibrahima would be appealing to charity after he left Natchez. These clothes would attract attention. The suit was also the colonel's touching attempt to distinguish the prince as a person. "The indulgence of appearing before [the President] . . . in the garb of his country and rank was a thing of but little moment as to expense and what he was only in justice entitled to."

If you can't have your years back, Marschalk seemed to be saying, at least you can have your clothes.

April 8 dawned beautifully clear, without the frost or winds of the past few mornings. It was still cool for spring, but the season was fully present. In a week Natchezians would be cursing gnats and making their usual offerings to mosquitoes.

Ibrahima, followed by his wife, children, and grandchildren, passed through the dirt streets of Natchez for the last time. Almost twenty people were in his procession, Marschalk included. "It was indeed a very interesting sight," wrote an observer. "The appearance of Prince was venerable and dignified. His whole family gave the strongest evidence that they are the property of a man who . . . feels the proper duties of a Christian master."

At the same landing where he had arrived forty years before, Ibrahima "bid them a final adieu." He was encouraging and told them he would get the money to purchase them soon. If he could "but realize his prospects and regain his property" at Timbo, he could "buy them free at ten prices." The family seemed outwardly calm. The sons, Marschalk thought, "are really the finest looking young men I have seen. They were all genteely dressed. They expressed themselves pleased with the freedom of their parents."

Yet, at this fateful hour, the colonel added, "there was a look of silent agony in their eyes I could not bear to witness."

Your young men shall see visions,
and your old men shall dream dreams.
—Acts 2:17

6. A Northern Campaign

The *Neptune* beat a noisy path up the Mississippi from Natchez, coughing white steam and rasping from its scrape pipe like a hoarse giant. The rain had stopped for a time. It was clear now, and even cool. As Ibrahima looked out, he saw a swollen river that had left its banks to cut off houses and drown thickets of cane in its rush. Abandoned cattle bellowed forlornly from newly created islands, and passing flatboatmen twirled their poles against the uncertain currents of flood. It was the yearly drama of spring on the river.

Travel on the *Neptune* was not as romantic as a later age might imagine. One hundred and twenty-three feet long, the *Neptune* was only seven feet longer than the first steamboat ever on the Mississippi. It boasted in the Natchez press of "superior accommodations for passengers," of course, but it was really just a squat little boat with a low single deck, a square stern, and a creaking paddle wheel on one side. The entire boat could have fit into the dining rooms of the showboats of later years, on which gentlemen with impeccable white bone buttons would win and lose plantations at euchre with thrilling insouciance.

The escort Marschalk had arranged for the trip was Nathaniel Ware, a planter and once acting governor of Mississippi. Ibrahima had known him for ten years as a neighbor of Thomas's. He was a handsome person, fair-skinned, with long, thin hair that fell onto his neck. Ware was selling his Mississippi farms and moving himself and his daughters to Philadelphia. His domestic life at Natchez had been shattered when his wife, Sarah, went insane at the birth of their second child. Now Sarah was to be left behind, sunk in a hopeless melancholy and occupied by painting the outlines of roses on the white walls of her apartment. This tragedy had turned Ware, already most reserved by nature, into a bitter and morose man from whose sarcasm even his own children were not always safe.

Ware had long had an interest in Africa, and he held Africans as slaves on his plantations. He would later travel on the African continent. Of black Muslims he would write, "It is a singular fact, that the further you penetrate into the desert or continent of Africa, the more intolerant and zealous are the Mahometans. The negro races who have turned Mahometans are intolerant to the faggot, and use brute force on all christian slaves or other christians that fall in their way." Ironically, these views were held by the same man who had heard and believed that "kind and hospitable attentions" were given to Dr. Cox by Ibrahima and his family. "I know the worth of Prince," Ware told someone who inquired, and he let the matter drop with much less attention than he would have given to compounding an interest or plaguing an overseer.

The *Neptune* labored on its way, soon passing Memphis, an experiment on a bluff where less than one thousand people lived. Later, in mid-April, it passed the confluence of the Mississippi and the Ohio, where the former, carrying the Missouri's drainage in its run, entered the clear waters of the latter looking as dirty as "a tub of soap-suds after a hard day's wash." Ten days after he left Natchez, Ibrahima arrived at Louisville, Kentucky. Here the *Neptune* refueled, dropped some cargo and passengers, and continued upriver the same day. It was to Cincinnati that Ibrahima's thoughts were turned, for the colonel had made it an important stop on his trip. Ibrahima's pocket was filled with letters of introduction to Mississippi expatriates living there.

The Queen City was reached in two days from Louisville on Saturday, April 19, 1828. Only a fort in the wilderness had been here when Ibrahima began in slavery. Now, Cincinnati was the young colossus of the West, from whose dingy red buildings a flood of flour, pork, and whiskey poured on the lower Mississippi Valley. With 22,000 people, it was ten times the size of Natchez and easily the largest, busiest American city he had seen. Perhaps more interesting was the fact that when his foot left the plank of the *Neptune* for the Ohio dock, Ibrahima came for the first time in his African or American life to a place where slavery was prohibited by law.

Dressed in his "Moorish costume," Ibrahima walked the city streets. It was the first day of ten months of appearances in what Americans believed to be "the costume of his country." Marschalk had guessed wildly about the fashions of Futa, but he did have an instinct for what would attract attention. The dress had created a sensation at Natchez. Some thought it "tawdry," some "handsome and respectable," but no one was going to ignore it.

"The grave looking elderly personage in Moorish dress, who has attracted the attention of many of our citizens for a day or two past, is stated to be, and there seems no doubt of the fact, an African Prince, who was taken prisoner in his youth, and has been nearly forty years a slave in the neighborhood of Natchez," wrote the editor of Cincinnati's *Republican*. The newspaper recommended Ibrahima to the local citizens by printing a letter that Marschalk had written to a "Miss Jane" of the city. It began, "This letter will be handed to you by a very extraordinary personage—no less than your old acquaintance Prince (or Ibrahim), who is now FREE, and on his way to his own country." The colonel continued at length, praising the African's character and detailing the events of the last eighteen months. Two other newspapers in the city, not to be outdone, published or excerpted Griffin's letter to the Colonization Society, which that organization had published in its nationally circulated magazine.

Marschalk's costume would more than pay for itself in the months to come, but the cost of it had taken almost one half of the State Department's advance. Barely was there money left to pay Ibrahima's passage to Washington, and nothing was on hand for Isabella, whom the government did not even know was coming. To make up that difference, Ibrahima paraded through the streets, accepting money from the charitable. The press accounts opened many doors, a writer for the *Daily Gazette* putting the matter plainly: "No provision is made to defray the expenses of his wife. It is earnestly hoped that the citizens of Cincinnati will contribute what may be necessary to aid her in that journey." The interest in this prince who became a slave and who was about to become a prince again was strong. It was the same attraction that had called the attention of Marschalk and the Natchez patrons to the old man—a "romantic and extraordinary case," as one Ohioan put it. And the dollars came in.

Toward the end of April, Ibrahima left Cincinnati and traveled up the Ohio to Wheeling, Virginia. The National Road, which led eastward to the Atlantic coast, had its western terminus there. Now followed a bone-jarring ride of about a week through Pennsylvania and Maryland toward Baltimore. Newsmen followed his progress, and their accounts, widely reprinted in Boston, New York, and other seaboard cities, have "the Prince of Timbuctoo" dashing through sleepy little villages in a coach-and-four. It did not seem to matter that the coach-and-four was the public stage. Griffin's letter to the Colonization Society, going the rounds of the press under the title "The Unfortunate Moor," was similarly being misinterpreted to mean that Ibrahima, by the death of his father, was already "King of Timbuctoo" and that he was on his way home to claim his royal rights. Even before he left Natchez, a writer in the Philadelphia *American Sentinel* insisted, "He is entitled to the Throne!" Thus, a useful if confused aura spread itself before him.

On their arrival in Baltimore, Ibrahima, Isabella, and Ware went to the home of Benjamin Lundy, editor of the antislavery newspaper *Genius of Universal Emancipation.* For some reason Marschalk had the idea that Lundy was an agent of the Colonization Society and had told Ibrahima to call on him for aid. Lundy was, in truth, the most conspicuous critic of the Society in the entire country. He had just been denounced in the North as "a great zealot" for opposing it. Slave traders did not like him either. Lundy had been attacked the year before in front of the Baltimore post office by a slaver who stamped on his face until it was a mass of blood. Lundy's popularity in the city was indicated when his assailant was brought to court and fined one dollar and costs. Still, he persevered, lecturing everywhere and publishing the *Genius,* of which half the subscriptions went to the slaveholding states, some even to Natchez.

But Lundy was not found in town. He had set off for the North a week before, leaving the *Genius* in the hands of William Swaim, his assistant. This bookish individual, whom Lundy had met when traveling in North Carolina, knew who Ibrahima was, for he had reprinted Griffin's letter a month earlier. Swaim greeted the old man kindly, and he made room in the issue of May 10 for a powerful plea: "Though this victim of ruthless misfortune has lately stepped into the enjoyment of his natural rights, he has children remaining at Natchez. While he related to us this painful truth, the tears gushed from his eyes and rolled down his cheeks."

At this time Henry Clay happened to pass through the city. Clay's health was not good, he had been to see physicians in Philadelphia, and they advised "abstraction from business, a journey, some attention to exercise, and a little medicine," as he wrote President Adams. He landed at the Baltimore wharf on his return to Washington and on a cloudy Tuesday proceeded amid cheers and huzzahs to the City Hotel. It was an election year, and the grayness of a spring day could never interrupt anything as important to American life as a partisan parade. The tall and fair-complected Clay was enveloped by friends of the administration everywhere he went. "Abstraction from business," however good as a personal prescription, would not check the ascendency of Andrew Jackson, or deny that "military chieftain" the Presidency in November. And on that outcome, both health and fortune depended.

Before Clay left Baltimore the next morning, Ibrahima came by and introduced himself. The Secretary, an ebullient, unaffected person, charmed the African with his friendly manner. Someone who spoke with Ibrahima afterward wrote, "He is highly delighted with Mr. Clay." The Secretary recommended he come to Washington straightaway so that the administration might mull over his situation.

Agreeably, Ibrahima left Isabella with Swaim and took the five-hour stage to the capital. It was a route through a comparatively barren country. Unfenced fields of tobacco fronted the road, and neighborhood dogs yapped at passers-by. There were some small towns on the way, but they "wore a miserable air," as James Fenimore Cooper noted on a similar trip. Near the District line the stage passed Bladensburg, last stop of the British army before it entered Washington in 1814 and now the favorite dueling spot of the *beaux sabreurs* of the city.

Washington itself was a sprawling place, still very much "the city of magnificent distances" it had been in Monroe's time. A French traveler of this period likened it to a town gone visiting in the country. Its dwellings were so scattered in bunches—a few at the White House, a few on Capitol Hill, and a few along Pennsylvania Avenue, which connected them—that it looked like a town rising out of the ground. The Capitol with its rounded dome was easily the most imposing sight in the city. From its grounds a double row of prim and shadeless Lombardy poplars ran along the avenue toward the White House. That fashionable street was then a gravel road from which weeds still had to be cut, and only chips of stone from new buildings thrown into its mudholes saved the unwary from sounding their depths. Without a sewage system, pavement, or lights, it was still the type of city from whose best windows droves of mules could be seen passing by at any time. And it only helped a little to hear Davy Crockett explain that the mules were going to Massachusetts to teach school.

Ibrahima did not choose to put up at the Indian Queen, where Southern and Western legislators boarded because of the good quarters for their horses and slaves. He had had a lifetime of that and wanted as little more as possible. Understanding that he would be treated respectfully at Williamson's Mansion House, he bid thanks and adieu to Ware and checked into this place, which regarded itself as "quiet and economical." As it was on Pennsylvania Avenue, only two blocks from the White House, and had a fine larder, Ibrahima picked wisely. Most important, he was not treated as a slave. "I have been treated a gentleman," he said of the hotel.

In this heart of the Republic slavery and the slave trade flourished. Though Washington was smaller than Cincinnati, with a population of less than nineteen thousand, there were about two thousand slaves in the District who worked on farms, in homes, and in boardinghouses. Some of those in the latter made acquaintances with national figures. One was mistress of the governorelect of Alabama, who was serving out a term in Congress. But clearly it was the trade itself that was the feature of Washington life most shocking to Northern and European sensibilities. "The public will be surprised to learn," read a letter in a Vermont newspaper, "that this District is made the headquarters for carrying on the domestic slave-trade. The prisons can not hold them all, and there are certain low taverns in town called pens where the slave dealers keep their purchases and when they have a drove, they take a chain like an ox chain, and on each side of this iron the slaves, over the right and left wrists together, & thus ironed [they] are driven off." Processions of handcuffed and chained blacks, moving glumly through the streets, were a common sight. It so infuriated one of Benjamin Lundy's subscribers that he attempted unsuccessfully to buy space in the *National Intelligencer* for this piece:

Cash!!   Cash!!   For Whites!!

Having good reason to believe that a cargo of the white sons and daughters of our republicans will bring a good price at Algiers, (seeing their yellow children sell so well in our Republic,) I am induced to offer a great bargain for twenty white boys, of any age, and for twenty-five girls, (those of ages and beauty to suit the pashas would be preferred,) if delivered in good shipping or driving order, that is, *chained and manacled at the door of the Representatives Hall, Washington.*

The capital was an anxious city. Spring had begun early and with great beauty, but the greens of April were giving way to something hot and sinister. The twentieth Congress had its mind fixed on the fall presidential contest, but its hands wrestled with tariff reform, a discussion that seemed to get longer and less fruitful each day. The ladies were restless, the peak of the fashionable season had passed, the drawing rooms were thinly attended, and some congressional families had already left for home. The legislators themselves were looking for an excuse to follow them. Those who stayed did so because the tariff issue was one of the few aspects of the coming presidential campaign that would not be treated in terms of the moral shortcomings of the two candidates.

The fifteenth of May dawned in showers, as had the day before. "Rain," President Adams noted cheerlessly in his diary. It was a Thursday, and senators, soldiers, and favor seekers lined up early to see him. Ibrahima came too, passing the old wartime barn and stables where the horses and cows for the use of the First Family were kept. Near the Treasury building could be seen the ramshackle sheds where the commuters of State and Treasury quartered their horses. The wings of the presidential mansion had not been completed—what there was needed a coat of stucco, too —and only the south portico had been erected. Architect Charles Bulfinch said the mansion "was such as no gentleman of moderate property would permit as his own residence." The grounds were beautiful, however, for the President had an interest in arboriculture and had planted an array of fruit trees that were then in wildest flower.

Adams was sixty-one, still vigorous enough to ride horses and even take his spills with some style. A stocky man with square jaw and florid face, he had a high forehead that suggested correctly his classical intellect. Adams was a person who had the respect of the American people, but he had never known the adulation that poured forth wherever the chemistry of Clay or Jackson was in operation. "I found him as taciturn as the Lybian desert," wrote a visiting Englishman.

Ibrahima was soon before the President in his office on the second floor of the mansion. The meeting was a rather extraordinary juncture of people—Adams, impressive heir to a great tradition, and Ibrahima, son of a distinguished father himself, fresh from forty years in slavery, now meeting the President in relative equality. Grateful to Adams, there is no reason to think the African was awe-struck or obsequious in his presence. R. B. C. Howell, a Baptist elder who knew the prince, wrote that he "had nothing of the hesitating manner of persons in low life. However honorable, learned, or dignified any person present may be, he seems perfectly at ease, conversing with great freedom and much good sense."

The African had been admitted while Adams was with Secretary of the Navy Samuel Southard. The portly Southard would be responsible for Ibrahima's transportation overseas. He knew about the movement of American ships to Africa and was friendly with officials of the Colonization Society, which sent vessels to its Liberian colony on an erratic basis. In his diary Adams wrote, "Abdel Rahman is a Moor, otherwise called Prince or Ibrahim, who has been forty years a slave in this country. He wrote, two or three years since, a letter to the Emperor of Morocco, in Arabic, in consequence of which the Emperor expressed a wish that this man might be emancipated and sent home. His owner, residing at Natchez, Mississippi, offered to emancipate him on condition that he should be sent home by the Government. He came in while Mr. Southard was with me, and we had some consultation how and when he should be dispatched to his home, which he says is Timbuctoo." It had been Adams's intention for many months to have Ibrahima transported to Tangier and delivered to the Emperor. Indeed, that the Emperor had wished this was the single reason the government had interested itself in him at all.

But Ibrahima had come to the White House with something else in mind. His homeland was much closer to Liberia than to Morocco, and there was no way to guess the reception he might receive in the latter place. So, as Clay noted later, "he expressed a strong desire of going to Liberia, and afterwards proceeding to his friends [in Futa]." At last the administration discovered what Griffin had known and Marschalk did not want to know the year before. Though Ibrahima knew much about geography and customs south of the Sahara, he had never traveled north of it. Ibrahima had no connection whatever with Morocco other than sharing the religion of its people. When this fact was coupled to his insistence that he be sent to Liberia, Adams could do little but agree. "The President thought it proper to yield to his inclination on this subject," Clay wrote, the precise motives not committed to paper. It was a decent decision by Adams, and it was certainly less embarrassing than his two alternatives: send Ibrahima to Morocco against his will or send him back to Natchez.

Ibrahima used his access to the President to make a plea for something that had become central to everything he did. "He says," Adams wrote, "he has left at Natchez five sons and eight grandchildren—all in slavery; and he wishes that they might be all emancipated, and be sent with or to him." This was quite a request from a man in whom the administration might have no further interest. But whatever the President would decide on that point, Ibrahima let him know that the government's action in freeing him had ended one problem only to raise thirteen others. Obviously these were facts he intended for Adams even before he left Mississippi. At Natchez he had asked to be allowed to deliver personally to the President two letters pleading his case.

Later in the day Ibrahima plowed the same ground with Clay. It is more than possible he was a rather pathetic object to those in the executive branch—not who they thought he was, not wishing to go where they thought he would, not content to abandon his sons in gratitude for his own good fortune. Here he was now upon them, with his wife, his testimonials, his "native costume," and his high, high hopes. For the present no decisions were made, but, reassuringly, Clay was even more cordial than the day before. "Mr. Clay was very flattering to me," Ibrahima said. "He invited me to partake of the hospitalities of his house," certainly a mark of unusual regard. "I declined, telling him of my good treatment at Williamson's."

Official visits completed, the prince set off to deliver his last letter of introduction. It was a letter Griffin had written to the Reverend R. R. Gurley, Secretary of the American Colonization Society. The object of this organization, to send free blacks and emancipated slaves to Liberia, has already been mentioned. The Society hoped that the "free people of color" in the North would see the advantages they would gain in moving to a country where they could find the civil and economic liberty that prejudice now denied them. Southern slaveholders, the reasoning continued, would take the opportunity the Society presented to free themselves of the burden of slavery by sending their bondsmen to a country so remote they would never be bothered by them. This scheme, though not a dozen years old, had already encountered problems of finance and morale, but the feeling in the Society was that its plan was in ascendancy. The Society had an increasing number of workers, it took in money gathered yearly in churches and through bequests, and it was expanding its auxiliary branches. In Africa the dedicated Jehudi Ashmun, the Society's agent, toiled away with the settlers at Monrovia more faithfully than could have an army of mere hirelings. When its friends, such as Henry Clay, considered these facts, they were not at all unsure that the Society might bring forth something fantastic.

Most obviously lacking enthusiasm for the Society's goals, however, were the same free blacks the Society expected to export. "Massa Clay, he want de niggers go to Africa, let he go first and show de way," a Bostonian said. At large meetings in that city and in Philadelphia and New York, they had condemned the Society for its potential ability to deport them against their wills. A decade of naysaying this objection by the Society had changed few minds. "We have chosen rather to bear the ills we have than fly to those we know not of," one black explained. "Nothing appears to me more trifling," another wrote, "than to talk of repaying to Africa the debt we owe her, by returning her sons to her coasts. —I consider that the shortest way to accomplish this grand object is, to do her sons justice wherever we find them."

The Society was also on the defensive in the South. The influential Charleston *Mercury* labeled it "an insidious attack on the tranquillity of the south, a nest egg [of] northern abolitionists, that therefrom might be raised and hatched for the south, anxiety, inquietude, and troubles to which there could be no end." Many white Southerners saw no difference between the attitudes of extremists and gradualists on the subject of emancipation. For Colonel Marschalk to regard Lundy as an agent of the Society he had just criticized in a tour illustrates the confusion. The public funds spent to send to Liberia those Africans "recaptured" by government ships in the illegal international slave trade and to maintain them there also offered Southern congressmen a generous target. Mention of the symbiotic relation between the private colony of the Society and the public Agency for Recaptured Africans never failed to enrage a section of Southern opinion, which cared nothing for the former and actually hoped to destroy the latter. Agency funds had been cut in February, and a further attack was prepared in Congress the following week.

The national office of the Society was kept in rented rooms of a brick building opposite Ibrahima's boardinghouse. Secretary Gurley and his family lived upstairs, and here, too, lived John Kennedy, who was the office factotum. The downstairs was something of an attraction in Washington, for the Society had set up displays of African ingenuity from Liberia and the surrounding country. There were specimens of native cloth, iron implements, and a tiger skin sent from the colony. Coffee from Liberia could be tasted here as well.

When Ibrahima arrived at the office, he discovered that Gurley was in New York with Francis Scott Key, attempting to raise money for the Society. He was expected back soon, however, and had told Kennedy that the prince would visit. Kennedy met the old man, talked with him at length, and opened his letter of introduction. Griffin had written, in part, "It affords me the highest gratification to say the bearer of this letter is Prince the captive Moor, in whose behalf I addressed you in February last. Since the date of my letter, he has been manumitted and now proceeds to Washington at the expense of the U. States. He leaves this place, Sir, with many benedictions." Kennedy himself wrote to Gurley later in the day:

> To day the Moor (Prince) came to the Office. . . . Prince came fully up to my expectation, & to the accounts which have been given of him; there is something truly dignified in his deportment & manner, and he is acute and intelligent on every subject that was mentioned; I showed him the map of Africa & on pointing out Cape Mesurado [in Liberia] to him, he instantly mentioned in what direction Teemboo lay & the distance with surprising accuracy, mentioned the names of 2 places where he had been at school, both of which I instantly found as described, with the names of various towns & territories between Teemboo and Timbuctoo.

In the next few days Ibrahima met congressmen, a traveling free black, a visiting Oriental explorer, and a mass of local luminaries. Among the area residents was the Reverend James Laurie, a Presbyterian minister and Society ombudsman who lived next door to the office. Dr. Laurie, a native Scot, was a barrel-chested preacher whose voice rang out like a mill-clapper. He possessed as well a natural warmth not generally expected in one so orthodox in his views. At last the elusive Gurley appeared. A Yale graduate from Connecticut, Gurley was licensed to preach, but he had never been ordained, throwing all his energies into the Society's work. He handled its entire correspondence, met with its Board of Managers, did the editorial work for its *African Repository* magazine, and traveled on its behalf, once visiting Ashmun in Monrovia.

Ibrahima's personal worth and his value to the Society were

immediately recognized by both men. "We have repeatedly conversed with Prince, since his arrival in our City," Gurley wrote, "nor have our expectations concerning him, in any respect been disappointed. He is intelligent, modest, and obliging. Though he has been in slavery forty years, his manners are not merely prepossessing, but dignified." Dr. Laurie observed, "Teembo, the Capital of his own nation, is only about 300 miles distant from Cape Montserado. The benefit resulting to the Colony from the restoration of Prince, accompanied by his family, may be of the highest importance, and of incalculable benefit to benighted Africa."

With Gurley's help Ibrahima wrote a letter in English to Natchez.

> My dear Children, I wish to inform you that myself and your mother are tolerably well, only the fatigue of travelling to this place. In Washington, I visited the President's house and other public buildings. I will also inform you of my reception in Baltimore, the gentlemen there took me in a carriage around the town and shew me all the beauties thereof. The people of Washington are quite kind to me, and I have no cause to complain of them.
>
> My dear boys, Simeon [*sic*] and Prince, for God sake dont let Lee get a wife till you hear from me.

The closing was, in effect, a plea to keep the number of people who would have to be purchased small. The father remained optimistic, adding, "The President and Mr. Clay, they both received me very kindly, and I expect from their kind expressions to me, that they will pay every attention to my business."

Anxious for any help, Ibrahima agreed to talk with the Society's Board of Managers the following week. This was a body of local ministers and other benevolent souls who made policy for the Society. For the special meeting ten members came, the largest number in months. Among them were Dr. Laurie and attorney Francis Scott Key. Key had become well known when his poem, "The Star Spangled Banner," was fitted with success to an old English drinking tune. More recently he had assisted the government in arguments before the Supreme Court against some slavers whose ship had been seized on the Florida coast. His summation conjured such a horrifying picture of the slave trade that a listener in the courtroom felt it "would have done honor to a Pitt or a Wilberforce."

After the members were introduced to Ibrahima, a general discussion followed. "He told me if he should go with his wife to Africa, he was afraid he would think so much about them he had left that he would not long survive," Kennedy related. The Board determined at length to inquire precisely what Adams and Clay intended doing for him. Dr. Laurie, Key, and a third member were appointed a committee to "wait upon the Secretary of State and ascertain from him whether it is competent for the Government to provide for the purchase of the family of Prince."

The response was prompt and it could not have been more disappointing. The committee was informed that the best the government could do was pay his expenses while in the city and on his voyage to Africa. His children, it seemed, were beyond the reach of official benevolence. Board minutes give no reason for this lack of interest, but they are easy to surmise. Most important was Ibrahima himself, who had not proven as valuable as anticipated. He was almost worthless for diplomatic purposes, and whatever the personal feelings of government officers in the case, the government had little use for him. Had Ibrahima been the Emperor of Morocco himself, however, there might still have been a reluctance to make this type of gesture in an election year. The State Department had been hammered at throughout the month for its expenditures by the *United States Telegraph,* a pro-Jackson print whose argus eyes lost no opportunity to spot anything embarrassing to Adams or Clay. Even the mention of such a purchase would have fueled its fire uncontrollably. Adams's own antislavery views had already been sneered at by his critics in the South, and the controversy surrounding any large emancipation would have delighted his enemies there. Driving a final nail into any hopes of a purchase was the notion that it could not be accomplished, the administration willing, without a congressional appropriation, and in that case the plan moved directly into the temple of the absurd.

Ibrahima was hard hit by this refusal, but he did not despair. He knew it had been a possibility. Before he left Natchez, Cyrus

Griffin told him to forget his children, for the price Thomas would want for them would be as high as the stars above him. Still, there are hopes that a father cannot send away, and Ibrahima was prepared to beg in the streets and seek charity if he had to do so. On his first visit to the Society's office he had lain an alternative plan before Kennedy. "He entertains a hope that some of the leading men here," the bookseller wrote, "will commence a subscription & recommend his case to public notice in which event he feels confident that in Phila. NYork & the other cities he could raise enough."

"If the other cities treat me as kindly as they have treated me [here] in Washington," Ibrahima said, "I hope to get them."

The true wisdom of a connection with the Society now became clear. This national coalition of Southern liberals and Northern reformers was probably the one organization in the country that could help him from private sources. It could not make the purchase itself, for it did not buy its emigrants, only receive them. But it could offer its national machinery, a network of agents in the large cities, space in the *Repository,* and access to powerful newspapers. Ibrahima already had attracted vast attention without any promotion, and the money-drawing power of his "Moorish costume" had been demonstrated in Cincinnati. As he was willing to travel and make public appearances he might collect several thousand dollars. The Society would help him because it knew it could benefit from the attention he would draw to the colony. His relation to the ruling family of a powerful state near Liberia held untold dividends for the colony if he could be placed in the Society's debt. Critically, Ibrahima did not appear self-seeking. "He seems to think more of the benefits he could render to the Colony by his return to Temboo than of his own personal gratification," a supporter wrote.

Interestingly, the board had committed the Society to help him already. During his meeting with it, one enthusiastic member proposed that Gurley "write Mr. Foster & expostulate with him, on the propriety of his disposing of the children of Prince the Moor, at a price at which the benevolent public might be induced to contribute for their emancipation, & to urge upon him . . . to place their emancipation at a moderate price." The motion was tabled,

and fortunately, too, for Thomas, who had not corresponded with
the President previously, would hardly have replied to this type of
nonsense. He would only have become incensed that people in
Washington were meddling with his property. The task of drawing
water from that stone was left to Gurley, and instead the board
authorized Dr. Laurie to prepare a paper recommending the Pullo
to the charity of the public.

The subscription-book method was adopted. It allowed a generous individual to put down his name and amount of contribu-
tion in the heat of philanthropy and not have to worry about
paying until he was tracked down a few days later. Dr. Laurie
bought a leatherbound book with blank pages and at the front of
it wrote a condensed history of Ibrahima's life, capped with an
appeal to the liberal-minded: "He has the feelings of a father, and
cannot bear the thought of leaving his offspring in bondage,
while he is restored to freedom. He is therefore making an effort
to raise as much as will procure their emancipation; and it is
hoped that the interesting case of this meritorious individual will
be regarded in a favorable light by those who are blessed with liberty and the means of enjoying it." To these paragraphs Dr.
Laurie signed his name, and Ibrahima followed this with an inscription in Arabic.

"We are requested to state that Prince Abdraman, of Timboo,
will attend, in Moorish Costume, at the Panorama of the Falls of
Niagara, today, from 10 o'clock A.M. 'til 6 P.M. —Where the
public will have an opportunity of seeing this interesting Personage, who has been the subject of singular and extraordinary vicis-
situdes." So ran the Society's announcement, faithfully inserted in
the administration prints. "The Falls," a painting of the original
on five thousand square feet of canvas, was displayed at a
rotunda near the White House. For an admission fee of twenty-
five cents, a viewer could see this panorama, which was said to
mimic nature so well that patrons came away wet. Ibrahima, by
special arrangement with the management, got half the gate for a
full day's appearance in costume.

Many ladies who saw him here requested he put his autograph
in their albums. For the curious and for those incredulous at the

thought of a literate African, he wrote the opening sura of the Qur'an, called the Fatihāh. It was the sentiment written so many times in slavery:

> In the name of God, the merciful and the compassionate.
> Praise be to God, the Lord of the worlds, the merciful,
>   and the compassionate.
> The King of the day of judgment.
> Thee do we adore, on Thee do we call for succor.
> Lead us into the right way, the way of those to whom Thou
>   hast been gracious, of those toward whom Thou hast
>   not been angry, and who have not erred.

"It must be evident to everyone," wrote a Northern black who met him, "that the Prince is a man superior to the generality of Africans whom we behold in this country. He is a fine Arabic scholar, and even now, at his advanced life, writes an elegant hand." The tall, spare African soon appeared on Capitol Hill, where his erect bearing and tangled mass of white hair caught the eyes of the legislators. He was admitted to the presence of committees of Congress, drawing even the attention of the slaveholding Southerners. One person who saw him felt "his deportment would have been thought that of a gentleman in any company, however refined." In a committee room where he presented his subscription book, Congressman Edward Everett saw Ibrahima write "the Arabic character with the fluency and the elegance of a scribe." So impressed was Everett that he still remembered the moment when he was Secretary of State in 1853, and he recalled it then in a speech: "I must allude to the extraordinary attainments of that native African prince, Abduhl Rahahman. If there was ever a native-born gentleman on earth, he was one. He had the port and air of a prince, and the literary culture of a scholar." In Everett's mind Ibrahima ranked with Paul Cuffee as a representative of the great capacity of Africa.

Visits to individual homes in these weeks netted Ibrahima a few dollars more. "The African prince called to see us," Congressman Everett noted in his journal. "I gave him $5. His story is exceedingly curious." President Adams was less charitable. "Abduhl Rahaman brought me a subscription book to raise a fund for purchasing the freedom of his five sons and his eight grandchildren, to which I declined subscribing." Adams gives no explanation in his diary for this refusal, but two conjectures come quickly to mind. Perhaps Adams did not wish him to suffer from the bitter party emnity, as he might if Adams appeared his advocate. Less generous to the President is a notion more probable, that he was tired of being dunned by strangers from every section of the country, many of whom acted as if he had an obligation to help them.

Congress ended its six-month session on May 26, and in the next few days its members paved the roads out of town with wheel spokes and harness leather. As Ibrahima had exhausted local charity, he decided to go north in their wake. Clay was not only agreeable to his plan, but the Secretary did a kind thing for him. Like Adams, it seems Clay recalled only that Thomas had freed him "on condition that he should be sent home by the Government." What Thomas had insisted upon, and what Clay had agreed to, was much more restrictive—"that he should only enjoy liberty in his native country." Forgetting or ignoring this, Clay prepared the following recommendation.

Washington, 5th June, 1828

> The bearer hereof, Prince, is a Moor, reduced to captivity near a half century ago. The Executive of the United States, has obtained him from his master, with a view of restoring him to his friends and country.
>
> He and his wife, Isabella, intend visiting some of the Northern Capitals of the United States.
>
> I take pleasure in recommending him to the kind and friendly offices of all in whose company he may fall.

H. Clay

With this note and with letters from Gurley, Ibrahima traveled back to Baltimore during the second week of June. Upward of seventy thousand people lived in this city, and its ships traded to every quarter of the world. Yet the blacks here enjoyed little personal or economic security. "I observe that a good deal has been said of the propriety of allowing the blacks to drive hacks, carts, &c.," someone wrote editor Lundy. It is a comment that throws flares of light on the uncertainities of their existence. From just such causes the Society had made some friends among Baltimore blacks. A handful had actually emigrated. *Voices from Africa,* a colonization history for black children, had been published recently in the city, and a member of the Society of Friends was circulating three thousands copies at his own expense to promote the Colony.

Ibrahima rejoined Isabella in a room that Swaim may have provided them and rested a few days. On the clear, sunny morning of June 10, he called at the Gay Street office of Charles Harper, a young Harvard-educated attorney who handled the local agency of the Society. "A man of brilliant talents, charming manners, refined and generous," Harper was a simple-spirited person much offended by the "Prince of Timbuctoo" stories. "If what I have read in the papers about his being paraded through towns in Moorish costume and treated as a fallen sovereign be true," he complained to Gurley, "the injudicious zeal of his friends has well nigh made him ridiculous." Sight of the Pullo ended his fears. "He is quite a respectable looking old man," Harper conceded. "I was glad to see him dressed and behaving so properly." Ibrahima had a long conversation with the attorney in which the subject of the course of the Niger River came up. Here, as in Washington, Ibrahima stated that the river disappeared into the earth and never rises. Harper was unconvinced, but had little doubt "the question will be settled by some explorers from Liberia."

As such assurance suggests, Harper was completely dedicated to the idea of colonization. In a letter written in 1827 from South Carolina he had said, "John, we must not die until we find some place of refuge for the blacks. [Otherwise], a fearful conflict is in preparation for posterity." "John" was John H. B. Latrobe, son of the noted architect Benjamin Latrobe. An attorney like Harper, who was his most intimate friend, he was the person who coined the word "Monrovia" for the capital of Liberia, in honor of James Monroe, President when the town was founded.

"Mr. Latrobe and I gave [Ibrahima] a certificate to take around with him, in which we set forth his claims and called upon the charitable," Harper informed the Society. Again, Ibrahima walked the promenades, visiting the public fountains, the Washington Monument, Fell's Point, and the city buildings. The hand that had brandished a sword and scattered the Bambara to their headwaters a half century ago now thrust a subscription book at the high chokers and silks of the Baltimore gentry. This commercially minded place and entrepôt of the domestic slave trade scarcely noticed. By week's end he had collected here and in Washington but a total of $420. It was a small and not a cheering amount for the need at hand. It was less than half the price of Simon or Prince alone.

This fact turned his efforts to Philadelphia, where he arrived in mid-June. It was a city that impressed visitors as clean, well paved, and open. The streets ran at right angles, and the houses had a well built and comfortable look. The white marble banks and public buildings had a strength and character that pointed back to the Quaker origins of the town. Some people still insisted the city's most prominent aspect was "a grave decorum" inherited from the time of Father Penn. This must have been exaggerated, but it was true that at the Academy of Fine Arts an unknown person had mutilated the statues of the nude males by removing from each that feature which offended.

Colonization affairs here were among the healthiest in the United States. The goals of the Society had much support in white business and professional circles. Influential friends included Gerard Ralston, merchant and treasurer of the Pennsylvania Colonization Society. There was also the trader John Hanson, whose receipts of gold dust from the colony attracted much attention. One of the Delaware River wharves was crowded with his Liberian ivory and camwood piled up like cords of firewood. Another supporter was Dr. John K. Mitchell, a physician and lecturer at the Medical Institute of Philadelphia. Recently Dr. Mitchell had been urged by Gurley to take a young Liberian named Washington Davis as a medical student. He had been agreeable, "but on consulting my pupils, several of whom are from South Carolina," Mitchell reported, "I find prejudice too strong to permit me to take the course dictated by my own feelings. To give him a public regular medical education in America seems out of the question." Davis had been sent to New York for the present.

Ibrahima brought to Philadelphia his Mississippi and Washington testimonials, the subscription book, Clay's passport, and a satchel of *African Repository* issues. The latter contained biographical details suitable for republication by interested editors.

Ralston and Dr. Mitchell met with him, inspected his credentials, and read the letters he brought. The men were, as Ralston phrased it, "convinced of the correctness of the statements made concerning him." With five other Philadelphians they prepared a lengthy certificate for him to use in his local solicitations. It leaned heavily upon the rescue of Dr. Cox: "We join in commending him to the benevolence of our fellow citizens, trusting that the son of a man by whom one of our countrymen was befriended in time of need, at a distance from his home, will not be denied by this wealthy people the small sum requisite to redeem his children from bondage." Nathaniel Ware was in town and added a laconic endorsement.

Dr. Mitchell had wanted Ibrahima to come to Philadelphia for some time and had even written Gurley asking it. Meeting him at last, Mitchell was highly pleased. He took him around the city to see several wealthy friends, confidently making it known at Washington that "Prince will get at least 1000$ in Phila." Later Ibrahima patrolled the streets alone, haunting the Coffee House, where merchants had gathered since 1754. On his walks others shuffled in competition, including a man who claimed charity because the Indians had cut out his tongue. One call took the prince to the office of Mayor Joseph Watson. At the mayor's writing table he penned autographs for onlookers, writing, as a newsman said, "with much facility, in the Arabic manner from right to left. This is all the more remarkable as he had been forty years out of practice." His outfit drew much attention. It was observed "he appeared in the costume of his country"; "a dignified looking man of full African colour & visage"; "a tall genteel person, of genuine dignity of manners."

The custom of the Society was to call on Christian ministers in Philadelphia and elsewhere to preach sermons and gather collections in behalf of its activities every July 4. In this request the Society was encouraged by those who thought youth first tempted into vice and ruin by the drumming, fiddling, dancing, firing of cannon, and drinking of toasts that always accompanied the day. Episcopalian and Presbyterian churches in the city agreed to cooperate with this plan, and an arrangement was made for the collection at the Sixth Presbyterian Church to be donated to Ibrahima. He would be present on that day, as would the Reverend

John Lewis, a Baptist preacher from Liberia who would outline the prospects of the colony. Center stage, however, would belong to the Reverened John H. Kennedy, the church's minister, who was preparing a sermon titled "Sympathy, Its Foundation and Legitimate Exercise Considered, in Special Relation to Africa."

Kennedy was an individual whose life typlified the feverish reformism of the times. He labored daily to send Bibles to the "priest-ridden" Catholics in South America, to stem intemperance, or in some similar work. But all zeal burned low compared to his interest in Liberia, where he wished bark to core to be sent as a missionary. A man of prayers and fasting, Kennedy had seen slavery in Virginia and North Carolina, and he loathed it. "Mr. Kennedy is warmly engaged in our good cause," Gurley was told at this time, "with *all his heart, head & both of his hands.*"

Friday, July 4, turned out cool and pleasant in Philadelphia. Country farmers abandoned their hayfields, and so many stores closed in the city that the place exhibited the usual appearance of a Sunday. General Jackson's friends by the hundreds went to a celebration at Lebanon; equally numerous were the administration diners in the Masonic Hall. At ten in the morning several dozen people assembled at the Sixth Presbyterian Church on Spruce Street. Ibrahima was introduced to them. In his best English he told them of his African life, his captivity and slavery, and his wish to redeem his family. Lewis spoke next and then took his seat, and John Kennedy mounted the pulpit for his appeal. He began it with a call for Christian benevolence and charity. He believed in the essential unity of all races. Africans, he said, "are men, rational and immortal beings, possessed of feelings and rights and hopes and souls. Shall we remain unmoved while they are reckoned up as the beasts of the field?" The fruits of such an attitude would be terrible. In the South, "in process of time, the slaves must gain the ascendency. The scenes of St. Domingo will be acted over in our land." Kennedy predicted civil war unless slavery was ended. "*Lover of our country!*" he shouted, "slavery if not remedied will prove our ruin. Already a line broad and deep divides between the slave States and the Free. Animosities exist in almost every form; and widely separated as these sections of our country are in habits and interests we hope for nothing better, until a righteous Providence, for our own crime of withholding from others what he has freely bestowed on us, shall sweep this promising empire with the besom of destruction!"

For the charity of the moment, Kennedy made a direct plea: "We ought to feel kindly and to act kindly towards others, to sympathise with the sufferer and to lighten if may be, his burden. There is an obligation on all persons to give suitable expression to their sympathy." At the conclusion of his sermon, Kennedy circulated a collection plate to call forth those "suitable expressions." But, for this well-publicized and arranged meeting, the contributions were disappointing.

The aspect of the press was also discouraging. Coverage was thin to nonexistent. Prominent newspapers printed nothing about Ibrahima and in one of them even the space to announce the church meeting had to be purchased. Interest in Africa, though greater than in the South, was low. This was one reason why Enoch Lewis's *African Observer* magazine had failed here in the spring. But beyond this, few literary men in the city had an appreciation of Ibrahima. The editors of *The Casket* ("flowers of literature, wit, and sentiment") devoted much of their August issue to explorers seeking Timbuktu as if unaware there was a man walking the city streets who had been there. Weekly newspapers ran scraps from African explorers such as Clapperton or Laing as if ignorant that Ibrahima could have kept a row of clerks busy with his knowledge of the western Sudan. Most Philadelphians seem simply to have missed him, and science missed the unique opportunity of his visit.

It was true that many in polite society had fled the heat of summer for Germantown or other correct places. Those who remained were drawn to other matters such as the visit of the English writer Captain Basil Hall. The clergy's eye would not leave Charles Grandison Finney, the startling evangelist, and as for charity, there were more appeals to it than ears to hear them. Money was being sought for schools, for orphans, for the deaf, and for the "lunatick." A drive was under way to raise funds for churches and to purchase Bibles for destitute families. Charitable "houses of refuge" needed support. Most topical of all was the appeal of the committee to aid war-racked Greece. Even before the death of Lord Byron in 1824, but especially after it, this cause made remarkable headway among the fashionable. Nor had the

Ottoman slaughter and slavery of the Christian Greeks elevated opinions of Islam in the United States. In the face of all these claims to charity, the Colonization Society itself suffered. Over-all July 4 collections were poor, and Ralston was forced to write Gurley on July 22, "the contributions this year are much smaller and fewer than I expected."

Dr. Mitchell's assurance of "at least 1000$" now appeared foolishly optimistic and inflated. Not half that had been pledged, and not all that had been pledged could be collected. "Prince Abduhl Rahahman's subscription is not as prosperous as I should wish it to be," Ralston confessed. There was no doubt the season was wrong, the demands on the charitable high, but equally important was the fact that few people took the time to help him. Some members of his own committee even failed to attend his meetings. Alexander Plumley, an itinerant agent of the Society who was in the city, summed it up: "I was very much pleased with the Prince, but sorry to hear that no more exertion had been made for him. Dr. Mitchell observed to me that he succeeded very well in soliciting donations when he called with the good old man, & nothing was wanting but the aid of other gentlemen to do the same, to raise a respectable sum for him; but you know how reluctant gentlemen are to go on begging errands." For six weeks' labor Ibrahima collected $350.

To counter his disappointment, everyone pointed him northward. "I am inclined to think he would do much better in the Eastern States," a member of his committee wrote Gurley. Agent Plumley, the wandering *marabout* who had just traveled one thousand miles by coach and five hundred by foot for the Society, was also convinced that New England was the place for Ibrahima to go. "The case of the old man excited much interest in the east when I was there," he informed the national office, "& I am confident that, if the proper steps were taken, any sum, that is anything within the bounds of reason necessary to liberate his family might be raised." The bounds of reason included ten thousand dollars, Plumley speculated, "so confident [am I of] my knowledge of public sentiment in N-E."

Dutifully, Ibrahima departed Philadelphia in late July, making his way by steamboat and stage toward Boston. His time in traveling was passed in part by writing in a book he had purchased.

Though it might not appear so to observers, Ibrahima was being embarrassed by some of the requests he received to write literary passages. The years of slavery had taken their toll in both calligraphy and grammar, had taken it so thoroughly that now only his early lessons in the Qur'an came to him without effort. The pressures to appear "a scholar of no ordinary acquirements," as one Boston editor phrased it, were terrific, however, and he felt it so important to his fund raising that he practiced continuously at copying lines from a Qur'an and a second book in Arabic that had been given him in Washington. Thus occupied, he sped away to New England, passing through New York, but declining to stop for now. His health was not good, he had been ill in Washington, and he wished to visit farther north before the winter began.

Ibrahima reached Boston during the first week in August. When he had become a slave in 1788, it had been a comfortable, uncrowded seaport of eighteen thousand people. Now the city had more than tripled its population and expanded everywhere on the hilly peninsula that was its home. What had been back lots and wastes were filled with buildings. The one bridge from the "tight little island" now had four neighbors. On the site of John Hancock's pasture was the State House, a most imposing structure with "a high moslem-looking dome." Around it, the cowpaths of the Revolution had become narrow and crooked streets lined with markets, churches, and homes. Across macadamed Beacon Street was the Commons, where Quakers had been hung in the seventeenth century. Nearly within the shadow of State House was "Nigger Hill," home of Boston's black community. Here, too, was centered what a local minister called *"Satan's Seat,"* a Beelzebub's delight of drunkards, harlots, and outcasts who influenced "multitudes of coloured people into habits of indolence." Such a charge did not suggest that many respectable black tradesmen and laborers lived in the area, that public begging in the city was infrequent, or that Boston's citizens considered it a safer place to live than New York.

Ibrahima had received, perhaps from Gurley, a letter of introduction to Charles Tappan, a local merchant. This somewhat pompous individual was the principal partner in the firm of Tappan & Mansfield, a piecegoods business on State Street. A member of

a large Connecticut River Valley family, Tappan was a conservative with a reformer's instincts. He found the colonization ideals
well in harmony with his own and was no friend of those who
wished a hasty, turbulent emancipation. He stood aloof from
means that were not moderate. It was a disposition shared
with Edward Everett and many white Bostonians and it gave little
comfort to Benjamin Lundy, then in town speaking on the "fallacious reasoning" of the Society.

In a now familiar routine, Ibrahima began his appearances. It
was advisable to see the newspapers first, as a bit of editorial sarcasm or doubt could ruin the propsects for charity. And it was
important for the editors to distinguish him from some of the imi-
tators he was inspiring, such as "Abdullah Mohammed," who
claimed to have been taken from his native Syria by pirates.
"Abdullah," with *his* certificates and *his* doleful story, hoaxed a
governor, a professor of Eastern literature, and other influential
persons for free meals and lodging before being exposed as a lark-
ing college student. "Almourad Ali" had also popped up, collecting $1500 for "my passage home to Turkey" before it was discov-
ered the only home he had was in Albany, New York, and he was
wanted there by the police. "People now-a-days had rather be
swindled by ten pretended foreign noblemen, than to render assistance to one needy and deserving fellow citizen," an editor
lamented.

Fortunately, Ibrahima had no trouble clearing away suspicions
of imposture. His visits to the newspaper offices, made in the
company of Tappan on Saturday, August 9, 1828, scored impres-
sively for him. Editors liked the tall and well-formed African. He
appeared to them "a tall, venerable looking black, with an intelligent countenance," "a striking face and a clear and intelligent
eye." One editor wrote, "We had the pleasure of an introduction
this morning, through the politeness of Mr. Tappan, to *Abduhl
Rahahman,* the celebrated African Prince, the story of whose misfortunes has recently been developed in the public prints, and is
doubtless fresh in the recollection of every friend of suffering
humanity. —The object of his visit to this city, is to avail himself
of the benevolence and charities of this community. This appeal
we are confident, will not be made in vain."

Ibrahima planned to appear in costume the following Monday,

and this day's visits were purposeful, since the stories they generated would appear in Monday's editions. When the new week arrived, the editors did all they could for him. The *Evening Bulletin, Columbian Centinel, Daily Advertiser, Patriot, Commercial Gazette,* and *New-England Palladium* took up the case simply and humanely, accompanying their articles with such fetching items as Clay's passport or one of Griffin's letters to the Society. Even the local campaign organ for Jackson was sympathetic. Despite this overwhelming introduction, Ibrahima was not found on the streets as promised. A fever had hit him again, and it was not until the afternoon of Tuesday that he felt strong enough to venture out. For this purpose he dressed in the blue frock coat and full trousers drawn about the ankles. A broad crimson sash was put around his waist, the white muslim turban was replaced with a green silk Turkish cap, and although the crescent remained, the scimitar was sensibly retired. With his long blue cape thrown over one arm, he paced State Street, an excellent location leading to busy wharfs. "His dress gave to his figure a fantastical appearance," someone later reminisced. "There was a novelty in the arrival of such a person in Boston, as this coloured Prince of the Blood, and, of course, he attracted the gaze of our citizens as he passed along."

Gaining strength in the following days, he lengthened his walks, visiting the Exchange with Tappan or stopping at the Mall, where concerts were carried on several evenings a week at the expense of public-spirited individuals. His clothes made him an object of amusement to some. Children gathered at corners and in parks to look and shout at him. Neither could William Clapp of the *Evening Gazette* resist a few pokes at "The Prince Errant." "The most of our citizens have seen a tall, sedate, sable son of Africa, walking about the streets, dressed in the costume of his country, if such are the fashions at Tombuctoo. It is doubtful if King Woolah himself, on the high festivals of his court, could make a more imposing show." Clapp wished "*His Highness*" a safe return to Africa, "if such are his own wishes—though he seems to be doing very well where he is." Others who saw him had more sober reflections. "We have as a people used the Africans so ill—our dainties have been so connected with their privations and blood, that we think it but a drop in the bucket to do a kind act to *one* of them," "Gambia" wrote to the *Evening Chronicle*. "I felt ashamed to see a man begging money to redeem his children in the streets of our *free* and happy republic," an authoress noted, "and [I] blushed for the dishonor of my country."

Appreciation of Ibrahima was not confined to whites. Prominent blacks had learned straightaway of his arrival in Boston and lost no time in offering him their help. Within two days they were escorting him on the Mall and elsewhere about the city. Their excitement was evident in the remark of one: "The day of my anticipation has arrived, and I now have the pleasure of being in the company of an African Prince." As these individuals almost without exception feared and opposed the Colonization Society, Ibrahima demonstrated his own independence by associating with them. The connection shows true integrity in the African. He was ready to help and be helped by the Society, but he did not consider himself a ribbon on the tail of its kite. Further, in the face of the realities of fund raising, for which he needed many friends, his own prejudices against darker people continued to erode. Just as slavery had worked to destroy his Pullo concept of superiority by its devastating and arbitrary leveling, now the blacks of Boston, freely assembling their few resources for his use, were doing the same. His presence in the city had caused their neighborhoods to be swept with what a white friend called an "enthusiastic feeling." Residents even decided on a public dinner in his honor.

A Rhode Islander once said enviously that "the Bostonians, when they set out to do a thing, never do it by halves." Ibrahima could see what he meant. In a weekend of frantic planning, the African Masonic Hall was chosen as the site for a banquet, a route for a street parade established, and fifty blacks joined to underwrite the cost of the affair. The celebration was held on Wednesday, August 20. By four o'clock in the afternoon of that day, several hundred people had gathered before the African School. Arranging themselves in the order of a marshal, young men, chief marshal, committee of arrangements, president and two vice-presidents-of-the-day, the prince, two more vice-presidents, clergy, elder citizens, and another marshal, the procession marched off to the airs of a local band. Arriving at the African Masonic Hall on Cambridge Street, they enjoyed "a well provided dinner and dessert." Songs followed, including one written especially for Ibrahima. "The whole ceremony," wrote a Boston editor, was "characterized by a spirit of urbanity and decorum highly honorable to all concerned."

If anything seemed absurd about a parade and banquet of hair-dressers, tailors, handcartmen, laborers, waiters, and barbers honoring an old slave, it soon gave way. These were men with serious thoughts, concerned not only about their own fates in Boston but about such great issues as the continuance of Southern slavery and the regeneration of Africa. One of the marshals happened to be David Walker, a clothing dealer, who, as a passionate advocate of freedom, was within a few months of issuing his incendiary *Appeal* for liberty through insurrection, which would infuriate the South and widen the sectional cleavage. "Our worthy guest," Walker said of Ibrahima, ". . . was by Africans' natural enemies torn from country, religion, and friends, and, in the very midst of Christians, doomed to perpetual, though unlawful bondage. May God enable him to obtain so much of the reward of his labor, as may purchase the freedom of his offspring."

The sense of the banqueteers was given in a string of toasts. Ibrahima's fortitude and character were lauded and he was called "fellow countryman" and "great and noble patriot" by the speakers. The sharpest toasts were pointed south:

> May the Slave-Holders of the world be like the whales in the ocean, with the thrasher at their back and the sword fish at their belly, until they rightly understand the difference between freedom and slavery.
>
> The Manumission Society. —May complete success attend their philanthropic undertaking.
>
> Southern Gentlemen, are you not alarmed? Methinks I hear Dame Fate exclaim, Africa shall be free without the aid of the Colonization Society!

Ibrahima and the company applauded each sentiment. Shouts of support ran through the hall, and messages from those unable to attend arrived to be read and heartily approved. For his hosts' unexpected demonstration of warmth and friendship, Ibrahima rose to toast them. "Brethren," he said simply, "the token of respect which you have this day been pleased to confer, will ever be held by me in grateful remembrance."

There was an exhilaration in the day's events, and when the

banquet was ended, it could not have been apparent that the toasts and cheers that were raised would fly to the rafters and commence an echo that would ring in Natchez and New Orleans. What concerned the diners and what pleased them, too, was the fact that it had not been Mississippi's planters who raised testimonial glasses to the son of Sori. That had been done by the children and grandchildren of his own part of the world. Ibrahima had looked old to them as he sat at the table of honor, and the marks of hard labor were on his face. To reflect on what had happened to him, one diner said, "excited the indignation of all." But it was strangely true that despite his forty years of slavery, he was still man enough to be a matter of consequence to them, his character striking enough to be a matter of pride. And in that case it was not trifling of Ibrahima to take their charity. By being himself he could leave in its place a small inspiration.

7. "The Almoner of His Bounty"

Cyrus Griffin was sinking deeper into the bogs of Natchez. A few weeks after Ibrahima left for the North, Griffin became editor of a new newspaper called the *Southern Galaxy*. Handsomely printed on an imperial sheet, it drew praise throughout the country. The name was suggested by his brother Joseph's *Eastern Galaxy and Herald* of Brunswick, Maine, though the columns of the *Galaxy* would owe less to Joseph than to Boston's lively and literate *New-England Galaxy,* whose mixture of wit and solvency Cyrus admired greatly. At any rate, the paper certainly could not bring in less money than his law practice, and the crutches forbade anything more active.

His effort to attain a circulation was novel. Sending out the first issue, he asked those who did not like it to send it back. Those who failed to do so would be considered subscribers. "No gentleman could be so impolite as to return the paper," a fellow editor wrote, and so by July four hundred, willing and unwilling, were joined by his enterprise.

"What a happy fellow must the editor be, who conceived so good a plan to give circulation to his paper," said a writer in Boston. "He must be a Yankee, and we hope the paper will not turn out to be a wooden nutmeg."

The notes from Cyrus's talks with Ibrahima were written into a series of articles that Cyrus published in May and June. It was one of but two or three accounts of African life and opinions collected from a slave ever to run in a Southern newspaper. In the third installment, Ibrahima scorched the rapacious planters. "You

no pray often enough—you greedy after money," the Pullo told
the cotton lords. It was not flattery designed to win readers and it
did not help the paper. "It may be thought—it has even been
hinted," Cyrus wrote, "that we have already attached too much
consequence to the incidents of this man's life. We cannot help
it." Still, when the series concluded, Cyrus ignored the flow of
news from the North and fell silent on his friend.

At the plantation he listened gloomily as Thomas outlined the
terms for the sons' manumission. The old man had seen the gold
in hand at last. "He states explicitly he shall claim $8,500 for the
children and grandchildren," Cyrus wrote Gurley. "Comparing
these slaves with others, the price claimed for them is exorbitant;
but, estimating them by their intrinsic value—their moral habits
and physical ability, the sum claimed would scarcely be considered extravagant here." Ibrahima's letters to his children had
arrived and been read to them ("Every letter passes through the
hand of their master"). Instead of calming them, the letters,
offering word of the fantastic world beyond the gullies of the children's nativity, added to the unsettled feeling that had run on
the bluff since spring. Ibrahima wrote only of the kindnesses he
had received, but news of any progress was turbulent. Quickly
Thomas complained "in relation to the language used by Prince,
as tending to excite insubordination. I would suggest the propriety
of cautioning Prince upon this point," Cyrus added, "as it may
increase a feeling of hostility, which, as you are well aware,
already exists to no small degree, toward the Colonization Society
in the South."

The summer crawled along awaiting more word from the
North. Clouds seemed to desert Natchez, the sun burned orange,
and dust assumed its customary arrogance, billowing up from the
boot into the unsuspecting mouth. Mosquitoes fed on the citizenry
until it was said they were so heavy they fell straight from the
flesh to the floor. Yellow fever was imminent, and the city fathers
wisely prohibited excavation of building sites, since "yellow jack"
might escape through holes dug into the earth. So many whites
left town for the country it seemed to Cyrus that the place was
"overrun by Negroes and Indians." Of all human endeavor, it was
only politics that did not evoke the most genuine cynicism.

Early August found Cyrus at the courthouse, challenging those who lacked the residency to vote. Hobbling about the polls, he brushed against Judge John Maury, a Jackson man whose recent election to the criminal court he had opposed.

"Stand back, Sir, until I am done!" Maury shouted, and he sent Cyrus sprawling with a shove. The editor said nothing at the time, but that evening sent him a note requesting an explanation of his violence. The judge, replying through a friend, said "that it was a singular question to ask him—that his conduct on all occasions spoke for itself."

Now publicly humiliated, Cyrus seemed in no position to teach the judge his manners. He was unable to walk without crutches or a cane, "as Maury well knew." "So far as regards physical ability," wrote Cyrus, "I might easily be overcome by a boy of fourteen." Still, a public jostle and rebuke were treatment no one who wished the respect of the nabobs could ignore. Two days later Cyrus posted this notice:

> Circumstances require me to denounce the Hon. John M. Maury as a SCOUNDREL and a COWARD, possessing the malignity to inflict an injury, but destitute of those principles of honor that should induce him to afford *satisfaction*.

> Natchez, 6th August   C. Griffin

Only twenty-four months in Natchez, and Cyrus had fallen into one of its worst habits.

The following day, armed with three pistols, he went cautiously from his apartment to the *Galaxy* office. There was no incident. But on returning to the Mansion House for lunch, he heard his name called as he approached the hotel door. Turning, he saw Judge Maury aiming a pistol in each hand at him. It was obvious His Honor did not intend to observe the rules of the *code duello*. Both men opened fire immediately, the bullets smacking everything on the street but their targets. The judge then rushed Cyrus, who fumbled wildly in his trousers for a concealed pistol while he dragged himself through the hotel portals and into the bar.

"Now is your time, Maury, damn him! Kill him!" shouted a spectator, as each exchanged another round in the hotel. The editor merely aerated Maury's coat, but the judge's ball chewed into the thigh of Cyrus's lame leg. His foe disarmed and wounded, Maury drew a sword cane and fell on him. Parrying two or three thrusts, the editor seized the sword, but the judge's superior strength drove the blade deep into his chest. Cyrus thought the stab fatal, and, crying "Murder!" fell on a chair and then on the floor. Maury wanted more and came at him again, but a bystander aroused himself at last and intervened.

Cyrus was carried upstairs to his room. There Dr. Cox dressed his wounds and found them not as serious as they looked. Though confined to bed, the editor still cranked out the *Galaxy,* giving columns and columns of his views of what had happened. Maury began to glower again, so much so that he offered Cyrus a second opportunity for satisfaction in September. By then, however, the editor had contracted dengue in his convalescence (courtesy of Natchez's famous mosquitoes), and, with joints so painful they could scarcely be moved, "that reparation which gentlemen of honor have a right to demand" seemed distinctly less important than it had the month before.

Peter Butler, the clothier who helped organize Ibrahima's Boston banquet, asked at that dinner, "Southern gentlemen, are you not alarmed?" He would not have believed their reply.

Southern gentlemen were alarmed indeed. As the circumstances and extent of Ibrahima's tour became known in Natchez by late summer, Thomas grew livid. Why had the government not sent him overseas? "I consider the contract entered into by the Government, thro' the agency of Henry Clay, Secretary of State, entirely violated, and I would not have entered into it for two thousand dollars," he wrote, "if I had known that the business would have been conducted as it has been, inasmuch as the said Prince has written several letters to my slaves, stating he would procure their freedom." Thomas covered Marschalk with complaints, and he told the mending Cyrus to demand that the Colonization Society send Ibrahima off. He was worried particularly by the news that Ibrahima would return to Natchez during the winter. Cyrus informed Gurley in mid-September, "I write you at the request of Mr. Thomas Foster, the former master of Prince. He has been recently informed that it is the intention of Prince to visit Natchez. He wishes to say to you, or rather to him through you, that he objects to this arrangement. He would remind him of the condition of his manumission, which was that he leave the U-

States with the least possible delay. He thinks the contemplated visit would be attended with the most pernicious consequences—and that should Prince persist in his design, on his arrival here, he would be remanded to servitude."

The planter seemed to be in a second childhood to Cyrus, but his power to injure Ibrahima through his family had to be respected. "We are to make due allowances for the actions and feeling of a man," he wrote, "in whom self-interest has, perhaps, swallowed up every other consideration." Recalling Gurley had published two of his earlier letters, he added, "I speak, of course, confidentially." One duel a year was enough.

The situation at Wall and Franklin streets was even more awkward. Colonel Marschalk had been his champion, mailman, agent of liberation. It was he who had given Thomas assurance there would be, as Clay had promised, "no difficulty in acceding to the conditions." It was to him that Thomas delivered Ibrahima under a deed so drawn. And it was to him that Ibrahima expressed the desire to return with the money he raised. The colonel's hope that Ibrahima might find some funds in the North had encompassed no tour so extensive nor interest so public as was occurring. His discomfort became a deepening chagrin as Indian Summer rolled over Natchez. Each mail from the North brought more and more news of Ibrahima's activities. Embarrassed, still smarting at the charge of having sold himself to the Jackson campaign, he considered throwing the entire mess into presidential politics. An enmity toward Adams and Clay, who had sent the public printing to Captain Cook at the *Ariel,* made this an obvious remedy. Thomas, knee-jerk supporter of General Jackson, could not object if he did, for the administration had ignored him cavalierly. News arriving in late September of the banquet in Boston settled his determination. The dinner seemed brazenly political, its toasts revolutionary, and Ibrahima wildly truant. Then, about the first week in October, yet another letter from the Pullo arrived. Although innocence itself in content, it coolly announced the prince's intention to visit Providence, Hartford, New York, and elsewhere. If a last straw was needed, that was it.

The colonel prepared a methodical attack. A full two weeks were spent in gathering ammunition. He had the clerk of the county court draw up certified copies of Clay's January letter to himself. Other documents were sent out for the imprimaturlike signature of a prominent notary. Even Thomas was persuaded to drive into town and give a statement of his woes. From these items, from letters, transcripts, and abolitionist items in the nation's press, Marschalk penned a *coup de main* for the Jackson campaign. The very night that Ibrahima's tour reached its high point in New York, the press of Marschalk's *Statesman & Gazette* struck off fifteen hundred copies of a handbill titled, "Mr. Adams and the Emancipation of Slaves and the Violation of the Faith of the Administration." This five-thousand-word broadside was soon distributed at Natchez and in Louisiana, from Concordia across the river down to Pointe Coupée, Baton Rouge, and New Orleans, passed eagerly along by supporters of General Jackson. For those who might miss this "extra," Marschalk reprinted it in the October 16, 1828, edition of his newspaper.

"The facts which we are about to lay before the community are of a most alarming character," the handbill began. "Citizens of the South! We entreat your attention, whilst we proceed to prove a shameless violation of a written contract of Messrs. Adams and Clay with Mr. Thomas Foster of this state, which violation has done and is now doing more to cause the massacree of St. Domingo to be reacted here, than any other thing which has ever occurred in the union!" After demonstrating what was true, that Clay was permitting Ibrahima to enjoy his liberty in the North, the colonel laid the most incendiary toasts of the Boston banquet before his readers. The sentiment of Domingo Williams, who hoped "the slave holders of the world would be like the whales in the ocean, with the thrasher at their back and the SWORDfish *at their belly,*" was highlighted and repeated three times. "The slaves of the south," Marschalk deduced, "are openly invited to revolt and to murder their masters. Look at the last census of the white and black population of Mississippi and Louisiana, and ask yourselves what must be the consequences if our blacks are inoculated with the doctrines contained in the toasts." Disingenuously including pieces from Lundy's *Genius of Universal Emancipation,* Marschalk played on the ever present fear of slaves "revelling in *white blood.*" Adams and Clay, "the emancipating Administration," must bear the responsibility and consequences if this happened, for they "violated a most solemn contract in permitting this dinner." The effect of Ibrahima, "their travelling emancipator," and his Boston cronies would be "to excite the Negroes in the southern states to rise and massacree their masters. . . . Has [Ibrahima] not already inspirited the 'thirst for liberty' into 15 of Mr. Foster's slaves and several others? . . . Anxious that our deluded fellow citizens who still adhere to Mr. Adams, should awake to a knowledge of the real questions now at issue," he concluded, he would open all his letters and related papers for public inspection. "Unite with us in the cause of self-preservation!"

Could the colonel have been serious? Was he frightened, or was this just another trick from an old, much-battered editor? There is no doubting the answer. Marschalk, who had harried what he now termed "the emancipating Administration" into emancipating Ibrahima, had caught Clay in a clear oversight. But the remainder of his handbill, the bulk of it, was the sheerest sophism, and everyone knew it. Cyrus, a violent Adams man, was astonished when he read it. Another anti-Jackson figure in the city wrote, "The apprehension and alarm of its author is manifestly *affected* and *unreal*." For yet another, the colonel was "hypocritical [and had] a zeal more than suspect." People were not worried by his news; they were surprised by it. Most cared less what the opinions of Boston were than that he had given them publicity. "Regretful," "dangerous," "inflammatory" were the early reactions. "Who would have heard of the dinner and toasts of the free blacks in Boston if this production had not issued from the press of this city?" it was asked. The colonel's handbill seemed calculated to produce the very effect he alleged to dread.

Administration men were certain he had overstepped himself by disturbing the racial peace, a crime electioneering would never excuse. Partisans talked angrily of indicting him for sedition. At least they hoped to present for signature "to every inhabitant in the city and county" a statement condemning him. Time permitted only twenty people to gather for the endorsement, but among those who signed were Francis Surget, Dr. Stephen Duncan, Job Routh, Alvarez Fisk, William Dunbar, and Adam Bingaman—taken together, the very wealth and aristocratic marrow of Natchez. Their denunciation was printed in an *Ariel* "extra" of October 24, headed an "Address to the Citizens of Louisiana and Mississippi."

"The undersigned have seen with alarm and painful regret a publication in the 'Statesman & Gazette' of the 16th inst. and also in the form of an 'extra,' " the paper read. "We most seriously lament, as citizens of slave-holding States, that a publication of this nature should have been deemed necessary or proper in the present electioneering contest. . . . We were not prepared for a resort to means in this quarter, which we consider dangerous in their tendency; mischievous in their consequences; and totally unworthy of the friends of any honest cause. . . . Those who have dragged this most delicate subject so rudely before the public . . . have therby trifled with, if not jeopardized, the peace and security of the country and perhaps the lives and happiness of our families."

Cyrus, at the request of Dr. Duncan (who would become the nation's largest slaveholder by the 1850s), gave a statement designed to clear Clay and refresh the public mind as to Marschalk's activities in Ibrahima's behalf. He claimed boldly that Clay's manumission was a private and not official act. Further, as no ships had left the United States for Liberia since the emancipation, Clay could hardly have been expected to send Ibrahima without one. As for the colonel, he stated, "I must confess that it serves to illustrate to me very forcibly, with how little ceremony a man can turn a moral somerset when under the influence of deep political excitement."

The sharpest contempt was a piece of *Ariel* satire.

Off to the Alligators in the Swamps!!!

BLOODY MURDERS

Horrible!–Horrible!!–Horrible!!!–who would have thought of such a dreadful conspiracy against the people of the South by the Jackson party. It seems by an extra sheet published at the *Statesman* office, and which appears as an editorial by Andrew Marschalk, that Marschalk [has] been accused of joining with John Quincy Adams and Henry Clay to make a Bargain with Thomas Foster of this county, to raise a Rebellion amongst the Slaves–that the said Andrew did write a letter to Mr. Clay beseeching him to get Prince a Moorish Slave, the son of a mighty King of Africa, or Asia or some other hot country, liberated

with a view to send him through the Eastern and Northern
states, to eat, drink, and get drunk with all the great men,
white and black, of those parts, in order to rouse the free
negroes, and raise a mighty Army, and march through the
Southern states, and murder the sleeping babies in their
cradles, and take the wives and sisters captives, and reserve
for them a more horrible fate; and that Mr. Clay with the
consent of Mr. Adams, did authorize the said Andrew
and gave him money for that purpose, and that said
Andrew, after the liberation, brought Prince into Natchez
and dressed him up in a Moorish costume, with a Turban
on his head and a broad Cimeter at his side.

Oh! Fellow Citizens of Louisiana and Mississippi, all ye
people of the south, prepare yourselves for the dreadful
scenes that now await you, for deny it as ye may, it is
well known that Prince is now marching at the head of his
Black Troops with the Moorish Cimeter at his side, and
that the said Andrew is to be second to Prince only, &
has been for some time cleaning & sharpening for that
purpose the trusty sword which drank so deeply of Indian
blood.

Rouse up, fellow citizens—rouse up, for Prince cometh
with his mighty army and the *sword of Andrew is thirsting
for* BLOOD.

Such sarcasm suggests that the controversy was changing few
votes. Marschalk claimed gains, but some members of the Jackson party confided the affair was doing them more harm than
good. It was pushed on until the presidential election, however,
the *Statesman & Gazette* giving as much as half of one issue to
the subject. Opposition opinion Marschalk dismissed as "the arrogance and intolerance attendant on the possession of Bank Stock
and Cotton Bales." Ibrahima, in April "a dignified captive, a
man," was now "a personage not fitted to the United States, even
when subjected to the restraint of a master." As for the administration, "it is believed Prince will be retained for years in this
country if Messrs. Adams and Clay are retained in power."

The *Ariel* rebutted by attempting to pass the Boston toasts off
as lampoons made up by students at Harvard College, while from
the *Galaxy* Cyrus threw enfilades on the colonel's "consummate
hypocrisy." "With what unblushing effrontery [has] this man

turned about and affected to criminate and condemn what he alone was almost solely instrumental in effecting," he wrote. The attorney remained calm when Marschalk published a letter to Gurley pilfered from his files, but the colonel's attempt to label him an abolitionist and so ruin his future in the state brought pistols to mind again. His attacks became "unjustifiable and dishonorable" in Cyrus's view, and had not election day on November 3 made further bile unnecessary, the regulars at the Mansion House bar might have been treated to a second "reparation of honor" in one season.

It was in Louisiana where this bugbear was designed to have its impact. Scene of two insurrections in living memory, the state was close enough to Natchez to be alarmed, sufficiently distant not to know the truth. The Jackson press of the state, particularly the *Courier* and the *Louisiana Advertiser* of New Orleans, seized the story on its appearance and spread it sensationally. A notice in the latter illustrates how inaccurate and violent were the charges there:

> Louisianans! We deem it our duty to inform you that this same Negro who is travelling through the Northern States in a splendid carriage at the expense of the Government, is almost daily employed in inundating the Southern States with private letters. Many of these letters were written at the President's House. The Negro is well educated in English.
>
> Read, Frenchmen of Louisiana, and remember St. Domingo! Read, Americans of Louisiana, and remember the Frenchmen of Hayti! Read, Freemen of the South, and shudder at the bitter cup that Northern bigots would have you drink!

Supporters of the President answered along *Ariel* lines. They were appalled that the business was seeing print in the South. "A more daring attempt to raise the slaves to deeds of insubordination in this state was never made," said one. As if to fulfill such fears, a group of free blacks were heard shouting in the streets of New Orleans, "Long live the Northern States! They protect our rights!" There was considerable commotion in the city that weekend, and the night watch had to use the flats of their swords to remind the disaffected where they were.

The incident was the fruit of Marschalk's *"libelle inflâme."* "Had an incendiary missionary set out to preach rebellion and disobedience to the black population there could not be a more alarming prospect to the slave holders." A writer in the bilingual *Argus* of New Orleans charged the Jacksonites would involve Louisiana in *"le sang et le carnage pour triompher de leurs adversaires."* The editor of the *L'Abeille* demanded the Avocat-Général of the state arrest the Jackson editors for inciting insurrection by reprinting Marschalk's handbill.

Editor P. K. Wagner retorted:

> The people of the South ought not to permit a cruel and vindictive African tyrant, crafty, deceitful, proud, and ambitious, to march through the Southern as he is now doing through the Northern States. This travelling emancipator is coming among us, with Mr. Clay's passport in his pocket, impatient to propagate [the Boston toasts] here. Should he ever set foot in Mississippi or Louisiana again, it is to be hoped that a band of patriots will seize upon him and secure him in irons.
>
> Louisianans! Remember that ANDREW JACKSON is a man of the South, a slave-holder, a cotton-planter. Recollect the iniquitous and profligate PLOT OF ADAMS AND CLAY to excite the prejudices of your Northern brethren against the SOUTH by employing an emancipated NEGRO TO ELECTIONEER FOR THEM. Yes! They thought they could not be withstood when they had
>
> AFRICA AT THEIR BACK!!
>
> But we WILL withstand them and their COADJUTORS OF THE HOUSE OF TIMBO, and conquer them too. TIMBO AND QUINCY! QUINCY AND TIMBO!
>
> EBONY AND TOPAZ! TOPAZ AND EBONY!

On election day, 1828, Andrew Jackson triumphed as easily in both states as he had four years earlier.

It was August, the month of duel and dengue in Natchez, and the tall, fine-featured minister, only thirty-four years old, took to the bed from which he would never rise. "I have come here to die," Jehudi Ashmun had said on his arrival home in New Haven.

Seven times as colonial agent in Monrovia he had buried the last whites in the colony besides himself. His wife had been one of them. Now he had returned from Africa too late to recover from his own case of fever. While friends sat around his bed, he rolled and grimaced with pain. Yet he endured remarkably, never complaining or even mentioning his suffering except to apologize to those near him for his agony. "There was something to remind one of the last hours of Socrates," wrote a friend.

On Monday evening, August 25, 1828, "the founder and defender" of colonial settlement in Liberia died. The Wednesday next, Ashmun's body was taken from Miss Miller's to the Center Meeting-House. It was followed through the streets only by the Reverend Gurley and by Cecil, a little African boy who had been Ashmun's companion since the agent wrested him from a Spanish slaver several years before. As the funeral discourse began, Ashmun's mother, who had learned of his death only minutes before when she arrived at the steamboat landing, drove to the church, entered it, and threw herself in tears on the side of the bier.

His was a tragic end, well known and much lamented, for a missionary to any benighted latitude was the *beau ideal* of every right-thinking child of New England. "A correspondent informs us he has seldom seen such evidences of universal and unaffected sorrow," wrote an editor at Hartford. The Colonization Society's officers donned black armbands of crape, a color reflecting well the inward gloom felt at the loss the colony had sustained. But the time was equally propitious for the Society to make headway. Attention fixed strongly on colonization for the moment, as stories of Ashmun and the colony were featured in many newspapers. For the old Pullo, too, the time was at hand for a last harvest of Northern philanthrophy.

Ibrahima was in Boston when the agent died. It was shortly after his banquet there. "I came to this city five weeks ago," he wrote to Natchez, "and have been kindly welcomed and have by much toil succeeded in collecting a few hundred dollars. But the cold weather is coming on, and I think of leaving." As a gesture of farewell, the blacks of the city decided to form a cavalcade and escort Ibrahima to outlying Dedham. A flush of white hostility to the idea developed. "This escorting business will reflect no credit on them," "A Friend of the African Race" complained to the *Evening Bulletin.* "It will have a tendency to destroy the favorable impression made by their recent dinner." As Ibrahima would just as soon have the cost of the parade as the parade itself, the idea was dropped and an amount equivalent to the escort entered in his book.

He left the city in mid-September, having already visited Charlestown, Salem, and other places nearby. Autumn was rushing over the country as he called to the south. A Friends' meeting house, a Baptist church, and a lyceum hall provided stages for his appeal. "This aged Moor is dignified and imposing," wrote someone in New Bedford, where he collected $182. The Society of Friends' members in Providence, Rhode Island, were especially helpful. One venerable Quaker gave him fifty dollars and others another hundred. A few gave him grumbles. Ibrahima, said a writer in the *Rhode-Island American,* "appears too much elated with the public notice he has attracted. It is idle to carry our philanthropy to that false refinement which would overstep the barrier nature has placed between the two species of mankind." Neighboring editors reprinted the remark in approval. A handful were unimpressed on any account. "The Prince exhibits no traces of education or mental ability to distinguish him above the common blacks which we meet every day," a cynic noted.

The first of October found storms over New England, floods in the Connecticut Valley, and fevers on the coast and far inland. Freshets laid waste to a year's farming, and the rivers looked chocolate under their loads of topsoil. It was raining, as it had been for the better part of two weeks, on the day that Ibrahima arrived in Hartford. Though a thriving town of about ten thousand, Hartford still had a rural elegance and simplicity, an impression fostered by dark freestone churches, sleepy residential rows, and peaceful seminarians frolicking in Hog's Creek. To Ibrahima's delight a Pullo lived in the neighborhood. He was a very old man named Sterling, "a countryman of his, formerly a slave." A meeting was arranged, and the two, an observer wrote, "conversed with great animation on incidents and persons well recollected by each."

Do you remember such-and-such a war? Ibrahima asked.

"Oh, yes," Sterling responded, "I was in it—under the command of your father."

Ibrahima drew the attention of another person, too. Back in April the newspapers of the city had printed his remark that Christians did not follow Christianity's precepts. The statement had bothered the Reverend Thomas H. Gallaudet, a graduate of Yale and of Andover, who lived on a hill west of the State House. For his pioneer work as superintendent of the American Asylum for the Education of the Deaf and Dumb, later generations would know him as the founder of deaf-mute education in America.

"My venerable friend," he had written then to Ibrahima, whom he knew only through press reports, "remember . . . that it is the religion of Jesus Christ alone which leads men to do good to the souls of their fellow-men. What other religion does this? I know there are those who call themselves Christians (and it is easy for men to call themselves by any name), and yet act directly contrary to the commands of Jesus Christ. Do not judge the religion of Jesus Christ by such men. Read attentively, I beseech you, the New Testament." By the hand of a Palestinian missionary he sent Ibrahima the long-sought Arabic Bible and himself sent an Arabic translation of Hugo Grotius's *On the Truth of the Christian Religion.* "My venerable friend, how important it is that we should find and embrace the true religion! You, whose soul will so soon be in eternity . . ." Ibrahima received the books while in Washington.

Quiet, diminutive in size, and scholarly by temperament, Gallaudet seemed frail or even feeble on first sight. His great energy took its source not so much in his strength as in his will, in his conviction that it was his duty to be useful to humanity. "Gallaudet never rose in the morning without having in his mind or on his hands some extra duty of philanthropy to perform," wrote Henry Barnard, a friend. In classrooms and workshops on Asylum Hill, he and his assistants taught "the natural language of signs" to about 130 black and white pupils and instructed them in crafts and other employments. The cleanliness and order of the hill were impressive, and even Margaret Hunter Hall, an English visitor who discovered little to like in the United States, had found no faults when she visited there the previous year. "Mr. Gallaudet's soul is wrapped up in sharpening the remaining facilities of his interesting charges," she observed. Yet he still had time to preach at the county jail, help the local schools, and serve as manager of the Connecticut Colonization Society.

Anyone who was impaired or imperfect in some way had a claim on Gallaudet that more normal people were denied. "The field of human wretchedness which some visit from a sense of duty, he delighted to explore," wrote Horace Hooker, "and never seemed so happy as when inventing schemes to relieve the suffering or to raise the fallen." Gallaudet knew, as Paul had told the Corinthians, that God picked the most obscure and insignificant instruments to accomplish His designs. "He selects some neglected and perhaps despised individual to become the Almoner of His Bounty," Gallaudet said in an 1820 sermon, because "a long and sometimes a severe course of discipline is necessary to teach us how worthless and how weak we are in the sight of God." Bleeding Africa claimed a special share of his sympathy, and the miseries inflicted upon it by the slave trade made it a premier object of Christian charity. It was Ibrahima's arrival that brought these old feelings to their feet. Within the past week the Asylum had been through a harrowing attack of fever that killed two pupils, put five near death, and set the board of directors talking of moving to a healthier place. With all this on his mind, how did Gallaudet have time to become involved with Ibrahima?

"Are you fully acquainted with his very interesting history?" he wrote to the Society after meeting him. "Were you aware when Prince left Washington of the deep interest he would excite with regard to the colony at Liberia? Have you thought of the various bearings which his return, with all his descendants, is to have upon the Colony at Liberia & upon all the interior of Africa in a commercial, as well as philanthropic & missionary point of view?" By prevailing upon the Pullo to spend a few days in the city he was able to learn much about his life. An officer in the American Peace Society, Gallaudet was appalled by the succession of violence and slavery that unfolded. "I think I see Africa," he said, "pointing to the tablet of eternal justice, making us Americans tremble, while the words are pronounced, 'Vengeance is mine, I will repay, saith the Lord.' "

At early candlelight on the evening of October 2 a large audience in the Center Church heard Gallaudet appeal for his latest cause. In an anecdotal and sentient way he told the prince's story and outlined his prospects. The "Brick Church," as it was known, had hosted his sermons on prisoners, missions, Indians, deaf-mutes, colonization, and who knows what else. Ibrahima had a veteran exhorter at work, and on his own ground, too, a man whose homilies had won even the praise of John Quincy Adams. One moment a Mungo Park, the next a Wilberforce, Gallaudet spoke that night with a confidence and a feeling no one had reason to expect from someone who had known Ibrahima two whole days. A stream of well-wishers came to the front at his finish. Their charity was considerable. Added to that collected in several churches the following Sunday, it amounted to $156.

But it would have been a failing in Gallaudet to put Ibrahima on the New Haven stage with the money and a mere Godspeed. Who would help Ibrahima elsewhere in New England? Or in New York? "It is somewhat to be regretted that you did not send some one with Prince," he wrote Gurley. "It would have greatly benefited the great cause of Africa . . . and procured twice as much money as has [been] obtained for Prince." Most importantly, who was going to steel Ibrahima in Christian tenets? "It is most earnestly to be wished that he should have the cause of the Redeemer at heart."

Gallaudet's large and expressive eyes, irradiating his face as they fixed over his spectacles on the great gray African, lighted at last upon "that obscure instrument" which God had marked for the portentous. "The finger of God seems to point to great results arising from the return of Prince," he said. "It would seem as if Providence had taken him under His peculiar care, and destined him . . . to be the means of opening into the very interior of Africa 'a wide and effectual door' for the diffusion of that Gospel to which we are indebted for so many invaluable blessings." "Age has mellowed his youthful vigor; servitude has softened his heroic spirit; and, we hope, Divine Grace has touched his sorrowing heart. . . ." "We see in these events that God's

ways are not our ways, nor His thoughts our thoughts. We see why
Prince was not permitted to return with his Moorish disposition
and his Moorish sword; that Providence continued him here so
long until grace had softened his heart."

On Saturday, October 4, Ibrahima left Hartford. Despite an
illness, Gallaudet was with him. "Blessed be God," wrote the
minister, "that we are permitted the honor of cooperating with
Him."

Its harbor, wrote Caleb Cushing, "was an immense forest of
masts stretching as far as the eye can reach." Its wharves, a
chaos of vessels, draymen, wagons, boxes of merchandise, loads
of coal, of cotton, of lumber, and of tea. The walk to Broadway
was a cautious one, for the sidewalks belonged to wheelbarrows,
or to piles of stones, sandheaps, and banks of bricks thrown up
by construction crews or by the Manhattan Water Company, re-
placing pine-wood waterpipes with new lead ones. There were
shops of every variety, parks, churches, streets upon streets of
fine brick and stone buildings, lighted by gas lamps at night.
Where else could a person, on the same day, buy one of twenty-
odd newspapers, see an Egyptian mummy, witness an execution,
browse through the latest European novels, and have coffee with
the likes of James Fenimore Cooper or Fitzgreen Halleck? Among
the innovations welcomed recently were a French opera company and a street vendor selling roasted chestnuts. Time would
tell if they belonged in New York, home of two hundred thousand people, largest city in the United States.

Ibrahima arrived on Saturday, October 11, after a forty-eight-
mile trip by steamboat from New Haven. He spent little time
here in August while traveling to Boston. It was reputation only
that preceded him the following Monday to a gathering at One
Rector Street, the home of the Reverend Jonathan M. Wainwright. A meeting of this type would hardly have seemed proper
unless sponsored by Wainwright, the Episcopalian clergyman who
was a patron of the African Mission School of Hartford. This
night Wainwright was host to about twenty-five people. In a letter
to Gurley, Gallaudet described them as "the most respectable citizens" and observed they represented several religious denomina-

tions. The group listened to his remarks on Ibrahima's life, asked a few questions, and appointed five of their number as a committee-of-arrangement to prepare a public meeting in his behalf.

Gallaudet sent their inquiries on to Washington, but added, "We all believe fully the truth of Prince's history, & if satisfaction is given [on the sum demanded for his children] & Col. Foster's demands are fair, the money can all be raised. It would have been well if Prince had brought with him more specific documents as to the sum necessary to ransom his descendants. I meet with some difficulties on this account, but still I go forward." In the margin he scrawled a postscript: "In confidence, suppose our Directors will release me this winter, & I come to Washington, & set down with you & we make a book? It would interest literary men in the cause of Africa. Prince knows all the chain of ports from Timbo to Timbuktu. He has seen the places where the Niger disappears."

The first and most important member of the committee-of-arrangement was Arthur Tappan, a man who would be as important as Gallaudet to Ibrahima. Younger brother of Charles of Boston, Tappan was forty-two years old, a slightly built man whose hazel eyes, sheltered beneath massive brows, had an intelligent though preoccupied look. He had been in financial straits in 1820—one who knew him described him as "poor" then—but by 1828 his company was flourishing, the largest importer of European and Eastern silks in the city. Annual sales amounted to one million dollars, and Tappan's personal income was twenty-five to thirty thousand dollars a year, conservatively estimated. He worked compulsively for these fruits. God had given him no facility with the pen, no arresting manner of speech, only the ability to make money. It was a talent he pursued diligently. The story was that he had one chair in his Pearl Street office. When a visitor called, both stood, and little time was wasted.

But if time was money, the money was God's. Humorless, colorless, self-righteous, Tappan was the legitimate heir to his family's Connecticut Calvinism. "I regard myself as the steward of the great Giver of all I possess," he wrote brother Benjamin in 1829, "and all that He has entrusted to me as sacredly devoted to the carrying forward of the great work of spreading the Gospel of Jesus Christ." Those crippling headaches to which he was subject stemmed perhaps in part from his own sense of guilt at being a weak and imperfect Christian, but his failings were not obvious to the world. Brother Lewis and many others thought him a model of spiritual concern and endeavor. "Saint Arthur," he was called, the pocketbook of missionaries, reformers, unfortunates. "Money was his passion," a historian observed, "to give it away his security." He was New York's most generous philanthropist, not because his wealth was the most immense but because he believed in giving away great amounts of what he had.

Tappan knew who Ibrahima was. The *Journal of Commerce,* his daily newspaper, had featured a story on the African in August. Still, Ibrahima came around to the store and presented a letter of introduction from brother Charles. There was little so impressive as the man in person. "Abdual Rahaman was . . . well educated, tall and dignified in appearance," brother Lewis wrote in his 1870 biography of Arthur, "and read the Arabic language fluently and wrote it with elegance. His princely bearing and intelligence excited much interest. . . ." For Tappan they excited strong notions of compassion, charity—and fortune. Imagine what might happen if Ibrahima contrived to open trade between Monrovia and Timbo, or even beyond with Timbuktu. It would strike at the slave trade, it would elevate the Africans, perhaps lead to their Christianization, and it would mean new wealth for the one who dared the dream.

Gallaudet wrote the Society of Tappan's interest in the commercial aspects of Ibrahima's return to Africa. The merchant wished, he said, to train "some coloured youths to go to Africa, even to its very interior, to become *Commercial Agents,* & possibly (inter nos) to induce the Government of the United States, to appoint a Consul to reside, if practicable, at Timbo." Tappan claimed that "the spiritual good of the Africans" was his sole concern, though certainly the importation of coffee, ivory, gold, and indigo would not have been objectionable.

Ibrahima, who had decided to become a trader on his return

to the coast, was pleased in several ways by Tappan's intentions.

The prince spent hours with another New Yorker, the Episcopalian intellectual John Frederick Schroeder. An 1819 graduate of Princeton, the Reverend Schroeder was the senior assistant minister of Trinity Church. High-tempered and sensitive, he was nonetheless a popular man and even more an admired one. Sitting in his study, Schroeder gave Ibrahima a thorough grilling on languages. Proficient in Arabic and Hebrew, Schroeder allayed any fears that Ibrahima's manuscripts might be of the quality of "Almoured Ali" of Albany. Ibrahima read the Qur'an, he wrote, "with correctness & fluency, and writes it with neatness and rapidity. He has read and written for me a great deal of Arabic." Among other information, the prince gave Schroeder extensive lists of Pular and Mandinka words.

Tappan, Schroeder, and especially Gallaudet bombarded Ibrahima in his spare moments with their Christian beliefs. Arabic Bible in hand, he could no longer plead an ignorance of their meaning. The intense, multifaceted pressure to embrace Christianity mounted, at long last, to its highest level. Many of the reasons to do so, as earlier at Natchez, had nothing to do with its religious merits vis-à-vis Islam, so affected was he by feelings of isolation, obligation, gratitude, and self-interest. Ibrahima listened attentively, seriously, to the preaching and, to an undeterminable degree, accepted some of what they said. But Gallaudet, who worked steadily with him (or better, on him) was never comfortable with the depth of his new convictions. "I have *hopes* that he is a Christian," the minister wrote, "but his means of religious instruction have been very limited. He requires to be talked with in a very simple, easy style." Gallaudet would reminisce in an 1848 letter to William McLain of the Colonization Society, "I saw in him some tincture of his Mahommedan faith, but not enough so as to neutralize his belief in the Gospel. I made the same allowance for it that Paul did for the Hebrew converts, who still retained some of their Jewish notions and prejudices."

The public meeting arranged by Tappan's committee was held at 7:00 P.M. on Wednesday, October 15, at the Masonic Hall. This huge Gothic building on Broadway, not one year old, contained what a Boston Mason boasted was "the most extensive and magnificent Hall in the United States," a beautiful room of arches, chandeliers, pendants, and mirrors. The meeting had been well advertised, but attendance was larger than expected. Hundreds of people passed the great gas lamps at the entrance and climbed the stairs to the second-story hall. There were people of fashion on hand, literary and religious figures, artists such as Henry Inman, even a man from Natchez, Thomas Servoss, who had known Ibrahima in less exalted days.

"Mr. Chairman, and ladies and gentlemen," Gallaudet began, after being introduced by Dr. Wainwright, "before I attempt to give you this evening any statement relative to the history of the prince, I propose to lay before you the testimonials now before me; and I am sure that if any one present will take the trouble to examine them, he will see clearly that the prince is what he has represented himself to be. . . ." The opening was typical of Gallaudet. Be cogent first, fervent later. As a speaker he did not assault. He wore and wore. A Hartford neighbor thought the technique that in which "the hearer was borne along by a constantly swelling tide, rather than swept away by a sudden billow." But when the moment for emotion came, he would deliver it. He could be so expressive in his face that, without speaking, without moving his arms or body in any way except to flex his facial muscles, he could communicate to a deaf-mute child the rapture of the saved and the torments of the damned on Judgment Day.

"The account which I have received from Prince is that he is a native of Timbuktu, that interesting city in the very heart of Africa. . . ." Ibrahima sat next to Judge Jonas Platt, the official chairman of the meeting. He was wearing something "his master's indulgence" had allowed, a blue coat with gilt buttons. From beneath it, a full white collar reached up to the bottom of his ears. Erect and alert, he managed what few could, to look dignified while seated. From time to time he gazed down at young Inman, who was sketching him from a front seat. The Pullo's face was wrinkled with age, and, against his collar, looked "quite black" to the audience.

"His life appears like a romance," Gallaudet was continuing, "and the incidents would be incredible if the evidence was not so undeniable." He had recounted Ibrahima's African years, the war, the meeting with Dr. Cox, and the manumission.

> I would now ask if this is not one of the strongest cases that can be presented to our feelings. After an absence of forty years from his native country, during which long period he has been a slave in this land, Prince has a desire to see once more the land of his fathers and to lay his bones among those of his kindred. . . . The object of Prince in returning, is not to assert his right to the throne; he has seen too much of the dangers of the situation to attempt it at the advanced age of sixty-six. He has found, too, what indeed might be found by any one, that happiness does not depend on one's rank. He proposes to have no other desire than to fix himself as a colonist at Liberia; to live and die under American protection; and to render this country what aid he can in promoting an intercourse between our colony and the interior.

> When Prince arrives there, it will soon be known that old Abduhl Rahahman is alive, and is come back, with his family. His relations at Tombuctoo will hear of it. Think you his son will not go to see his aged father, whom he supposes dead? He doubtless will, and when the peaceful intentions of the old man are ascertained, no apprehension will be excited among his relations. They will invite him to visit the land of his youth; an intercourse may be opened between Liberia and a territory as large as New England, the capital of which, Teemboo, is as large as Baltimore; and probably this intercourse may be extended through a line of posts, where the relations of Prince are the chiefs, even to the city of Tombuctoo. It may be the means of securing advantages to our trade, to scientific curiosity, and to benevolence.

> I would ask, then, if humanity and patriotism do not urge us to render assistance to Prince for the hospitality afforded one of our own countrymen. . . . We may be able to extend our commercial relations to the very heart of Africa, and the influence of our institutions also. As Christians, we must especially rejoice that an opportunity will be afforded for diffusing the blessings of Christianity to that dark and benighted region. . . .

> Methinks I see [Ibrahima] like a Patriarch crossing the

Atlantic, over which he was taken a slave forty years since, with his flock around him, happy in the luxury of doing good. I think I see benighted Africa, taking her stand among the nations of the earth. I think I see Egypt, as heretofore, pouring a flood of light into Greece, and Carthage arising in former glory. I think I see Africa, pointing to the golden rule of the gospel, which if all practised, happiness would result to individuals as well as to nations, and the efficacy would be felt throughout the world: 'Whatsoever ye would that men should do unto you, do ye even so unto them.'

The last remarks "excited repeated applause." It was a professional performance, made in a hall thought difficult for public speakers. "A powerful appeal to the sympathies of the meeting, as Christians and patriots," a writer would say in the morning's *New-York American*. The audience voted him its thanks, and then had Judge Platt appoint a "Committee of Five" "to obtain from our citizens the sum yet needed to free the family of Prince Abduhl Rahhahman from slavery. . . ."

On the list of the committee's members was the charmed name of Arthur Tappan.

I come to these shores to die,
and anything better than death,
is better than I expect.

—Samuel Bacon

8. A Single Plank

Dr. Richard Randall arrived in New York during the week of October 20, 1828. He was a native of Annapolis, Maryland, schooled in Philadelphia, and was a former army surgeon and doctor in private practice in Washington, D.C. Andrew Foote, later a Civil War hero, wrote that Randall "possessed great firmness of purpose and benevolence of disposition, superadded to extensive scientific knowledge." Because of his empathy with Africa and his medical and military experience, he had been named to succeed Ashmun as colonial agent. He was in New York to take passage with Dr. Joseph Mechlin, the new colonial surgeon, on the U.S. schooner *Shark,* soon to leave for the West African coast.

Dr. Randall closeted himself with Tappan and Ibrahima. The merchant was interested in establishing a company to ferry immigrants to Liberia and conduct a regular trade between there and New York. The new agent caught fire at the idea, although Tappan cautioned, "My project has from the first been predicated on Abduhl Rahhaman's being able, through his family connexions with the aid he might receive from us, to open a friendly intercourse with the interiour."

The Society's board of managers had instructed Dr. Randall, while sounding out Tappan, to have Ibrahima write a letter to the current *almaami*. Randall was to deliver it when he arrived in Liberia. From information Ibrahima and Cyrus could gather at Natchez, they had concluded that Abd al-Qaadiri still reigned. In Boston, however, the prince had met a colonist from Sierra

165

Leone who told him that his mannerly, gray-bearded brother
was dead and a forty-two-year-old nephew, Bubakar Mawdo,
wore the turban. On that evidence Gallaudet had told the Masonic
Hall audience that Bubakar was *almaami*.

Ibrahima had his own ideas on the subject. For some reason,
when he wrote the letter Dr. Randall wished, he addressed it to
his brother anyway. It was a remarkably simple letter, but it
would create a sensation at home. Whoever the recipient, from
the perspective of Timbo it would be little short of a letter from
the grave.

> To Abdul Guadilly [Abd al-Qaadiri] and Mohammado
> of Foulah Jallow, Teemboo:
> This letter is sent by me, Abdul Aramana [Ibrahima], to
> Abdul Guadilly, to inform you that the good people of
> America have redeemed me and the whole of my family
> from slavery. I have therefore forwarded these few lines
> by the favour of [Dr.] Richard Randall, and have desired
> him to forward it, if possible, to my country, to you. I
> expect, by the help of God, to visit my country again in
> a short time; and I write to let the whole of my country
> know the generosity of the American country, which I
> shall be more able to express myself, when I have the
> blessing to revisit my country.
>
> Abdul Aramana

Gallaudet left for Hartford toward the end of October. "Do
instruct [Ibrahima] this winter in the doctrines of the Gospel,
& enforce them upon his conscience & his heart," he wrote
Gurley. From Tappan came a letter to the Asylum dated November 1. "We are doing something for Prince, and I doubt
not shall make up at least one thousand dollars in this city,"
the merchant wrote. "If I could be sure of having your assistance
in raising the money in other towns, I should say we might
calculate on all that is required, even $8500. . . . But, to effect
this, it is absolutely necessary that you reengage in the work,
say for two months this winter and two months more in the
Spring. As soon as you can say positively that you can make this
service, I will on my own responsibility open negotiations for
obtaining the liberation of Prince's family."

In New York, as in Boston, Ibrahima was well received by

local blacks. He became friends with the Reverend Benjamin Paul and also with the Reverend John C. Murphy. The latter preached a sermon and took a collection in the prince's behalf in his Abyssinian Baptist Church. The gentlemanly Samuel Cornish was a third friend, also a clergyman, but best known as the founding senior editor of *Freedom's Journal,* the first black newspaper in the United States. "The Prince is a man possessed of more discernment, sound judgment, and decision of character," Cornish wrote in 1829, "than one half of the emigrants who have gone [to Liberia] from this country put together."

It was with Cornish, an agent of the African Free School, that Ibrahima made a tour of its brick building on Mulberry Street, where three hundred black children were instructed daily. One of the students was the young Liberian Washington Davis, whom Dr. Mitchell of Philadelphia, it will be remembered, had been unable to accept as a pupil due to the prejudice of his other students. Davis sketched a map of Africa on the blackboard and pointed out Liberia to Ibrahima. "Their conversation on the various subjects of the Colony appeared to be very interesting," said C. C. Andrews, the principal.

The African's most important and far-reaching friendship was formed with John Russwurm, a young black editor. Russwurm, the son of a white Jamaican planter and a black woman, had lived in the West Indies, Canada, and Maine. From Bowdoin College, where he was a friend and classmate of Nathaniel Hawthorne, he received a Bachelor of Arts degree in 1826, one of the first two blacks in the United States to do so. He came to New York and served with Cornish as junior editor of *Freedom's Journal.* When Cornish retired in September, 1827, Russwurm took over the paper.

As recently as January, he had announced himself "opposed to the plans of the American Colonization Society," a view agreeable to Cornish, Paul, Murphy, and the great majority of his readers. "Abide in the ship or you can't be saved!" as Cornish preached. For Ibrahima, however, Russwurm wished the support of both "the friends of the cause of Abolition *and* those desirous to promote the Colony at Liberia." He liked the old man, spending time with him and listening to him pray. The prince's imminent return to Africa had come to have a personal meaning for the editor. His disavowal of colonization had been sincere —as late as the spring of 1828, he seems not even to have received the *African Repository*—but as the year went on, he grew more and more dissatisfied with the position of blacks in the North. "I consider it a mere waste of words to talk of enjoying citizenship in the United States," he would write that winter. "It is utterly impossible in the nature of things. All, therefore, who pant for this, must cast their eyes elsewhere." Haiti was one place to look. With Ibrahima as a catalyst, Africa emerged as another. Before the year ended, Russwurm was seriously considering immigration to Liberia.

The Abyssinian Church meeting of December 14 was the last event held for Ibrahima in the city. He was already anxious to leave. Tappan had been thinking of going south with him to push his commercial and diplomatic plans for the colony. Now, however, he decided to await a response to Ibrahima's letter to Abd al-Qaadiri. "I want the information that I shall probably get from Dr. Randall, before moving in the business," he wrote. Neither could Gallaudet go. "The Committee of the Directors & my colleagues, after mature deliberation, gave it as their opinion that I ought not," he informed Gurley. Unexpressed concerns over his family's health also held him back. Ever considerate, he sent a package of goods down for the Pullo.

The Society faced the winter owing seven thousand dollars, having an empty treasury, more than seven hundred applicants for emigration, and urgent requests for supplies from the colony. While a number of private trading vessels had visited Monrovia during the year, there had been no ship of immigrants. Gurley had attempted to mount an expedition for months. "We only await the funds," he wrote in August, and he was waiting yet in October. To end the dilemma, a series of meetings was held in November and December to raise the hire of a ship. With the funds collected there and with some loans, including five hundred dollars from Francis Scott Key, enough was brought together to charter a ship then at anchor at Norfolk, Virginia. Notice was given by the Society in late November that the immigrants should rendezvous at that place.

"Prince Abduhl Rahaman says he is desirous of going to Liberia by the first vessel," Tappan wrote Gurley, "and I have

promised to write you for information." This letter was dated
December 9. It was composed in time for the unpleasantness at
Natchez to have come to Ibrahima's attention. The African may
not have realized how fully he had become a point of controversy,
but the acrimony of the election there had been noticed in the
nation's press and letters written northward by Cyrus and the
colonel. Ibrahima would have been aware of the bitterness and
ill will let loose. It was also time for the thought that Andrew
Jackson, the newly elected President, would be inaugurated in
three months. There would be no passports from that old slave
trader, unless it were one to Natchez. Everything considered, it
would be wise to be overseas when the new administration took
charge in Washington.

Consequently, Ibrahima left New York on Saturday, December
20. "Abduhl Rahaman came among us as a stranger," Russwurm wrote, "but he departs from our city with the well wishes
of thousands. . . ."

Returning to Philadelphia after a five-month absence, Ibrahima was reunited with his wife. Isabella had been there since
July, apparently. He also renewed the tiring rounds of interviews and applications to the charitable. From Dr. Mitchell, the
colonization enthusiast, came twenty dollars. From Dr. Edwin
James, chronicler of the Stephen H. Long Expedition, another
ten. From Robert Wharton, fifteen-time mayor of the city, five.
Nathaniel Ware gave him ten.

Ibrahima took their money and pocketed it. It was a natural
instinct after forty years of penury, but it irritated his sponsors.
"The old man should have brought all the money to me," Gerard
Ralston complained, "and then I could have made the receipts
of money conform with the book—but not having done so—the
accounts as per his book are not correct, and he will probably
lose some 20 or 30 Dolls., for I observe several sums on the books
which are not marked paid, and which he does not recollect
whether or not he ever collected." His inexperience with cash was
evident, Tappan writing in another context, "Prince is not competent to manage money concerns."

An interesting visit was made to Condy Raguet, late U.S.
chargé d'affaires in Brazil. "Prince Abduhl Rahhahman . . .
related to me in detail the circumstances of his abduction from

his native country, and of his remaining for forty years, in slavery near Natchez," Raguet wrote in a memorandum. The diplomat asked Ibrahima to fashion the Lord's Prayer into Arabic on a quarto sheet. The request being too difficult, he wrote instead the opening sura of the Qur'an, hardly an appropriate substitute. The manuscript was placed in the collections of the American Philosophical Society, not to be translated and identified for several years.

On the morning of January 1, 1829, Ibrahima joined the blacks of Philadelphia in their New Year's Day parade. The route of this annual event was up Lombard, up Walnut, down Chestnut, down Spruce. The African marched along through the heart of the city, an honored guest. Later, he sat prominently in Wesley Church, where the program of the day was presented. Newspapers in the city, in New York, and in Boston mentioned his appearance. Despite the tumult at Natchez, he was making no effort to be less conspicuous.

Signs of the voyage were evident at Baltimore, where Ibrahima called on C. C. Harper and John H. B. Latrobe, the young Society agents who had helped him in June. They were busy buying stores for the ship—on credit, of course. Forty-two barrels of prime pork, twenty-five of beef, thirteen of cornmeal, twelve of flour, two hogsheads each of molasses and tobacco. Once inspected, the goods were taken to the wharf and loaded on the steamboat *Virginia,* which made weekly runs down Chesapeake Bay to Norfolk. Gurley had authorized sixty dollars for Ibrahima's personal provisions, but Harper, otherwise diverted, referred the matter to Norfolk with a request he be attended to there.

The steamboat left Fell's Point on Wednesday, January 21, at 3:00 P.M. The day was clear and cold, with snow on the riverbanks and an enervating wind from the northwest. Besides Ibrahima and Isabella, the *Virginia*'s living freight included four other couples, three with children, a total of thirteen emigrants. Harper's supplies were on board, as were seeds, crockery, and clothes "provided by several charitable ladies" of Baltimore. "I have this moment returned from the Norfolk steamboat which I saw underway before I left the wharf," Latrobe wrote to

Gurley that afternoon. "The emigrants went off in high spirits, and those who were on a visit to this country with real joy." He referred to William Draper and wife, passengers then visiting from Liberia. Natives of Fredericksburg, Virginia, the Drapers had emigrated in 1824.

The *Virginia* was to stop in the bay and take on board fifteen slaves liberated for the voyage by Margaret Mercer, their owner. There was no other way to pick them up, as a delay involved in bringing the steamboat to nearby Annapolis for them, felt Latrobe, "would infuriate the regular passengers." "The Norfolk boat does not," Harper wrote, "and *will not* stop." Problems arose when Miss Mercer attempted to find a way to take them out, for the rivers were choked with ice, the wind was elevating everyone to the purple, and no master would stir to help her. The one person interested in a fare was Captain Ducrot, a sleazy old waterman. He offered a boat recently sunk to kill the rats infesting it. Having no other choice, Miss Mercer accepted. Raised, hastily dried, and launched, the little vessel entered the bay. The *Virginia* having already passed, it rendezvoused with darkness and salt water. The passengers had to pump steadily just to keep themselves afloat. While Captain Ducrot fed himself from their modest stores, they pushed on up the bay to Baltimore.

Latrobe, roused from his breakfast by their arrival, ran from wharf to wharf hunting a conveyance to carry them to Norfolk. Finally he secured passage on a packet schooner. The emigrants boarded on Sunday morning, January 25. As it was the weekend, many other blacks were in town, mingling among them and witnessing their departure. The cheerfulness of "Miss Mercer's people" seemed inappropriate to one observer, who remarked that they were going to land where many of them would die.

"So shall all of us have to die," someone replied. "People die everywhere."

A third spectator said that anyone watching them pass would see their skins and think, "There goes a boat-load for Georgia."

"Yes," said a fourth, "but this is in the opposite direction."

A very old black watching the commotion spoke last. "Heaven will protect them; to whatever land they go, God is there."

Young Harper, who overheard these remarks, went home after seeing them sail and turned philosophical. "It crossed my mind

that the old man's exclamation was prophetic," he wrote to
Gurley. "The time will doubtless come, when the name of some
of these people will be recorded and their memory revered, as
are those of the early Pilgrims of our country. Some formal history will relate how they sailed, while a crowd of their own colour
watched them from the shore. . . . How few of those that gazed,
if any, comprehended the novelty and moral grandeur of the
scene!"

The *Harriet* drifted restlessly at Old Point Comfort. It was a
handsome vessel, built at Bath, Maine, in 1819 by the noted
shipwright James McLellan. It had two decks and three masts,
and it measured 275 tons. The dimensions of the ship were ap-
proximately ninety-five feet in length, twenty-five in breadth,
and twelve and one half in depth. The *Harriet* had been fretting
at anchor near Norfolk for a month since taking two companies
of troops to Fort Moultrie, South Carolina. The Society learned
of the ship and paid $2,400 to charter it for the emigrants. A
murder among its crew in September followed by the drowning
of several hands in October had attached no stigma of "death
ship" to it. William Johnson, the *Harriet*'s captain, was a respectable and competent sea dog who had skippered it for years. His
ship had a reputation as a fast sailer, and that was good news to
the board of managers, which had apprehensions "that a long
voyage may affect the health of the Colonists." Since the emigrants themselves preferred the *Harriet* to the *Nautilus,* a second
ship offered the Society, there had been no difficulty in selecting
it.

The loading and dispatch of the expedition were the cares of
Glasgow-born John McPhail, an officer of the Society's local
affiliate. A person of "zeal, energy, and diligence," McPhail was
a businessman with considerable property in Norfolk and Monrovia, and he had provided the ships for the Society's Liberian
expeditions in 1826 and 1827. McPhail not only had to get the
colonists, their goods, and those sent from Baltimore happily
arranged on the *Harriet,* but also purchase and lay aboard more
than a thousand dollars of additional provisions, too. Tappan
had arranged to buy Ibrahima a house frame and some additional building materials ("Do see that he is made comfortable"),

and the board of managers ordered McPhail to provide them. Plank was scarce, but the agent did find him a sixteen-by-eighteen-foot frame and saw to his personal needs.

Ibrahima and his friends from Baltimore were actually the last colonists to reach the ship. About thirty "well known and honest" blacks from Norfolk itself were sailing, and they had been waiting impatiently to depart since December. Seventy-five people "of a very respectable appearance" had arrived from Richmond in two steamboats on January 18. They had left their homes amid "emotional farewells," while perhaps two thousand other blacks looked on. These colonists were moving principally due to the influence of the Reverend Lott Carey, a former neighbor. Born a slave and raised at Richmond, Carey had purchased his freedom partly with money he got by collecting and selling scraps of tobacco from the warehouse where he worked. He became a Baptist minister and went to Africa early in the decade. "I wish to go to a country where I shall be estimated by my merits, not by my complexion," he had said. In the absence of Ashmun, Carey had taken charge of the colony. His friends from Richmond did not know, as they turned their steps after his, that Carey would not be there to greet them. In November he and a number of others had been at the agency house in Monrovia preparing cartridges to use against a slave trader. Somehow, a stock of gunpowder had been ignited and a tremendous blast ripped the building. Human torches, the survivors ran from the place shrieking, "Lord, save me!" "Lord, help me!" Inside, Lott Carey, the Richmond slave boy, had been blown to pieces.

The *Harriet*'s passengers totaled 152, of whom the great majority were from Virginia and Maryland. "They all appear cheerful and contented," McPhail wrote. "Amongst them are several well-educated schoolmasters. Also a well-educated Presbyterian minister and his family, and a Methodist and a Baptist preacher, of more than ordinary talents. Also a number of valuable mechanics, viz., carpenters, cabinet-makers, turners, blacksmiths, brick-makers, stone-masons, a gun-smith, a brass founder, and a printer. Take them all together, I think them by far the most intelligent and discreet set of people that the Society have ever set out. . . . More than half of these people can read and write.

One hundred of them can read. And what is extraordinary, I have not heard an oath nor an indelicate expression among them, nor seen any of them use spiritous liquors, although I am constantly with them." From a writer in *Niles' Weekly Register:* "They are spoken of as very orderly and decent people; and many of them, except for the color of their skins, would have been valued members of society in the United States."

The Secretary of State had been informed by the Society of Ibrahima's departure by letter. Clay's reply was a sigh of relief: "I am *very glad* to receive this information, being desirous that Prince should be sent to Africa in conformity with the engagement entered into with his former proprietor *before* the close of our present Administration." Dr. Laurie and Reverend John N. Campbell, the tall, slender pastor of Washington's Second Presbyterian Church, met with Clay during the second week of the month to learn precisely what the government would do for him. "A reasonable sum for his passage and subsistence" was promised.

Clay also gave Ibrahima another passport. Its full text follows.

Department of State
Washington, 17th January 1829

The President of the United States, having been informed that the bearer hereof, Abduhl Rahhahman, was held in a state of slavery by a citizen of the United States, that he was of Moorish descent, and a person of much consideration in his native country of Africa, and that his emancipation from slavery would be very agreeable to the Emperor of Morocco, the undersigned Secretary of State of the United States was directed by the President, to adopt measures for the liberation of the before-mentioned Moor, Abduhl Rahhahman, and for his transportation to his family and connections and native country. His manumission was accordingly procured from the citizen of the United States who held him as a slave, and he came to this City, at the public expense, last spring. It was the President's intention to have him transported to Tangier, to be delivered to the Emperor of Morocco, but as Abduhl Rahhahman prefers going to the American Colony of Liberia, on the coast of

Africa, from whence he expects to be able to reach his
relations, the President yields to his desire, and accordingly
he proceeds to Norfolk, in company of his wife, to obtain,
at the expense of the United States, a passage in the ship
Harriet, a vessel chartered by the American Colonization
Society, which is preparing to sail for Liberia, about the
20th of this month.

In testimony of the foregoing I have hereunto set my
hand and affixed the Seal of the Department of State this
17th day of January, in the year of our Lord 1829.

H. Clay

McPhail had hoped the colonists could sail about January
20, but late arrivals, plus the time to load, postponed the day
again and again. By January 15, the house frames belonging to
the Norfolk colonists had been placed below. Then followed the
two barrels of personal baggage each passenger was allowed.
Additionally, McPhail let every person stow in six months of
provisions freight free. Agreeable to a suggestion by the late
Ashmun, boxes of farm and domestic utensils, particularly scarce
in the colony, were put aboard. Not until the morning of January
28 was the lower hold of the *Harriet* filled. All the colonists took
possession of their berths then, and distribution of ship's rations,
a harbinger of departure, commenced.

Gurley visited the immigrants from Washington and "at a
meeting attended by all those attached to the expedition, had an
opportunity of impressing upon their minds the great and solemn
duties to which they were about to be called." Following him,
the Reverend James Douglas gave "a very interesting discourse,"
suggested by the verse in Hebrews, "For they that say such
things, declare plainly that they seek a country." His theme was
"that City which hath foundations, whose builder and maker is
God." Two colonists, one a Methodist minister and one a Presbyterian, also spoke, and the Reverend James Nimmo, President of
the Norfolk Colonization Society, concluded the service with a
prayer.

It was Ibrahima's farewell, appropriately religious, to America.

On Saturday, February 7, 1829, the *Harriet* cast off and
dropped down to the forts where Hampton Roads and Chesa-

peake Bay meet. On February 9 it rode the strong winds of the bay to sea.

The unforgettable motions and smells were present, the creaking masts and thumping hull, but there was little else to recall the crossing of so many years before. The real difference lay inside him. There was no terror this time, no anger or sense of betrayal. If his pulse quickened now, it was not in fear but in anticipation and wonder of journey's end. Great changes had taken place in Futa, he knew, and it would require patience and tact to go home. He had no illusions of wielding great power again, or any real wish to do so. But at least he was free. His self-respect had returned, and he had something to live for. The sea would never be a neutral place for him, but the *Harriet* had no nightmares in its hold. Rather, league by league, it dropped them with the familiar stars over the horizon.

As guest of the Unied States, Ibrahima had been assigned a cabin, the most convenient, private spot on board. It was a proper consideration for the oldest male passenger, someone almost sixty-seven years old and in uncertain health, someone who, statistically considered, should have died a quarter century ago. The remaining immigrants camped in fifty berths six feet square each. The space was small, but adequate in a well-ventilated vessel like the *Harriet,* whose ceilings were six feet two inches. The ship seemed uncrowded, and, just as McPhail had thought, there was room for at least another thirty people. All, including Ibrahima, had been required to submit to a smallpox vaccination before sailing, and all "continued healthy during the voyage."

If the *Harriet* was no *Africa,* Captain Johnson was no John Nevin, either. "There were no complaints made of him by any of the immigrants," McPhail wrote later. The weather was good for mid-winter, with "fine, pleasant gales all the voyage." The easy passage of the ship, the health and common goals of the colonists, the play and excited doings of the children made the trip less than toilsome. It was the time and occasion for friendships, and for enmities, and few of either made on the sea were ever changed ashore. One of the three or four people on ship who knew what lay ahead, Ibrahima was understandably a center of attention for the purposeful, anxious adults. "In this company were several persons who became distinguished citizens of Liberia," wrote a physician about 1852. One of them was J. J. Roberts, who was from a free black family of Petersburg, Virginia. As a man, Roberts would become the first President of the Liberian Republic.

On the thirty-seventh day from Norfolk, the passengers sighted land. It was Cape Mesurado, a majestic promontory covered with a rich mantle of green. "Except for a narrow strip of beach with a few outlying rocks at the water's edge, all is one mass of foliage," wrote a spectator. Behind it, near the mouth of the Mesurado River, was Monrovia, the capital of Liberia. On March 18, the thirty-eighth day, the colonists reached their goal. The *Harriet* moored under the guns of the city, its immigrants in good health and great hopes.

Monrovia was located about two miles from the point of the Cape on an elevated ridge originally covered with forest and brushwood. It was a dry, sandy site, well open to sea breezes. From the ridge the roads of the town, where there was always a vessel or two at anchor, could be seen to the north, while the ocean appeared about a mile away to the south. When Ashmun arrived in 1822, he found 130 immigrants living in native houses. Now the town contained eighty to one hundred homes, "some very excellent," with others being erected daily. The rocky streets of the place led to a church, a school, a small library, and even a jail complete with a fugitive English debtor. The agency house was built on the most commanding spot in town, and it had an attractive piazza on all sides. The city was protected by two forts of twenty guns and two companies of richly uniformed volunteers. "The country is beautiful," wrote a colonist from Norfolk, "and nature has strongly fortified the Cape for a city." From its roads Monrovia looked for all the world like a small West Indian port town.

"I assure you that the first appearance gave *me* a very unfavorable [impression]," wrote Abraham Cheeseman, a Norfolk mechanic, "by seeing a parcel of naked beings presenting themselves before us, which had a very uncouth appearance." He referred to the Kru boatmen who met the *Harriet* in the river. Present on the landing were hundreds of welcoming settlers ("most of the people seem to be quite happy"), as well as Drs. Randall and Mechlin, who had arrived in December on the *Shark*. Dr. Randall was convalescing from a fever, but had insisted on greeting Ibrahima and the others personally and superintending their debarkation. "Comfortable shelters" of bamboo had already been erected for the passengers against the rains that would commence soon. They were conducted to these or to the homes of friends. As this was going on, Dr. Randall collapsed and was taken to his bed in the agency house.

Soon after his own arrival, the agent had met a Mandinka from Solima, which bordered Futa on the south. With the help of a European-educated African named Gomez, he spoke with him about the letter that Ibrahima had written in New York, the letter intended for his relatives in Timbo. "I inquired of the Mandingo, whether he could take charge of the letter," the doctor wrote the board, "but finding that he spoke doubtingly, and did not expect to return to his country for many months, I determined not to entrust him with it." Dr. Randall gave him a copy of the letter instead and promised him "a handsome compensation" if he would obtain an answer to it.

The first letter may still have been resting on his desk when the *Harriet* arrived. At any rate Ibrahima wrote a second time immediately. Timbo was hundreds of miles north-northwest of Monrovia. Rather than trust the letter by land, the African arranged to send it by way of Freetown, Sierra Leone, which had better connections with Futa. Ibrahima's arrival received additional publicity when Dr. Randall had his passport translated into Arabic and circulated up the rivers.

Fretting in his convalescence, the agent soon "broke from his immediate attendants" to see after the *Harriet* immigrants again. Since he was unable to walk, he was borne about Monrovia on a chair. When he found the government schooner grounded on a sandbar, he could not be restrained from going on board. Sunstroke resulted, and he was carried home completely delirious. "A most violent and fatal fever" seized him, and, despite a brief rally, he died on April 19, a month and a day after Ibrahima's arrival.

The passengers of the *Harriet* seemed about to follow him. Within a week of their arrival, a woman passenger died. Within a month six or seven others were gone, twelve within six weeks, thirty over the course of the summer. Nearly all the *Harriet's* crew fell sick, too, and the second mate, a man named Phoenix, died. A long spell of dry weather was the official culprit, together with the irregular modes of living, fatigue, and imprudent exposures. The free indulgence of the immigrants, bursting from a North American winter into an African spring, of oranges, bananas, and coconuts did not help, either. Pineapple, thought Dr. Mechlin, himself ill, was especially deleterious, "the oldest settlers not being able to use it freely without feeling its ill effects." Ibrahima, who had been in good health when he landed, was also attacked with "the coast fever" in April. "He, however, soon recovered . . . and continued to enjoy excellent health," Dr. Mechlin wrote.

By tragic oversight, the *Harriet's* mailbag did not contain instructions from the board for Ibrahima and the others to be sent to Millsburg, a more healthy place inland, and not be allowed to remain in Monrovia. The mortality was, at least in part, a consequence. Ibrahima was appalled with the succession of funerals. He had a letter written for him to the Reverend Paul in New York. "I beg you not mention to come to Africa, you must stay where you are, for the place is not fit for such people as you." For Russwurm, whose health was never robust, there was a special warning in the letter. "Please to tell Mr. John B. Russwurm that if he do come here, he will certainly be a dead man, he must stay where he is."

Gurley was incredulous to see Ibrahima's advice printed in Cornish's new anticolonization paper *The Rights of All.* "You speak of the letters sent by the prince . . . and you wish to know whether or not he did wrote [them]," the Liberian Frederick Lewis replied to an inquiry from Washington. "I firmly believe he had it wrote by some one who wrote for him, for you know he could not write in English himself, but my reason for saying this is that he talked with me on the subject of his letters that he entended to send. I found him like many both in america and this, untill they have been heare and have had the fever and then remain at least one year." "I believe," Russwurm wrote Gurley, "that the writer has said more than A. Rahaman intended he should. We have had considerable discussion con-

cerning its authenticity. Wash. Davis will not believe that it was
ever written at the Colony. It has not caused me to waver in
the least . . . and if A. R. were to send me one dozen such—it
would all be labor in vain."

Discreet or not, Ibrahima's alarm was valid. The passengers'
grumbling about the health of the colony was widespread. Benjamin Brand of Richmond echoed it in a letter to the Society. "I
cannot with a clear conscience have any hand in sending emigrants to Africa unless they can immediately on landing be
sent up to Millsburg," he said. "The bearer of this [letter],
Mr. Francis Taylor . . . is now on his way to the Colony. I have
told him that if he stops in Monrovia before he gets acclimated,
I shall expect to hear of his death by the return of the same
vessel in which he goes out."

The unloading of the *Harriet* gave Ibrahima another shock.
He was not allowed to take possession of his house frame. He
explained why in a letter to the Society. Announcing his safe
arrival, he continued, "I am sorry to say that McPhail diser-
pointed me, he told me that he had purchased a house fraim
for me and it was on board, but when I arrived here, I found
that he had not paid for it." A colonist named Cooper, to whom
it belonged, "would not let me have it." A keg of nails, also
promised, was not delivered. "I have no house nor can not
build one for there is not one nail in the Colony for sail, nor can
I get one for love or money."

Someone was at fault, but it may have been Cooper and not
McPhail. On January 27, before the *Harriet* left Norfolk, McPhail
wrote Gurley, "We had progressed two [*sic*] far when your
last letter came to hand to take a frame on account of Prince, but
I purchased one that was already on board." The conscientious
McPhail, treasurer of half a dozen businesses and organizations,
would not be likely to have made so plain a misstatement. His
record of consistently high performance for the Society, coupled
with the resolution of thanks voted him by the board for his
dispatch of the *Harriet,* suggest that Ibrahima's criticism was mis-
directed.

Whoever was to blame, it was small comfort. "I shall be in
the colony all the rains with out a house," he mused.

Ibrahima's plans now were twofold. "I . . . shall be of[f]

as soon as the rains are over, if God be with me," he wrote in May. At home he hoped to obtain the money yet needed to liberate his children. "I shall try [also] to bring my country men to the Colony and try to open the trade."

Interior trade was not a new idea. It was an old one, a fascination the colonists indulged to the definite neglect of agriculture. Linen worth fifty to seventy-five cents yard in the United States could be sold for two dollars in the interior. A "bar" of tobacco, worth pennies in Virginia, brought up to a dollar. Equal profits could be made on sugar, combs, pins, knives, and twine, not to mention the old favorites like powder, arms, and rum. In return, the colony could export ivory, gold dust, palm oil, rice, and certain woods from its part of the coast. When the *Harriet* left Monrovia to return to the United States in late April, there were a schooner from Philadelphia and a brig from Boston in the roads loading with colonial products.

Obstacles to trade were numerous, however. There was the "fickleness" of the indigenous population, who would enforce embargoes against the colony, claimed Baltimore colonist Remus Harvey, "whenever they feel disposed to enhance the prices of their produce." The previous year a boycott had put the colonists on rations of a pint of rice and a pound of meat per person per week. "A man coming here without money had as well be dead," wrote *Harriet* alumnus James Lund, "for they will starve him to death." A further complication was the international slave trade, which, though widely illegal now, was active within one day's sail. Near Gallenas to the north, Baltimore-built vessels flying Spanish flags hovered about in search of cargoes. Wars from slaving raids had nearly engulfed the colony at Christmas and were the reason for the military preparations at the time of Lott Carey's death.

Ibrahima hoped to ameliorate both problems. He wished to divert some of the Fulbe trade south from Sierra Leone and establish it on a regular basis. Futa was a powerful state, which, it was hoped at Monrovia no less than at Sierra Leone, might not suffer itself "to be bearded and insulted by such petty chiefs as inhabit the tract of country lying between them." Moreover, his brother Abd al-Qaadiri had expressed religious scruples about slaving to the coast. He might be prejudiced further against it by Ibrahima, who was determined "to lend his aid in annihilating that trade in human flesh, the horrors of which he had felt so deeply."

A momentary difficulty loomed when Ibrahima learned beyond question that the information he had gotten in Boston was correct—Abd al-Qaadiri no longer lived. He had died in 1825 and lay buried beneath the great trees by the mosque in Timbo. But Yaya, another brother, had succeeded him as *almaami*. "My brother is the present King, having been enthroned three years since," Ibrahima wrote to Tappan, "and his benign and placid qualifications endear him to all his subjects." Yaya, in fact, while *almaami* in title, alternated control of the country between himself and a grandson of Karamoko Alfa in an effort to avoid civil war.

"I found one of my friends in the Colony," Ibrahima wrote to the Society. "He tells me that we can reach home in 15 days and promises to go with me." Dr. Mechlin was prepared to spend five hundred dollars outfitting his expedition. Ibrahima would get under way as soon as the rains were ever.

As soon as the rains were over.
"The rains" started in mid-May. June was the wettest month, the streets becoming gullies and a great wash taking place. The chill of the nights was easily felt through the bamboo walls of his house.

"I am unwell, but much better," he wrote in the last letter to bear his name. Gurley had scarcely time to receive and read it before the writer was no more.

In late June, Ibrahima was "attacked with a diarrhea." Thinking it a trifle, he did not bother Dr. Mechlin about it. The decision was fatal, for the wear of the last two years now took its toll. The diarrhea progressed, sapping his appetite and energy. "An overflow of bile" resulted. Dr. Mechlin, called for at last, found "his system too weak on account of age to admit the necessary medicines." The doctor would not even attempt it.

The end was at hand and Ibrahima knew it. He made his last requests, one of which—that his manuscripts be sent to Timbo—was the act of a true Pullo. An unidentified colonist who saw him sink under wrote, "He had every attention that could be afforded. . . ."

On July 6, 1829, Ibrahima died. He was sixty-seven years old.

The old man never returned to Futa. Unlike the familiar Moses of his Qur'an, he never even saw the long-sought land from a mountain. But if he never regained his home, it must be said that there was a part of it he never lost, a part that he had carried away with him and, somehow, despite a life of degradation, had managed to bring back intact.

When the *Harriet* hove in sight of Cape Mesurado, at that precise moment, Ibrahima recommenced the practice of Islam. His friends in the United States were surprised and irritated.

Forty-one years in North America had chipped away at his personality with great effect. Cruelty and kindness by turns had brought him to many accommodations. The years demanded their compromises, most of them unpleasant. He dealt with the years as best he could, and he survived them. But there was one thing he never forgot or gave away. He clung to the God of his youth, seeking to understand and accept what had befallen him. The son of Sori was clinging still at the end.

After all that had happened to him, it was not meaningless to say, "He died in the faith of his fathers—a Mahometan."

Epilogue

Ibrahima's life was over, but not his story.

Shortly after his death, a commotion kicked up in the backcountry. It was rumored that a Fulbe caravan approached Monrovia from the interior. It came as close as Boporo, a large, well-fortified town about 150 miles north of the capital. There its members learned of the prince's death. They turned about and went home. Their cargo? Six to seven thousand dollars in gold dust for Ibrahima.

Only the money raised in the United States, a total of about $3,500, would be available for purchasing the children.

"Their emancipation would be paramount to every other consideration," Ibrahima wrote Tappan in a pleading letter from Monrovia. "Poor fellow!" the merchant confided to Gallaudet, "I fear his gray hairs must go down to the grave without the solace to be drawn from their presence. My friend in Natchez writes me that Mr. Foster now *refuses to sell.*" Stung by the election controversy, the planter was simply shutting them out. "The only hope of obtaining any of the children," Tappan continued, "arises from the prospect that he will not live long and that they may be obtained when the estate comes to be divided among the heirs."

That time was already at hand, for Thomas's health was failing. He appears to have had a type of heart disease. In January, 1829, he made out a new will and in March, as if prescient of his death, had his plantation resurveyed and platted for division. By the summer he required extensive, almost daily, visits from the doctor. His condition continued to worsen, and he passed away on September 1, 1829. Born the same year as Ibrahima, he died the same year, too. He left an enormous plantation, over one hundred slaves, and a five-figure bank account, yet ironically he lacked something Ibrahima had. A lifetime in Adams County and he did not even receive an obituary in the local newspapers.

In February, 1830, Thomas's wife Sarah and their thirteen children met to receive shares of his estate, a share worth over ten thousand dollars apiece in personal property alone. Of the children of Ibrahima whom we know, the following division was made. Sarah received Prince, his wife Bridget, and their five children. Cassandra received Lee. Simon, his wife, Hannah, and their five children went to daughter Frances.

Ibrahima's sons had been restless in his absence. Their anxiety was reflected in the quality of the plantation cotton, a large amount of which was returned in 1829 by Thomas's factor as too trashy and inferior to be marketable. Happily, the Foster heirs were anxious to sell them. Soon after the division of the planter's estate took place, Simon and his family and Lee, by an arrangement not detailed, were purchased by Tappan's New York committee for $3,100. The eight left Natchez in the summer of 1830, traveling to New York via New Orleans and arriving at Tappan's doorstep in late July. He placed them temporarily "in a pious family in Brooklin." The balance of Ibrahima's money, some four hundred dollars, was used for their board and the schooling of the children. All made the most of their new opportunities except Lee, who was briefly jailed for theft. By October, 1830, however, the eight were together on the *Carolinian,* bound for Monrovia. In December they were reunited with Isabella after a separation of two and a half years.

To aid the sons was the last favor Tappan ever did for the Colonization Society. His idea of a Liberian trading company perished with Ibrahima, and so did much of his interest and support for the colony. In time he broke with them and patronized their adversaries. Gallaudet remained true, as did John Russwurm, who emigrated in 1829 and ultimately became governor of Maryland-in-Liberia, but Tappan became an exterminating enemy. In 1833 he lectured Gurley, "Satan sometimes uses good men to promote his purposes." He died in 1865.

In Mississippi, Ibrahima's other friends went more quickly. Broke but beloved, William R. Cox was killed in a fall at his home in Natchez in September, 1831. The equally insolvent Cyrus Griffin, who abandoned the *Southern Galaxy* in disappointment, died of a fever while still in his thirties at a farm near Vicksburg in September, 1837. Colonel Marschalk, whose Jacksonianism in the 1828 election had been rewarded with a postmastership, died in August, 1838, at Washington, Adams County.

As part of the age itself, the old plantation was also destined for eclipse. Its worn-out and eroded lands could never again give as they had for Thomas and Ibrahima. Sarah Foster continued to live there until her death in 1837, and one of her children for several years longer, but most of the family sold their shares of the farm soon after receiving them. They moved on to Louisiana, to Texas, or to developing areas elsewhere in Mississippi. By 1865 Foster Fields was mostly memory. The Foster home, deserted now, served as a refuge for itinerant blacks of the Reconstruction era. When the bulk of the plantation passed into other hands, "the old house had become a warren for niggers," according to a granddaughter of Thomas's, "and was torn down" in the 1870s. Gravestones from the family cemetery, including Sarah's, were carried away and used as steps for neighborhood cabins. Time, as it always does, had worn down the proud.

That, more or less, tells it all, except for Prince and his family, who had been left behind in 1830.

Prince, the son of a prince and the grandson of a king, was never to see the land of his father. Still living on the plantation in 1834, he disappeared soon after from the records. When Sarah died in 1837, he was not counted among her property. The possibility seems remote that he was purchased by his brothers or by friends of his father and sent to Liberia. The Colonization Society has no record of his having emigrated. It seems out of character, anyway, for him to do what his father would not—desert his family. It is more likely that he perished.

It is certain that in 1838 his wife Bridget and his sons Alfred, Elijah, Edmund, and Lee were moved to Franklin County by

Sarah's heirs. There, amid the piney woods of southwest Mississippi, Ibrahima's grandchildren began new lives as the slaves of Thomas's grandchildren by his daughter Frances. They would know little of Africa, of holy war, of slave ships, tobacco, and kindly eccentric doctors. Only the grinding poverty was theirs.

The dream their grandfather had had for them would never be fulfilled.

Appendix

Genealogies

**Map of West Africa
in the 1780s**

Notes

The Family of *Almaami*

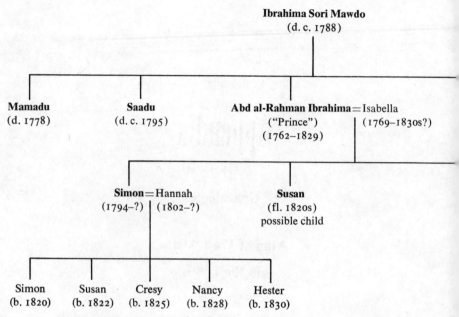

Ibrahima Sori Mawdo
(d. c. 1788)

Mamadu
(d. 1778)

Saadu
(d. c. 1795)

Abd al-Rahman Ibrahima═Isabella
("Prince")   (1769–1830s?)
(1762–1829)

Simon═Hannah
(1794–?) │ (1802–?)

Susan
(fl. 1820s)
possible child

Simon
(b. 1820)

Susan
(b. 1822)

Cresy
(b. 1825)

Nancy
(b. 1828)

Hester
(b. 1830)

This family migrated to Liberia in 1830.

The Family of Dr.

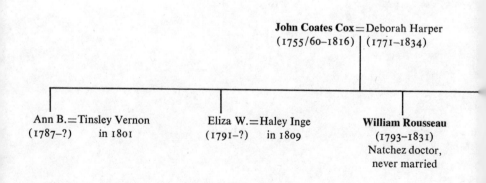

John Coates Cox═Deborah Harper
(1755/60–1816) │ (1771–1834)

Ann B.═Tinsley Vernon
(1787–?)   in 1801

Eliza W.═Haley Inge
(1791–?)   in 1809

William Rousseau
(1793–1831)
Natchez doctor,
never married

Individuals prominent in the text are listed in boldface type.

Sori (partial listing)

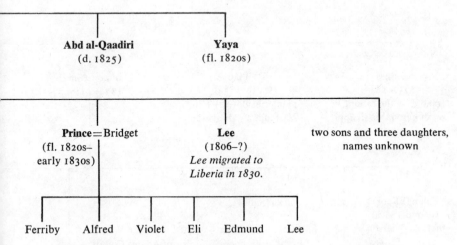

Abd al-Qaadiri
(d. 1825)

Yaya
(fl. 1820s)

Prince＝Bridget
(fl. 1820s–
early 1830s)

Lee
(1806–?)
Lee migrated to
Liberia in 1830.

two sons and three daughters,
names unknown

Ferriby Alfred Violet Eli Edmund Lee
This family remained in slavery in Mississippi.

John Coates Cox

Henry H.
(1795–1821)
Natchez attorney

Aurora＝Dr. John B. Lyons
(1798–1821)   in 1818

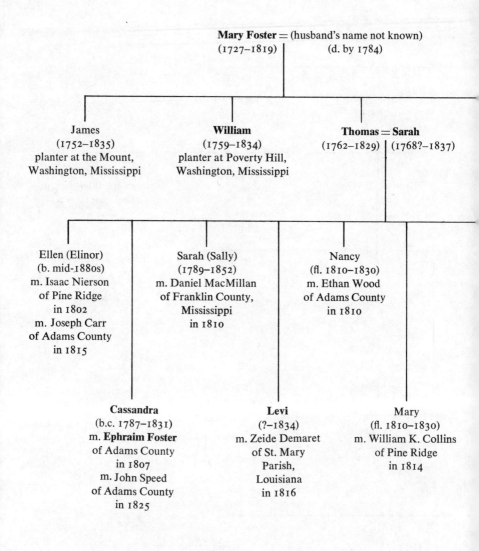

The Foster Family

Mary Foster = (husband's name not known)
(1727–1819) | (d. by 1784)

James
(1752–1835)
planter at the Mount,
Washington, Mississippi

William
(1759–1834)
planter at Poverty Hill,
Washington, Mississippi

Thomas = Sarah
(1762–1829) | (1768?–1837)

Ellen (Elinor)
(b. mid-1880s)
m. Isaac Nierson
of Pine Ridge
in 1802
m. Joseph Carr
of Adams County
in 1815

Sarah (Sally)
(1789–1852)
m. Daniel MacMillan
of Franklin County,
Mississippi
in 1810

Nancy
(fl. 1810–1830)
m. Ethan Wood
of Adams County
in 1810

Cassandra
(b.c. 1787–1831)
m. **Ephraim Foster**
of Adams County
in 1807
m. John Speed
of Adams County
in 1825

Levi
(?–1834)
m. Zeide Demaret
of St. Mary
Parish,
Louisiana
in 1816

Mary
(fl. 1810–1830)
m. William K. Collins
of Pine Ridge
in 1814

Individuals prominent in the text are listed in boldface type.

(partial listing)

John
(fl. 1780s–1820s)
planter and founder
of Washington

Frances Ann	**Thomas, Jr.**	**James**	Isaac H.
(b. c. 1795–	(?–1830)	(b. c. 1804–?)	(fl. 1820s–40s)
1837?)	m. Susan Carson	m. **Susan Alfhari**	
m. Colonel	of Natchez	of Louisiana	
Samuel W. Wells	in 1820	in 1833	
of Opelusas,			
Louisiana			
in 1814			

Elizabeth
(b. c. 1800–1831)
m. Captain
Samuel K. Sorsby
of Jefferson County,
Mississippi in 1816

Barbara
(1800–?)
m. Colonel
William Barnard
of Adams County
in 1818

Caroline
(1806–?)
m. **David S. McIntosh**
of Adams County
in 1824

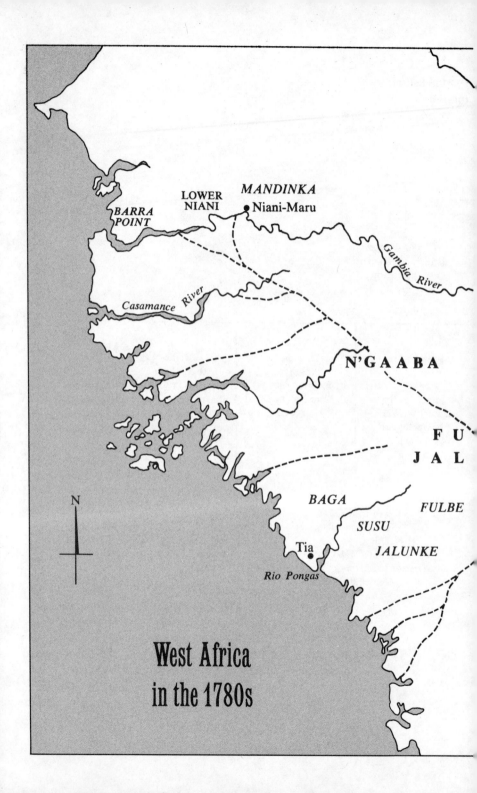

West Africa
in the 1780s

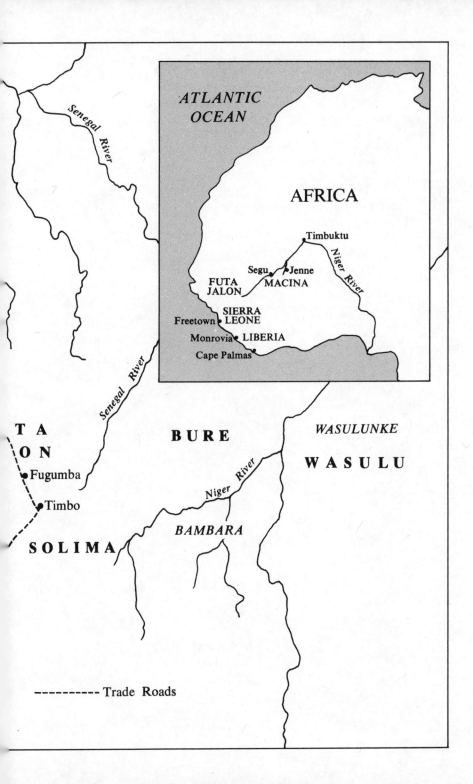

ATLANTIC
OCEAN

AFRICA

Timbuktu

Segu • Jenne
FUTA   MACINA
JALON

SIERRA
LEONE
Freetown •
Monrovia • LIBERIA
Cape Palmas

Senegal River

Niger River

T A
O N
• Fugumba

• Timbo

SOLIMA

BURE

WASULUNKE

WASULU

Senegal River

Niger River

BAMBARA

---------- Trade Roads

Notes

List of Abbreviations

ACS-DLC	American Colonization Society Papers, Manuscripts Division, The Library of Congress, Washington, D.C.
DLC	The Library of Congress
DNA	The National Archives and Records Service, Washington, D.C.
F.V., IFAN	Fonds "Vieillard," Institut Fondamental d'Afrique Noire, from translations in French generously made available by Professor Thierno Diallo, University of Dakar, Dakar, Senegal (source specified by *cahier* number).
MiDAH	Mississippi State Department of Archives and History, Jackson, Miss.
N*A*	(newspaper) *Ariel,* Natchez, Miss.
NAdCc	Circuit Clerk's Office, Adams County Courthouse, Natchez
NAdCo	Chancery Clerk's Office, Adams County Courthouse
NOL*A*	(newspaper) *Louisiana Advertiser,* New Orleans, Louisiana
N*S&G*	(newspaper) *Statesmen & Gazette,* Natchez
N*SG*	(newspaper) *Southern Galaxy,* Natchez
NY*JC*	(newspaper) *Journal of Commerce,* New York, New York
PHi	The Historical Society of Pennsylvania, Philadelphia, Pa.
P*MFJ*	(newspaper) *Manufacturers and Farmers Journal,* Providence, Rhode Island
PRO	Public Record Office, London

Statement   Thomas H. Gallaudet, *A Statement with Regard to The Moorish Prince, Abduhl Rahhahman . . . Published by order of the Committee appointed to solicit Subscriptions in New-York, to aid in redeeming the Family of the Prince from Slavery* (New York, 1828)

W*AR*   (periodical) *African Repository,* Washington, D.C.

W*DNI*   (newspaper) *Daily National Intelligencer,* Washington, D.C.

One of the most difficult aspects of writing this biography was the sorting of oysters from shells in Ibrahima's accounts of himself. While most of what he had to say is unexceptional enough, a few of his statements are at variance with the history of his country as found in the traditional chronicles and the writings of European and African travelers and historians. In the notes to Chapter 1 and in the text of Chapter 5 I have dealt with the question of *why* he gave misinformation on his African life. Enough is known of the biographies of other Fulbe slaves in the United States to indicate there was some tailoring of details to the interest of American hearers, and in that regard what Ibrahima did would be more surprising in its absence.

The question of *what* the misinformation was, however—a question so critical to a reconstruction of his life—may be dealt with here. Even at a distance of two centuries, a resolution of some of the questions his accounts raise is not as hopeless a task as might be imagined. Using those points where his persona and events connect with the history of Futa known from other sources, I have attempted to evaluate the former in the light of the latter and vice-versa, and then to move toward a synthesis of the two where they permit. Though I have tapped the knowledge of many colleagues in my struggle with his most controversial statements and obscure references, the conclusions I have reached and developed in this biography are my own. I am aware that relevant new evidence on Futa and its genealogy could cast more light on what he had to say about himself.

As an illustration of the difficulties posed by his accounts at points, it might be interesting to cite the prominent anomaly. Ibrahima claimed to have been born in Timbuktu, where, he said, his family had ruled for years. But the names given for his uncle ("the King of Timbuctoo") and for his father and the details given about them enable us to identify them beyond question as Karamoko Alfa and Ibrahima Sori Mawdo, the first two *almaamibe* of Futa. Though both men are giants in the history of Futa Jalon, neither has a known personal connection with Timbuktu as a ruler or even as a traveler. It is impossible for Sori to have lived on the Niger bend, after one chronology Ibrahima provides, and at the same time have been leading the struggle against Konde Birama in Futa, one thousand miles away. Loss of memory (Ibrahima was in his mid-sixties when he gave these accounts), exaggeration, language difficulties—all these things suggest themselves in his defense. But even taken together they cannot explain some of the discrepancies. Any person as intelligent as Ibrahima, who had never seen the sea and yet forty years later could remember the name of the particular West Indian island where he had landed after the Middle Passage, would hardly confuse Timbo and Timbuktu. It is clear he knows the difference. Such a defense is further discouraged because Ibrahima's statements of 1828 contain apparent contradictions though they were given only weeks apart. A comparison of what he told Cyrus Griffin and R. R. Gurley will prove that.

Clearly, then, a process of painstaking evaluation is needed in dealing with his evidence.

There are four principal sources for Ibrahima's life before 1788. They are Griffin's letters to the American Colonization Society, 1827–28, ACS-DLC; Griffin's NSG series, May–June, 1828; "Abduhl Rahaman's History," WAR, 4 (May, 1828), 79–81; and Gallaudet's *Statement* and speech (NYJC, 16 Oct. 1828). Although the WAR piece is autobiographical and one feels drawn to it, all accounts are equally "taken from his own lips."

Who did he say he was? Ibrahima maintained consistently that his father was Ibrahima, the second king ("Alman") of Futa. We cannot fail to identify this individual as Ibrahima Sori Mawdo. In a manuscript note of June, 1828, found in Watson's "Annals of Philadelphia" and translated for me by Thierno Diallo, Ibrahima wrote of himself in the third person, "His name Abd al-Rahman, his land Futa Jalon, son of our *almaami* Ibrahima. . . ."

We could deduce who his father was in other ways, however, even if he had not supplied us a name. Ibrahima told Griffin that when he entered the army in 1779, his father was king. By both Tauxier and Diallo and by any other reasonable chronology of Futa, 1779 was a year of Sori's reign. *Statement,* 1, contains the news that his father established the capital at Timbo, one of Sori's better-known accomplishments. By name and deed, then, Ibrahima claims the *almaami,* although he did not use the name "Sori," a *petit nom* for all Ibrahimas, in his accounts.

Who was he? Can his claims be confirmed? The political and genealogical information that he gave in 1827–28 was knowledge common to many Fulbe of Futa. Any man with Ibrahima's cunning and appetite for freedom, any Pullo, it might be argued, could have claimed royal blood to attract attention to himself. This possibility deserves consideration, but I think the evidence rebuts it effectively.

Ibrahima has not helped resolve the question by giving only his Islamic and common names and omitting his ethnic name (Diallo, Ba, Sow, or Bari). I do not feel this was due to any design of hiding his antecedents. No American of his time could have sorted him on the basis of his lineage. Once Gallaudet gave the name of *Ibrahima Jallo* (Diallo) for his father. I am of the opinion that this was a misunderstanding for *Ibrahima* of Futa *Jalon.* Fulbe royalty were Bari, so the distinction is vital. We cannot have the deeds of the Bari *almaamibe* performed by Diallo characters. If I were going to erect an alternative ancestry on the basis of this single remark, I would suggest Ibrahima was the son of a migrant Diallo family. This explanation, if stretched, might accommodate a Timbuktu birthplace, but it would also mean that Ibrahima lied about who his family was in order to make himself seem important. As the Diallo name is not mentioned by Gallaudet later in his pamphlet, or by any other sources, as there is much evidence for a Bari origin, and as there is some contemporary confirmation of who Ibrahima was, I leave this hypothesis for the one more probable: Ibrahima as a son of *almaami* Sori.

When I began this study in 1970, I decided to view his claims about himself objectively and to take nothing he had to say on faith. Such detachment is essential for all historians. Soon, comparing his narratives to the traditional and historical accounts of Futa, I noticed that the latter agree *almaami* Sori died about 1784. Ibrahima had maintained that his father was alive in 1788 when he was captured, then died soon afterward. Which was true? For two years I carried around the impression that Ibrahima had lied about the date of his father's death in order to heighten the effect of the story of his capture. It was that, or else he had to have another father altogether, which, in turn, meant he was being deceitful about a lot more. Not until I studied James Watt's journal at the Bodleian Library, Oxford, did I realize a date of 1784 for Sori's death was too early. Watt's information and the traditional reign lengths given in the *tarikhs* together suggested a death date of about 1788. Ibrahima had been correct.

I also doubted that Ibrahima had been enslaved on the Gambia. That river seemed too far from Futa. Books on the areas revealed little direct connection between the two in the late eighteenth century. Moreover, the English slaved on the Gambia and yet Ibrahima wound up in a Spanish province of North America. I suspected Ibrahima meant the nearby Kambia, or had gone down the Nunez, the Fatala, or some closer waterway. But Gambia it was, as the notes for Chapter 2 demonstrate. A juxtaposition of names and dates from colonial shipping returns in London and Spanish deed books in Natchez confirmed Ibrahima again. Even more surprisingly, he was right in identifying Dominica as his landfall in the Western Hemisphere. I was certain he meant Santo Domingo, an island with a more extensive New Orleans trade than small, foreign-owned Dominica in the remote Windwards. But Dominica was confirmed by the island's port records.

These are three instances in which, Ibrahima seemed to be wrong but was not. At the conclusion of five years of research on this man, I have developed a high regard for what he had to say about himself. While this is no carte blanche for him, it means that I have not been mislead by him often. He has earned the benefit of the doubt from me during our association, something that may be worthwhile to keep in mind in judging assertions on which no external evidence can be brought to bear.

African sources can neither confirm nor deny his claim to be the *almaami's* son. Despite my search in every record of Pullo life in the eighteenth century that I could find, I saw nothing upon which to judge his paternity. There may be no record that is definitive. There is no complete list of Sori's children, for example, or even an agreement about how many there were. Guébhard knows of seven, Farba Sek of twenty-two, Saint-Pére of fifty. One account states that Sori had thirty-three sons old enough to go to war in 1778. And then there are those children whom "the rigor of manners" would not permit Sori to acknowledge. We know details about few of either group.

In sum, Ibrahima is not recalled by name in any of the manuscripts, books, or traditional histories of which I know.

This does not mean he must be taken at his own word, however, for while Africa in Africa may not speak authoritatively on this subject, Africa in America may. There is some contemporary collaboration of Ibrahima's claims, given while he was in the United States, by a Pullo, a Jalunke, a colonist from Sierra Leone, and an African traveler. Their comments support him strongly. Sterling, a respected old Pullo living near Hartford, Connecticut, had a lengthy conversation with Ibrahima in 1828, and he "corroborated many things" Ibrahima told Gallaudet. When Ibrahima asked Sterling if he remembered a certain campaign waged in Sori's time, the Pullo replied, "Oh, yes. I was in it—under the command of your father." Certainly, Sterling seemed to have no doubt whose son he was.

Earlier, sometime in the 1790s, Ibrahima met at Natchez "a negro from his father's dominions. The negro cried Abduhl Rahahman and hid his face in the earth." The source for this story does not say, but we surmise this was one of Sori's slaves sold or stolen out of the country. Is this the reaction we might expect to the son of an obscure Diallo family? An unidentified man from Sierra Leone met Ibrahima in Boston in 1828. Far from disputing Ibrahima's identity, he confirmed it. And this person was intimate enough with the affairs of Futa to be able to give Ibrahima details about his son al-Husayn. Gallaudet considered this colonist "an authentic source" of information on Futa. Finally, there is the evidence of Dr. John Cox, who was in Africa about 1781. Dr. Cox was unequivocal in his assertion that Ibrahima belonged to "the royal family of the country." If the

doctor may be believed (see notes to Chapter I), his testimony
alone is proof of Ibrahima's lineage. His account, if nothing
else, is unsuspicious; what would he have gained by concoct-
ing such a story?

Contextual and circumstantial evidence also supports Ibrahima's claim to be the *almaami's* son. The slave name Prince
documents an assertion of identity upon his arrival in Natchez.
The clout he exerted on the plantation and the respect he received from other Fulbe at Natchez like Samba indicate he was a
man of authority at home. From motives of jealousy or ill will,
they could have undermined his claims, especially if they were
unfounded. There is no evidence or suggestion they did. White
Southerners, always suspicious of tales of royal birth, thought
slaves used them to enhance their status; yet the Natchez
planters did not doubt Ibrahima. They knew nothing of Futa,
but long association with Ibrahima led them to believe he was
truthful. It seemed unlikely to them, as it still does today, that
he could have successfully maintained a pose through forty years
of slavery. And there are the letters Ibrahima wrote to Abd al-
Qaadiri from New York and Monrovia. Why were they written
to the Bari? A pretext was surely unnecessary in Liberia, where
he would have to have written his own family. And what about
the stranger who visited Monrovia after his death and inspected
his manuscripts? This person was so moved by what he found
that he tearfully insisted that Ibrahima's widow return with him
to Timbo. Timbo was the seat of the Seydiyanke clan of the Bari,
the clan from which the *almaamibe* always came. And is it likely
that thousands of dollars in gold would be sent to Boporo upon
receipt of Ibrahima's letters had they not been signed with a
name that astonished the eye?

I believe, then, that both testimony and inference lead to the
same door. Abd 'al-Rahman Ibrahima was a son of Ibrahima
Sori Mawdo. He confused matters by connecting the ruling
houses of Timbo and Timbuktu and he exaggerated his own rank
in the family, but here, I feel, is a lost son of the Seydiyanke.
Additional evidence, from Africa, I hope, may one day clarify his
situation further. I suspect it will point in the direction established here. If not, then we are dealing with one of the greatest
confidence men of the age, who turned a hundred Natchez

Fulbe into an acting company, talked an Irish doctor into an insanely dangerous scheme, played cunningly upon the friendship of a few and the sympathy of a thousand, and ended up hoaxing a brother who had never heard of him out of thirty pounds of gold.

Either way, it is an incredible story.

A Note on Spelling

The use of *sic* has been avoided in the text, except in a few instances. I thought it more accurately portrayed the flavor of the times to present the misspellings and various renderings of names exactly as the characters of the story gave them. Most of these will be apparent to the reader, anyway. Timbo may appear as "Tembo" from the hands of one writer, for instance, or Abd al-Rahman as "Abduhl Rahahman" (or "Rahhahman"), etc.

Neither have I sought to standardize the grammar of the various quotations attributed to Ibrahima. He wrote no English, and so all quotes by him, except those translated from Arabic and Pular, are actually his words as written by other people. Naturally, the literary style and quality of each varies with the education of the writer. So, at the Boston banquet (p. 140), Ibrahima's reply is polished, while his complaint in Liberia about his house frame (p. 180) is not. Having explained this, I prefer to quote the original sources as they are, despite their variations, thinking the reader would rather see the exact wording than have me extensively copy-edit material inside quotation marks. The former seems preferable to an attempt to establish a uniformity of literary style for a person who, after all, did not even write the language.

1. The White Turban

"*S'il y a un peuple facile à aborder mais difficile à saisir, c'est bien le peuple peul,*" Thierno Diallo has written. I suggest one start with Diallo's *Les Institutions Politiques du Fouta Dyalon au XIXᵉ Siècle* (Dakar, 1972); Louis Tauxier, *Moeurs et histoire des Peuls* (Paris, 1937); William Derman, *Serfs, Peasants, and Socialists* (Berkeley,

1973); Alfa Ibrahima Sow, *La Femme, La Vache, La Foi: Écrivains & Poètes du Fouta-Djalon* (Paris, 1966), and Sow, *Chroniques et Recits du Fouta-Djalon* (Paris, 1968); Jules H. Saint-Père, "Création du Royaume Du Fouta Djallon," *Bulletin du Comité d'Etudes Historiques et Scientifiques de l'Afrique occidentale Française* [*B.CEHS*], 12 (Paris, 1929), 484–555; and Paul Guébhard, "L'Histoire du Fouta-Djallon et des Almamys," *L'Afrique Française, Renseignements Coloniaux et Documents publiée par Le Comité de l'Afrique Française et Le Comité du Maroc*, 1909.

page 3

early Fulbe history: Tauxier, 13–30; Herbert R. Palmer, *Sudanese Memoirs* . . . (3 vols., Lagos, 1928), vol. 3, 64ff.; Diallo, chapter 2. The Fulbe left Macina for Futa Jalon because of economic and religious discrimination. Joseph Harris's interview with Diallo Abdoul, 6 Feb. 1961, in Harris, "The Kingdom of Fouta Diallon" (Ph.D. dissertation, Northwestern University, 1965), 161–2.

Jalunke: Leland H. Holmes, "Changes in Yalunka Social Organization" (Ph.D. dissertation, University of Oregon, 1968), chapter 2. Jalunke was the collective Pular name for several different non-Fulbe people of Futa.

pages 4–5

religious tension: Saint-Père, 490–2, traces its course, which was near flood stage by 1720. Some would even start the *jihaad* at that date. Charles Reichardt, *Grammar of the Fulde Language* (London, 1876), xvii–xviii.

prayer prohibited: André Arcin, *Histoire de la Guinée Française* (Paris, 1911), 85–6.

Karamoko Alfa: Ibrahima Sambégo, called Karamoko Alfa ("the learned prince"), is the first great Muslim figure in the history of Futa. He is remembered as an almost fatidical holy man, instrumental in bringing about the *jihaad*. Arsène Lambert, who visited Futa Jalon in the mid-nineteenth century, wrote that he was the first person to break with the previous policy of peaceful conversion of the Jalunke.

circular letter: *cahier* #8, F.V., IFAN, reproduces long excerpts.

Sori: he was the son of Malik-Si, who died when he was an infant (Saint-Père, 524). Malik-Si's brother, Nuhu, was Karamoko Alfa's father. All belonged to the Seydiyanke clan of the Bari family. Guébhard, 53, provides a geneaology. Also see Tauxier, 289n; Diallo, 243. Jean Bayol, *Voyage en Sénégambie* (Paris, 1888),

102, places Sori's education at Fugumba. Guébhard, 50, terms him a "vigorous and lively fellow," accustomed to the physical life.

slashing the drum: tradition of Muhammad Sali, written in 1857, and translated in Charles Reichardt, *Three Original Fulah Pieces* (Berlin, 1859), 45–6.

the *jihaad:* 1653, 1720, 1725, and 1726 have each been given as the date for the battle of Talansan, which, most accounts agree, is the beginning battle of the *jihaad*. An exact starting date may be conjectural, but I think a good case can be made for 1730 as the closing date of the war. According to Guébhard, 51, Karamoko Alfa was installed in power shortly after the final Muslim victory. There is some concensus that he ruled for eighteen years. Since he was removed from power about 1748 (see the note below on his madness), one can conclude he must have come to power about 1730.

The *jihaad* by which the Muslim Fulbe established their power in Futa is beyond the proper scope of this work, but those who wish to investigate it should consult Guébhard, 49–51; *cahier* #8, F.V., IFAN; Omar Jamburia, "The Story of the Gehad or Holy War of the Foulahs," *Sierra Leone Studies,* O.S. #3 (1919), quoted in Christopher Fyfe, *Sierra Leone Inheritance* (London, 1964), 78ff.; Saint-Père, 500–10; Walter Rodney, "Jihad and Social Revolution in Futa-Djalon in the Eighteenth Century," *Journal of the Historical Society of Nigeria,* 4 (June, 1968), 269–84.

theocracy: for the organization of state and society see Guébhard, 51–2; Derman, 13ff.; and Rodney, 277–9.

Karamoko Alfa's madness: this occurred three years before his death (*cahier* #6, F.V., IFAN). Since Gordon Laing, *Travels in the Timannee, Kooranko, and Soolima Countries, in Western Africa* (London, 1825), 403–4, informs us he died in or about 1751, the madness must date about 1748. In N*SG*, 29 May 1828, Ibrahima states that when this occurred, he was deposed.

Sori chosen: Saint-Père, 529, details his election and the celebrations that followed. As Karamoko Alfa had forseen (*ibid.,* 523), with the army and numerous partisans to support him, Sori would have been difficult to stop.

regular campaigns: a prominent victim in this decade was Wasulu. Saint-Père, 538.

"as brave as Sori": *ibid.,* 522.

"found it close . . .": quoted in NY*JC,* 16 Oct. 1828.

tarikhs: an impressive collection of biographies, autobiographies, poems, genealogies, and historical chronicles has been assembled at the Institut Fondamental d'Afrique Noire, University of Dakar.

As already indicated, I have made use of a significant part of this set in reconstructing the African world of Ibrahima.

"the land of living . . .": Diallo, 115.

"[They] are handsome . . .": Golbery, quoted in Tauxier, 220–1.

trade to coast: Peter McLachlan, *Travels into the Baga and Soosoo Countries, During the Year 1821* (Freetown, 1821), 30, observed the Fulbe traded cattle, gold, butter, and clean or rough rice. Salt was carried away in baskets five and six feet in length. Assistant staff surgeon Brian O'Beirne's untitled journal of an expedition to Timbo in 1821, in Colonial Office Records [CO] 267:53, PRO, 183–4, mentions a mile-long caravan and notes the gold rings.

"They [say that . . .": "Journal of Mr. James Watt, in his Expedition to and From Teembo in the Year 1794 . . . ," Bodleian Library, Rhodes House, Oxford, entry of 9 March 1794.

"The people with . . .": *ibid.*

one of the richest . . . : a reputation enhanced by the gold that passed through their country from Bambouk. Many Europeans thought there were gold mines in Futa. Tauxier, 219–20.

Timbo: Gongovi was its original name. Ernest Noirot, *A travers Le Fouta-Djalon et Le Bambouck* (Paris, 1882), 177. Noirot provides a physical description of Timbo and the surrounding area. Also useful in preparing this sketch of Fulbe life were Theodore Canot, *The Adventures of an African Slaver* (New York, 1928 edition), chapters 14–19, and "Narrative of Mr. William Cooper Thomson's Journey from Sierra Leone to Timbo, Capital of Futah Jallo, in Western Africa," Royal Geographical Society, *Journal*, 16 (London, 1846), 106–38.

page 6

population: Watt, "Journal," 7 March 1794.

"They are remarkably . . .": *ibid.*

mosque: O'Beirne, 122, 154–5, observing that it was "remarkable for its size and age." Noirot, 176, said only the mosque at Fugumba was older.

two-furlong track: Watt, "Journal," 8 March 1794.

"Considerable attention . . .": N*SG*, 19 June 1828.

Individual libraries: Watt, "Journal," *passim.* Mungo Park, *Travels in the Interior Districts of Africa . . .* (London, 1799), 314, saw the Pentateuch circulated.

Most young Muslims . . . : Noirot, 212ff. The education was impressive enough in 1767 for a chief in Sierra Leone to send one son to Futa for studies, another to Lancaster, England. The latter became profligate. Testimony of James Penny, 6 March 1788, add. mss. #18272, British Museum, photocopy at DLC.

page 7

pilgrimages to Mecca: N*SG,* 12 June 1828.

mendicants: Natchez *Mississippi Republican,* 20 Feb. 1822, quoting an unidentified New York newspaper that mentioned a traveler from Egypt.

Spanish defeat: John Matthews, *A Voyage to the River Sierra-Leone, on the Coast of Africa* ... (London, 1788), 69–70, also mentions mendicants from Morocco.

Mediterranean convoy: *Proceedings of the African Association,* Vol. 1 (London, 1810), 381.

"The male Foulahs ...": all quotations in this paragraph are from Canot, 170–1. He also provides descriptions of everyday clothing.

clothing described: most travelers make some remarks. Noirot, 222–4, gives a good short description.

lack of markets: Canot, 171.

herders' disdain: see notes to Chapter 3 for citations.

One source states ... : Ibrahima, in N*SG,* 12 June 1828.

two working days a week: René Caillié, a traveler of 1827, cited in Derman, 36. Derman's book is especially valuable for giving a Jalunke perspective to life in Futa.

modi videndi: Gaspard Mollien, *Travels in the Interior of Africa, to the Sources of the Senegal and Gambia* (London, 1820), 299–300.

page 8

a law required ... : Watt, "Journal," 14 March 1794. "I learnt they have a law forcing every person to go armed, for fear of an insurrection of the slaves, and prohibiting on pain of death any slave from carrying arms. ..."

revolt of 1756: Laing, *Travels,* 405.

"eaten to the limits ...": expression in Guébhard, 54.

his appointees unpopular ... : Harris, "Kingdom of Fouta Diallon," 34–5.

Saalihu: Guébhard, 54, and *cahiers* #3, 4, and 6, F.V., IFAN, agree that Sori was deposed after an eleven-year rule. I believe mistakes in the chronology of Futa have been made by considering Saalihu's four-to-five-year rule part of Sori's total of thirty-three to -four. They should be figured separately. Thus, Sori (first reign, 1748/9–1759); Saalihu (1759–64); Sori (second reign, 1764 to his death *circa* 1788, becoming *almaami* again only about 1778 upon the final defeat of Konde Birama). This arrangement harmonizes the traditional reign lengths of the *tarikhs* with the chronology of Major Laing.

Sori deposed: *cahiers* #3–4, F.V., IFAN; Guébhard, 54. Watt "Journal," 19 March 1794: "the father of Ali Mami [Saadu] had been deposed and afterwards restored—I asked who deposed the old King —he said the chiefs. . . ."

exile: Guébhard, 54.

page 9

Ibrahima's date of birth: Cyrus Griffin to R. R. Gurley, Natchez, 13 Dec. 1827, ACS-DLC, giving 1762. The date seems correct. In 1828 Ibrahima claimed to be sixty-six years old and said his age at the time of his enslavement in 1788 was twenty-six. The question of his paternity has been discussed previously.

place of birth: Ibrahima told Griffin, Gurley, and Gallaudet that he was born in Timbuktu, where, he said, *almaami* Sori maintained two wives and a residence and spent a number of years. Dubious as that report is, however, I would not have the temerity to assert Timbo here, if it, too, had not been given. See Springfield, Mass., *Hampden Journal*, 8 Oct. 1828.

Ibrahima's account of close political and family ties between Timbuktu and Futa Jalon is one for which I have found no supporting evidence. I doubt there is any. In Chapter 5 I give my opinion as to why such a claim was made. It is worth observing, however, that some of the Americans with whom he spoke did not make adequate distinctions between the two places and must have garbled some of what he had to say about himself. Gallaudet once stated (*NYJC*, 16 Oct. 1828) that "the territory of Tombuctoo" was only one hundred miles from Sierra Leone. This, obviously, is a reference to Futa. Yet, on another occasion (*Statement*, 1), the same writer stated that twelve to fifteen hundred miles separated Timbuktu and Timbo. One would like to think that Ibrahima, in the broken English of his conversation, had been unable to make clear the distinction between those two places. But he himself said, "I born in the city Timbuctoo. . . . I moved to country Foota Jallo—I lived in the capital Timbo." Ibrahima's ms., 10 Oct. 1828, John Trumbull Papers, Sterling Library, Yale University.

It might be supposed charitably that Ibrahima intended to connect the two places in the same sense as the Pullo historian Mohamadu-Saadu, who told Noirot in the 1880s that certain early Fulbe immigrants had ruled at Timbuktu. Noirit, *A travers Le Fouta-Djalon*, 194. What Mohamadu-Saadu meant was that many of the Fulbe migrated to Futa from Macina, not far from Timbuktu, or, as Ibrahima told Gallaudet, and Gallaudet phrased it (*Statement, 6*), "Teembo, as it were, having been settled by a colony from Tombuctoo." But it is one thing to claim distant ancestors ruled on the Niger, another to say one's own grandfather and uncle did.

born on a Monday: conversation with Thierno Diallo, Dakar, 11 July 1974.

mother: she was a Pullo, apparently. *Statement,* 1. Her name is never mentioned.

dream: Sow, *Chroniques et Recits,* 34–5.

Saalihu's reign: he reigned but four or five years (*cahier* #18), and those under great stress (*cahiers* #3–4, 6, F.V., IFAN). Guébhard, 54, states that "a period of anarchy" occurred.

attack on Wasulu: the best account is Laing, *Travels,* 406–7. For the Wasulunke, see Diallo, 36n.

page 10

Solima: Laing, *Travels,* 407–8, giving all details cited.

deer: Saint-Père, 538.

Timbo razed, etc.: Laing, *Travels,* 408; *cahiers* #3–4, 6, F.V., IFAN; Guébhard, 54–5; Watt, "Journal," 17 March 1794. Arcin, 92, mentions the tradition that Karamoko Alfa's body was found miraculously intact. By 1763 it would have been buried twelve years.

returned in the spring: *cahier* #6, F.V., IFAN.

"Here is that . . .": quoted in Sow, *Chroniques et Recits,* 34–5.

Sori brought back: Watt, "Journal," 19 March 1794, mentions his restoration. Guébhard, 55, states that deputations were sent to Sori on his mountain, one from each of the nine provinces of the Fulbe confederation, to call him back to power.

page 11

less important title: it was at this time, apparently, that he held the title *shaikh,* which was voted him by an assembly of elders at Fugumba. Bayol, *Voyage en Sénégambie,* 102–3. He was not made *almaami* again until after the victory at Sirakoure. Guébhard mentions he accepted the recall "without bitterness."

stone and clay bank: Watt, "Journal," 12, 17 March 1794; O'Beirne, 153–4, contains the phrase "elevated by the labors. . . ." Watt, under the date of 24 Feb., mentions similar fortifications at Labé.

annual campaigns: Laing, *Travels,* 409–10, refering to this as "constant warfare."

to bring a rock . . . : Arcin, 92.

"Now I am . . .": Konde Birama quoted in Noirot, 195. "Fulbe" is inserted for "Poulas" in the original.

Ibrahima, Sori's son . . . : Ibrahima's claims to a Timbuktu birthplace make this period of his life difficult to reconstruct, as do his accounts of his early childhood and schooling, which contain few details and those varying among themselves at points. I prepared the reconstruction given here after a perusal and comparison of all the different versions of his life before 1781, with special attention to the chronology of events in Futa.

Edward Everett, "Abduhl Rahaman," *Orations and Speeches on Various Occasions,* vol. 3 (Boston, 1859) [hereafter "Rahaman"], 187, mentions that Ibrahima's schooling took place "partly at Teembo, his father's residence." For Everett's acquaintanceship with Ibrahima, see Chapter 6.

page 12

education in Futa: Ibrahima contributed the sketch in N*SG,* 19 June 1828. Also see Noirot, 212ff.

the stamp of his . . . : Charlotte Quinn, *Mandingo Kingdoms of the Senegambia: Traditionalism, Islam and European Expansion* (Evanston, Ill., 1972), chapter 3 (53–70), delineates the Muslim character and environment well.

"forty-eight hours . . .": Natchez tradition, probably reflecting Cox family history, related by Amanda Geisenberger, a local historian, in a conversation held 21 Aug. 1973 at Natchez.

his father decided . . . : *Statement,* 1. N*SG,* 29 May 1828, agrees, though having him leave at an earlier age. NO*LA,* 28 Oct. 1828, states that he "was at an early age sent from Timboo, of which his father was king, to Tombuctoo, where he was educated in Arabic literature. . . ."

titles of *tierno* . . . :Harris, "Kingdom of Fouta Diallon," 23n. The first two levels of achievement were learning to read and then to write the Qur'an. The second two, mentioned here, were marked with the conferment of these titles. It is important to note that the ages at which Ibrahima claimed important changes took place in his education are, appropriately enough, the same years that anthropologists have since marked as key ones in the intellectual development of young male Fulbe.

to follow his father . . . : "At twelve years of age [1774], Prince was sent to Tombuctoo, to obtain an education, being the rightful heir to the throne. . . ." *Statement,* 1.

The ancestral home . . . : Diallo, 34, based on historical and linguistic analysis, estimates that perhaps three fourths of the Fulbe came from Macina.

the trip could. . . . : Watt, "Journal," 23 Feb. 1794, lists five nations between Timbo and Timbuktu. "The intermediate nations are hospitable," he wrote, and "a person can perform the journey from Laby in four moons." For the route see Diallo, 98, and his map number 1, "Le Fuuta Dyalon: Situation Geographique." The tributary was the Tinkisso.

page 13

Macina and Timbuktu described: remarks in these two paragraphs are from Park, *Travels in the Interior Districts of Africa*, 208ff.; *Proceedings of the African Association*, vol. 1, 273–4, 374ff.; Heindrich Barth, *Travels and Discoveries in North and Central Africa* (3 vols., New York, 1857–59), vol. 3, *passim*. Also useful were the reports of Sālih Bilāli of Macina, Abū Bakr of Timbuktu, and Wargee of Astrakhan, whose accounts Ivor Wilks has edited for part 2 of Philip Curtin, *Africa Remembered: Narratives by West Africans from the Era of the Slave Trade* (Madison, Wis., 1967); and Tauxier, *Histoire des Bambara* (Paris, 1942). James Hopewell, "Muslim Penetration into French Guinea, Sierra Leone and Liberia before 1850" (Ph.D. dissertation, Columbia University, 1958), is helpful in illuminating the relationship between Futa and the Niger River cities.

"God, the Most . . .": Abd al-Rahman as-Sa'di, *Tarikh es-Soudan* (O. Houdas, trans.), (Paris, 1964 reprint ed.), 28–9.

Ibrahima in Jenne: N*SG*, 29 May 1828. He would have been there in the 1770s, when Jenne was ruled by a non-Muslim Fulbe dynasty that had compromised the sovereignty of the state with the pagan Bambara of Segu.

"Caravans . . .": Ibrahima, in NY*JC*, 16 Oct. 1828.

For all their alleged interest in Timbuktu, Americans of 1828 published few details from Ibrahima about it. This is unfortunate, since his facts might be used to check his credibility. On the whole, what he did say stands up very well. He was correct in asserting that the city is north of the Niger, not on it (New Haven *Connecticut Journal*, 14 Oct. 1828); that it was surrounded by a wall (NY*JC*, 16 Oct. 1828); and that there were other cities of equal size on the river (New York *Freedom's Journal*, 29 Aug. 1828). He did not know where the Niger terminated (he thought it was lost in the sand, *ibid.*), but neither did Amadi Fatuma, a great Niger traveler and Park's guide on his second expedition. Park, *Journal of a Mission to the Interior of Africa, in the Year 1805*

(Philadelphia, 1815), 74. Ibrahima spoke of five mosques at Timbuktu (NY*JC*, 16 Oct. 1828), Caillié of six, and Barth of seven (Barth, *Travels and Discoveries*, vol. 3, 325), but each saw the city at intervals of a generation. The only particular conflict is with Wargee of Astrakhan (see Curtin, above), who said there were no iron manufactories at Timbuktu in 1821. Ibrahima stated there were "several manufactories of steel and gold" (NY*JC*, 16 Oct. 1828), but then, he did see the city almost a half century earlier than Wargee.

three ancient centers . . . : Barth, *Travels and Discoveries*, vol. 3, 302, 323–5.

"They read the . . .": quoted in NY*JC*, 16 Oct. 1828.

page 14

"well versed . . .": NO*LA*, 4 Nov. 1828.

"He is very . . .": Schroeder to "Rev. & dear Sir" [Gallaudet?], New York, 21 Oct. 1828, drafts in the possession of Joan McDaniel, Washington, D.C. For the Reverend Schroeder, see Chapter 7.

When Ibrahima was seventeen . . . : NY*JC*, 16 Oct. 1828, reading in part, "At the age of 17, he was removed from Tombuctoo to Teembo. . . ." N*SG*, 29 May 1828: "At the age of seventeen, at which time his father was King of Footah Jallo, he received an appointment in the army."

Sori gained an even hand . . . : Arcin, 92, traces the reversal of fortunes.

"At length . . .": Laing, *Travels*, 410–11.

"God has punished . . .": Guébhard, 55, provides the quotation used and the reaction of the sons.

all the Fulbe and their allies . . . : Laing, *Travels*, 411.

page 15

Forty thousand: *cahiers* #3–4, F.V., IFAN.

"the honor of this . . .": Guébhard, 55, mentioning also his killing Konde Birama.

"A most sanguinary . . .": Laing, *Travels*, 411. For this battle also see *cahiers* #3–4, 6, F.V., IFAN; Bayol, *Voyage en Sénégambie*, 102–3; Noirot, 195; Farba Sek, "The Almaamibe of the House of Soriya," in Sow, *Chroniques et Recits*, 67ff.

"God! Help us!": Saint-Père, 544.

almaami again: Bayol, 102–3; Arcin, 95.

"*mawdo*": Harris, "Kingdom of Fouta Diallon," 36.

moved the capital: Hyacinthe Hecquard, *Voyage sur la cote et dans l'intérieur de l'Afrique occidentale* (Paris, 1855), 316.

opponents executed: *ibid.*, 314ff. Some writers place his second coro-

nation after the murder of the dissident councilmen, not before.
Watt, "Journal," 10 March 1794, mentions investing a *marabout*
with a fine robe.

page 16

"Until I was . . .": Ibrahima quoted in W*AR,* 4 (May, 1828), 79.
The year was 1781: all quotations and details in the next five paragraphs from N*SG,* 29 May 1828, which is based on Ibrahima's
recollection of the event. It is probable this battle took place in the
upper Niger region, possibly with Wasulu. Ibrahima informed Griffin that the Bambara war leader had made "repeated depredations
. . . upon the frontiers" of Futa.

page 17

John Coates Cox: of this individual before 1781 there are but two
pieces of information: first, a family tradition that he was from
Dublin (genealogical papers in the possession of R. Brent Forman,
Natchez, kindly shared with me); and, second, the Rockingham
County, North Carolina, census of 1800, by which it appears that
he was born in the period 1755–60. He would, then, have been in
his twenties when he visited Africa.
"Our people saw . . .": quoted in W*AR,* 4 (May, 1828), 80, containing most of the particulars of this visit.
no such creature . . . known before: Gaspard Mollien stated in his
Travels in the Interior of Africa, 257, that the old men at Timbo
remembered an Englishman who spent some time there, possibly
before the arrival of Watt and Winterbottom in 1794. Those
two are usually regarded as the first European visitors in Futa.
There is a temptation to think Mollien's old men mistook a mulatto
who resided at Timbo before Watt and Winterbottom's appearance for this individual. He claimed to be a white person. See
Thomas M. Winterbottom, *An Account of the Native Africans in
the Neighborhood of Sierra Leone* (2 vols., London, 1804), vol. 1,
185.
   But evidence for the unidentified European has continued to
mount over the years. Arcin, *Histoire,* 224, and Claudius Madrolle,
En Guinée (Paris, 1895), 33–5, both claim an unidentified Englishman visited Futa prior to Watt and Winterbottom. Madrolle
wrote that the visitor "stayed a long time in the country, married
there, and had a son." Arcin added that he "was married at Timbo
to a daughter of the almaamy." Research into Ibrahima's life has
now given us, I believe, the name of that individual. This knowledge is very useful in explaining why, when Dr. Cox met Ibrahima

in Mississippi years later, he "embraced [him] as if he had been a brother." Boston, Mass., *Evening Chronicle*, 30 Aug. 1828.

On the other hand, *almaami* Saadu told Watt ("Journal," 13 March 1794) that "no white man had ever visited him or his fathers before him." Unless Saadu was just being diplomatic because Watt brought gifts and promises of trade, this is a powerful dissent to the claim that the Cox visit took place, at least at Timbo. In W*AR*, 4 (May, 1828), 80, Ibrahima recounted the visit without stating *where* the doctor was entertained. *Statement,* 1, however, places it at Timbo.

Ibrahima and the doctor are the only direct sources I have found to affirm the rescue and hospitality described here, other than Cox's widow, who said in 1828 that her husband had visited Timbo. Griffin to Gurley, Natchez, 27 Dec. 1828, ACS-DLC. The Cox-Inge family record in *The Holy Bible* (New York, 1813), located at Ravenna, Natchez, indicates Dr. Cox did not come to North America until 1787. Any adventuring done in Africa, then, would have to have been done before that date, a date that is pre-Watt-and-Winterbottom and fits well into Ibrahima's chronology of the visit. The doctor's reputation as a specialist in fevers may be relevant here, too.

It would help to know what he was doing on the coast. If connected with a slave ship, as oral tradition suggests, or in the hinterland to purchase slaves (a detail Ibrahima would not care to have come out in 1828), another reason is added for Sori's solicitude. A Cox family account has him on an expedition to Timbuktu, a story he encouraged. Mildren Hamilton, "Notebook," kindly shown me by Leicester and Betty McGehee of Natchez.

For the present, at any rate, the possibility of his being the first European visitor in Futa is strongly raised.

found lying face down ... : Geisenberger interview, 21 Aug. 1973, cited earlier. Another traditional account is by François Mignon, undated clipping in the Roane F. Byrnes Papers, University of Mississippi Library, brought to my attention by Verbie Ann Lovorn.

O'Beirne: 117ff.

Canot: 169.

Park: *Travels in the Interior Districts of Africa*, 56.

Mollien: *Travels*, 81.

"Being the first ...": NY*JC*, 16 Oct. 1828.

"They brought ...": W*AR*, 4 (May, 1828), 80.

page 18

Dr. Cox recovered ... : NY*JC*, 16 Oct. 1828, reading, in part, "Prince

. . . had an establishment of his own, and Dr. Cox became an intimate at his house. His wound was cured, and he and Prince, became quite intimate." The same article indicates clearly that Ibrahima saw the doctor on horseback in Futa. *Biographical and Historical Memoirs of Mississippi* (2 vols., Chicago, 1891), vol. 1, 760, contains a Natchez tradition, clearly exaggerated, that the doctor taught Ibrahima "to read and write" the English language.

Mollien, writing in 1820 . . . : *Travels,* 257.

Easygoing by nature . . . : see Chapter 4, in which Cox's personality is delineated.

"for, if any . . .": Abd al-Qaadiri, quoted in O'Beirne, 132ff.

"What makes you . . .": Ibrahima reports this conversation in W*AR*, 4 (May, 1828), 80.

outfitted with clothes . . . : NY*JC,* 16 Oct. 1828.

gold: W*AR,* 4 (May, 1828), 81.

fifteen warriors . . . : *ibid.*

"not to go on . . .": *ibid.*

the same vessel . . . : *ibid.* The name of the ship is not given, of course.

page 19

al-Husayn: "Allusine, living in Teembo." *Statement,* 5.

next to his father: "Prince's house, adjoining that of his father. . . ." *Statement,* 1. O'Beirne, 153–5, mentioned the construction of the houses on the hill by Sori.

2. Across the Broad Casamance

An introduction to the peoples and time covered in this chapter may be gained from Georges Legrand, "La Gambia, Notes historiques et géographiques," *B.CEHS,* 11 (1928), 432–84; Henry F. Reeve, *The Gambia* (London, 1912); John M. Gray, *A History of the Gambia* (New York, 1966); Quinn, *Mandingo Kingdoms of the Senegambia;* and Curtin, *Africa Remembered,* both cited earlier; Board of Trade Papers [BT] 6:9–11 (Slave-Trade Investigations, 1788ff.), PRO; Frances Armytage, *The Free Port System in the British West Indies: A Study in Commercial Policy, 1766–1822* (London, 1953); Thomas Atwood, *The History of the Island of Dominica* (London, 1791); Caroline M. Burson, *The Stewardship of Don Estéban Miró* (New Orleans, 1940); John G. Clark, *New Orleans, 1718–1812: An Economic History* (Baton Rouge, 1970); and James A. Robertson, *Louisiana under the Rule of Spain, France and the United States, 1785–1807* (2 vols., Freeport, New York, 1969).

page 20

John Ormond: short contemporary biographical remarks by a former partner appear in Adam Afzelius, Diary, 26 Feb. 1796, Alexander Peter Kup, ed., *Sierra Leone Journal, 1795–1796* (Uppsala, Sweden, 1967), 76, 98n. Also see Canot, 78–9.

thirty thousand pounds: Carl Wadstrom, *An Essay on Colonization,* vol. 2 (London, 1795), 87–8, giving an extract from a report of the Sierra Leone Company.

"I felt an . . .": Zachary Macaulay, Diary, 6–7 April 1796, in Margaret J. Holland, *Life and Letters of Zachary Macaulay* (London, 1900).

well known in Futa . . . : *almaami* Saadu mentioned him to Watt and Winterbottom. "Journal," 6 March 1794. As Canot is witness (131–2), the Fulbe knew the individual traders on the coast and even the state of relations between them well.

"Riopongas . . .": Matthews, 13ff.

given Portuguese traders . . . : tradition says the Susu chief Manga Coumba Balla (Bangou) gave them the right to establish posts on the river. Jules H. Saint-Père, "Petit historique des Sossoé du Rio Pongo," *B.CEHS,* 13 (1930), 26–47.

page 21

portoobe: Pular for Portuguese and, in the early years, for Europeans in general. *Wojja noppi'en* ("red ears") was also used. Diallo provides a short but significant Pular-French word list.

trade: McLachlan, *Travels into the Baga and Soosoo Countries,* 30, gives the principal articles of trade: Watt, "Journal," 6 March 1794, mentions the flag.

ships were pillaged . . . : *WAR,* 4 (May, 1828), 79. Ibrahima may have meant to say that the factories where the ships called were attacked, instead of the ships themselves. At any rate, such things rarely happened on the coast except in times of great instability. These were those times, however, as will be seen below.

a turban of authority . . . : Saint-Père, 40ff., traces Sori's military, then diplomatic, maneuvers with Tia. Sori is well placed in this time by tradition's reference to his agent in the affair, Tierno Amadu Mawdo, the Alfa of Timbi, who was indeed his contemporary. See O. Durand, "Moeurs et Institutions d'une Famille Peule du Cercle de Pita," *B.CEHS,* 12 (1929), for the Alfa's genealogy. Matthews, 74, indicates that the Fulbe-sponsored *almaami*ship of Tia was well established by 1786.

a widespread war . . . : Matthews, 89, wrote, "When I first arrived at the Isles de Loss [in 1785], I found an almost general war raged throughout the extent to which we traded. The Suzees [Susu], aided

by the Mandingo slaves who had revolted from their masters, were
at war with the Bagoes and Mandingoes." Other passages by the
same writer make clear that peace had not been established by
1787. Also relevant is "Extracts from the Evidence of Jno. Matthews . . . 4 March 1788," add. mss. #18272, British Museum,
photostat copy at DLC.

Sori determined . . . : the disruption of trade "had annoyed his father."
NYJC, 16 Oct. 1828. The motive for the raid was retaliation. Statement, 2.

two thousand: Griffin to Gurley, Natchez, 13 Dec. 1827, ACS-DLC,
mentioning a figure of "about two thousand." The number varies.
Statement, 2, gives 1,700; NYJC, 16 Oct. 1828, 2,600.

"I was made . . .": WAR, 4 (May, 1828), 79.

location of Heboh country: Griffin said that the "Hebohs" lived north
of Futa. At the same time, however, they were near enough to
the coast to interrupt the trade of the Fulbe. That combination of
characteristics demands a great deal of geography.

Still, traveling north*west* from Futa, one came to the Mandinka
state of N'Gaaba (Gabu, Goobo, Khabu), historically an enemy
to the Muslim Fulbe. A trade road passed from Labé in northern
Futa through N'Gaaba to the Gambia. It seems unlikely to me,
however, that the blockage of trade occurred there. Sori attacked
toward N'Gaaba as early as 1751, again over the years, and even,
according to Guébhard, was mounting an expedition against it
at the time of his death. His sons continued this emnity. Mollien
discovered in 1818 that his Pullo guide would not enter that country because of the bad relations between the states. War between
Futa and N'Gaaba was too chronic for trade to pass regularly that
way.

It is important to remember that Griffin alone gives a direction
the Heboh country lay from Timbo. Neither Gallaudet nor Gurley,
perhaps significantly, does so, nor does Ibrahima in his WAR account of May, 1828. All the commentators do agree on is that the
Hebohs lived between Futa and the coast.

Ibrahima's expedition may well be connected with another
problem his father faced at this time, and from another direction.
I refer to the interruption of trade growing out of the war of the
Pongas' mixed-blood traders and their Baga allies against the Susu,
who, it has already been said, were allied with the Fulbe. This
struggle, part of the larger war that Matthews described above,
ultimately led to the refusal to pay the annual *sagalé* (payment in
tribute) to Timbo. That, certainly, was an action likely to get the
almaami's attention. Bruce L. Mouser, "Trade and Politics in

the Nunez and Pongo Rivers, 1790–1865" (Ph.D. dissertation, Indiana University, 1971), 22–3, sets the stage for those events in an admirable way.

"Hebohs": I have been unable to identify "Heboh" as an ethnonym or place name in Guinée of Guinée-Bissau. As stated in the previous note, they may be connected with the Rio Pongas difficulties reported by Matthews and found among the allies of the Baga in their war with the Susu. Matthews, 74, pointed out that "the Suzees . . . acknowledge subjection to the king of the Foolahs, whom they represent as a powerful prince . . . but the Bagoes . . . acknowledge no power superior to their own." Peter McLachlan, cited earlier, reported in 1821 that the Baga of the river were "brave and warlike people," full of deceit and danger (pp. 11, 19). About 1789 or 1790 they destroyed John Ormond's factory, according to Carl Wadstrom.

It is interesting to note that Joseph Hawkins, who visited the Pongas in 1795, located a people he called "Ebo" on the river in his *A History of a Voyage to the Coast of Africa* (Troy, New York, 1796). There are important flaws in this book, but, certainly, the similarity of his "Ebo," who were successful warriors, and Ibrahima's "Heboh" may be meaningful.

habe: C. W. Orr, "The Hausa Race," *Journal of the African Society,* 8 (April, 1909), 274–5. Orr stated that among the Fulbe in Yola Province, Nigeria, the word signified "the enemy." For its use in Futa, see Charles Reichardt, *Primer of the Fulah Language* (Berlin, 1859), 4, and Reichardt, *Vocabulary of the Fulde Language* (London, 1878), 43, 47. "Habe" would have to have been extensively corrupted to appear as "Heboh."

Ibrahima attacked . . . : Griffin to Gurley, Natchez, 13 Dec. 1827, ACS-DLC.

page 22

three hundred horse soldiers: NYJC, 16 Oct. 1828. Together with the source cited just below, this is the principal account of the events described. The one below contains direct, first-person statements by Ibrahima.

"We could not . . .": WAR, 4 (May,1828), 79.

"We saw the . . .": *ibid.*

"Men dropping . . .": NYJC, 16 Oct. 1828.

"I told everyone . . .": WAR, 4 (May, 1828), 79.

"They followed . . .": *ibid.*

"I will not . . .": *ibid.*

he . . . sat down . . . : New Haven, *Connecticut Journal,* 14 Oct. 1828, which also mentions the arrow wound.

reversed his weapon . . . : W*AR,* 4 (May, 1828), 79.

"I had a sword . . .": *ibid.*

gun barrel: *ibid.*

page 23

dragged from a pond . . . : *ibid.*

almost his entire . . . : Griffin to Gurley, Natchez, 13 Dec. 1827, ACS-DLC.

clothes stripped, etc.: NY*JC,* 16 Oct. 1828; W*AR,* 4 (May, 1828), 79.

bamboo hoops . . . : Canot, 146, mentions these.

"They made me . . .": W*AR,* 4 (May, 1828), 79. The distances, numbers, and sizes that Ibrahima gave were often exaggerated. So it happened that by 1828 the number of people on the *Africa* had nearly quintupled, Timbo had grown as large as Baltimore, and Timbuktu as large as New York. This "one hundred miles" is subject to use with caution.

no campaigns personally . . . : Guébhard, 55.

he raised an army . . . : W*AR,* 4 (May, 1828), 79.

slatees: Ibrahima was "stripped and sold to the Mandingoes; his captors, from revengeful feelings, refusing to except [*sic*] an exorbitant ransom which he offered." New York, *Spectator,* 21 Oct. 1828. Matthews, 13ff., observed of the Rio Pongas, "it is worthy of remark, that the same black merchants who visit Gambia come likewise to this place." Park, *Travels in the Interior Districts of Africa,* 8, remarks on these familiar African figures.

ransom: NY*JC,* 16 Oct. 1828, and the *Spectator* article, just above. NO*LA,* 25 Oct. 1828, maintained that when the ransom effort failed, Ibrahima attempted unsuccessfully to escape, murdering one of his captors in the process. Ibrahima would hardly have survived that, however. Perhaps whoever contributed this story was confused about the man he killed during the ambush at the pass.

"If they are . . .": "Examination of Robert Heatley," 19 April 1788, in Board of Trade Papers [BT] 6:10, PRO. Most often they were executed.

"refused to exchange": NO*LA,* 25 Oct. 1828.

two flasks of powder . . . : NY*JC,* 16 Oct. 1828, gives the list.

"My father came . . .": W*AR,* 4 (May, 1828), 80.

N'Gaaba and Casamance: Mollien, 315; Charlotte A. Quinn, "A Nineteenth Century Fulbe State," *Journal of African History,* 12 (1971), 427–40. *Daarul-harb* quoted in Diallo, 51.

page 24

The Gambia: details in this paragraph from Gray, *History of the Gambia*, 3, 273–6, 290–3, unless otherwise noted.

twelve hundred Africans . . . : "Examination of Heatley," 12 April 1788, BT 6:10, PRO, which also provides information on the navigation of the river.

French indulged . . . : "Minutes of the Committee of the Company of Merchants trading to Africa," entry of 9 Jan. 1787, Treasury Papers [T] 70:145; "Précis of African Papers," 14 Nov. 1785, BT 6:7, both PRO.

Robert Heatley: biographical details from "Examination of Heatley," 12, 19 April 1788, BT 6:10, PRO. Also of interest, "Examination of Thomas Nesbit," 3 May 1785, Home Office Papers [HO] 7:1; "Memorial of William Lyttleton," *et al.*, 21 Jan. 1791, BT 6:8; Daniel F. Houghton to Thomas Townshend, London, 24 Feb. 1783, 267:20, and "Minutes," 20 Aug. 1781, T 70:145, all PRO. For Lower Niani, see below.

page 25

"I have seen . . .": *ibid.*

Africa: details from the *Lloyd's Register* volumes for 1786, 1787 and 1789, National Maritime Museum, Greenwich.

"well-constructed": "Examination of Heatley," 19 April 1788.

1785 and 1786 voyages: Roseau port records for 1785 (*Africa* entered 25 Feb. 1785, CO 71:14) and 1786 (entered 24 April 1786, BT 6:41), PRO. The *Africa* landed only eighty Africans at Roseau in 1785. The prior arrivals in 1786 were the ships *Benson, Brothers,* and *Gascoigne.* The registry for foreign trade for London, 1786, (in which the *Africa* was listed) and the 1788 port rolls and muster rolls for London (which contained other valuable information on the vessel) no longer exist.

Africa: details from the *Lloyd's Register* volumes for 1786, 1787, lists "R. Heitly" as owner, but that for 1789 (1788–9) lists "Barnes & Co."

John Barnes: unless otherwise noted, all details are from his testimony of 26, 27, and 29 May 1789, in *Minutes of the Evidence [on the Slave-Trade] Taken before a Committee of the House of Commons . . .* (London, 1789), copy in the House of Lords Record Office, Palace of Westminster; and from "Testimony of John Barnes," 27 April 1785, "Minutes of Commons Respecting a Plan for Transportation of Felons to the Island of Leemaine in the River Gambia," HO 7:1, PRO.

governor of Senegal . . . : "Examination of Barnes," 18 March 1788, BT 6:9, PRO.

"a set of the . . .": Barnes to the Committee of the Company of Merchants trading to Africa, 21 Feb. 1764, T 70:37, PRO. 17 March 1765, contains "Every trader . . ." same to same.

page 26

Begging a passage . . . .: 19 April 1766, *ibid.*

wine merchant . . . : *Wakefield's Merchant and Tradesman's General Directory* (London, 1790). His association with the Company and with Whitehall, in "Minutes," 3 July 1781; 17 June 1783; 22 Sept., 6 Oct. 1786; 9 Jan. 1787; T 70:145, PRO; and BT 6:8 and 18, *passim.* For Barnes himself, see James Poirier to John Pownall, London, 1 Aug. 1769, T 70:69, PRO; and "Petition of Messrs. John Barnes and Richard Miles . . ," 20 March 1793, Lords Sessional Papers, Lords Record Office, Palace of Westminister.

"the best disposed . . .": "Testimony of Barnes," 27 April 1785, HO 7:1, PRO.

trading ventures: *Minutes,* 26–7 May 1789. He was also involved in the gum trade from the Senegal River.

opinions on slave trade: *ibid.* According to Barnes, the African lacked the "strong domestic attachments" characteristic of the European personality. In "Examination of Barnes," 18 March 1788, BT 6:9, PRO, he stated, "I believe that the principal source of slavery is Crimes.

"Q. Are not wars made for the purpose of procuring slaves?"

"A. I never heard so."

voyage in 1787: Carl Wadstrom, *Observations on the Slave Trade . . .* (London, 1789), 2–5, 19, mentioning both the war and the seizure of the English vessels; Roseau port records, 5 June 1787, BT 6:41, PRO; return date, Admiralty Papers [ADM] 68:205, PRO, under 4 July 1788.

page 27

John Nevin: The sole source of consequence is "Examination of John Nevan," 3 May 1785, HO 7:1, PRO. His last name is spelled various ways in the records.

Clarkson quotation: Thomas Clarkson, *The History of the Rise, Progress, and Accomplishment of the Abolition of the African Slave Trade by the British Parliament* (2 vols., London, 1808), vol. 1, 350.

"I have never ventured . . .": *ibid.*

"I was ill . . .": *ibid.*

set sail on the *Africa* ... : London *Public Advertiser,* 29 Jan. 1788; London *Daily Advertiser,* 31 Jan. 1788.

customary toll ... : "Examination of Heatley," 19 April 1788, BT 6:10, PRO. Heatley also remarked that from Juffure to Niani-Maru was a passage of six to eight days. An anchorage fee was customary at Niani-Maru.

about the first week ... : reconstruction, based on the dates of departure from Deal and arrival at Roseau.

Niani-Maru: short descriptions in "Some Account of Mohammedu-Sisei, a Mandingo of Nyani-Maru on the Gambia," *The Journal of the Royal Geographical Society of London,* 8 (1838), 448–54; William Gray and Staff Surgeon Dochard, *Travels in Western Africa, in the Years 1818, 19, 20, and 21* (London, 1825), 50. Gray observed that most of the residents were not Muslim. Also of value is "Testimony of Mr. Nepean," 27 April 1785, HO 7:1, and CO 267:21, *passim,* both PRO.

"Yanimaroo ...": "Nautical Map Intended for the Use of Colonial Undertakings ..." accompanying Wadstrom's *Essay on Colonization.*

place had become ... : Quinn, *Mandingo Kingdoms of the Senegambia,* 31–2.

pages 27–28

Ibrahima at Niani-Maru: W*AR,* 4 (May, 1828), 80. Ibrahima, without specifying a town, mentions being taken "to the Mandingo Country, on the Gambia." Niani-Maru is the trading station associated with Barnes, Heatley, and Nevin.

"They come in ...": "Examination of Heatley," 12 April 1788, BT 6:10, PRO.

With fifty of his ... : W*AR,* 4 (May, 1828), 80.

"The nature of ...": Barnes to the Lords of the Committee of Privy Council for Trade, London, 28 May 1788, BT 6:11, PRO.

for every four men ... : NY*JC,* 16 Oct. 1828, giving the proportions of sexes and ages. Ibrahima's figure of seven hundred aboard ship must be discounted, however.

"We should think ...": "Examination of Heatley," 19 April 1788, BT 6:10, PRO Heatley also described the standard process of boarding, feeding and transporting Africans.

"hospital": see sketch of "a Guineaman," thought to be the *Africa,* in *ibid.*

165 or 170 ... : 164 arrived at Roseau, according to port records. CO 76:5, PRO. The same records mention the beeswax and ivory.

captives not to understand . . . : "Examination of Heatley," 19 April 1788, BT 6:10, PRO.

fluent in Mandinka: N*SG,* 19 June 1828, stating he spoke "the Bambaria, Mandingo, Jallonkah, and Fouah languages, in addition to the Arabic." Schroeder, however, disputes the latter, apparently correctly. See Schroeder letter drafts, cited in Chapter 1.

Muslims and Fulbe in Lower Niani: Quinn, 18–21.

rapid loading . . . : to leave Great Britain around February 1 and arrive in Dominica April 21, the ship moved expeditiously. W*AR,* 4 (May, 1828), 80, gives the impression Ibrahima was sold as soon as he arrived.

page 29

descent downriver: river travel and scenery drawn from R. Maxwell MacBrair, *Sketches of a Missionary's Travels* (London, 1839), 202ff; Park, *Travels in the Interior Districts of Africa,* 4–7.

"It would be . . .": NY*JC,* 16 Oct. 1828.

75,000 other Africans . . . : the slave-trade investigations, cited in the introduction to the notes for this chapter, contain several estimates of the volume by year and by European nation.

his biographer did not . . . : this seems evident in Gallaudet's entire treatment of Ibrahima's story. He was no abolitionist, and he thought Foster in 1827–28 "made many sacrifices, and conducted himself very handsomely." NY*JC,* 16 Oct. 1828.

If the average height . . . : David MacPherson, *Annals of Commerce* . . . (4 vols., London, 1805), vol. 4, 145n.

six feet tall . . . : Griffin to Gurley, Natchez, 13 Dec. 1827, ACS-DLC. The irons were customary, Heatley thinking this "the only suffering the men are exposed to. . . . It is our interest to make them as light as it is possible for the safety of the ship's crew to admit." "Examination of Heatley," 19 April 1788, BT 6:10, PRO.

customarily . . . :the Heatley "Examination" gives the standard practices.

did not dance . . . :N*SG,* 19 June 1828; Watt, "Journal," 14 March 1794.

Nevin's quirt . . . : MacPherson's, *Annals of Commerce,* vol. 4, 145n, gives examples on other ships.

having tea . . . : Geisenberger conversation, 21 Aug. 1973, cited in Chapter 1.

page 30

at least five per cent: "Examination of Heatley," 19 April 1788. "The passage from the River Gambia is short, and we think an allowance of five p-cent for mortality a very large one."

"Tedious . . .": NYJC, 16 Oct. 1828.

"The horrors he . . .": Statement, 6.

"[The] Prince's . . .": NYJC, 16 Oct. 1828.

L'Aimable Louise, etc.: L'Aimable Louise from London Chronicle, 26–28 June 1788; Minerva from London Public Advertiser, 26 June 1788; Tartar from London Chronicle, 24–26 July 1788.

no deaths . . . : fifteen men and boys were usually employed on the Africa (BT 6:191, p. 11); sixteen made this trip (ADM 68:205, entered 4 July 1788). Both sources PRO.

164 alive . . . : the ship's cargo was inventoried by the Collector of Customs when it entered the port of Roseau. CO 76:5, PRO. Sale record is given below.

Dominica described: Joseph J. Gurney, Familiar Letters to Henry Clay of Kentucky . . . (New York, 1840), 55ff.; Atwood, iii, 72, 168–72, 276ff.

page 31

Twelve hundred whites . . . : MacPherson, Annals of Commerce, vol. 4, 156.

John Orde: Alan Valentine, The British Establishment, 1760–1784 (2 vols., Norman, 1970), vol. 2, 665.

"We are all . . .": Christopher Robert to Daniel Robert, Dominica, 3 Nov. 1787, Smith-Robert Family Papers, New-York Historical Society, New York, New York.

"free-port" designation . . . : Armytage, 56, 72. The decree establishing the free port at the island had been eagerly awaited by American merchants. Philadelphia Independent Gazetteer, 23 July, 6 Aug. 1787.

"Do not give . . .": Orde commission, CO 319:3, PRO.

6,254 Africans . . . : John Robinson, "Answers to Queries respecting . . . Slavery," enclosed in Orde's letter of 4 Oct. 1788, CO 71:14, PRO.

pages 32–33

The Spanish had . . . : ibid. Robinson observed that the traders were "obliged to take the proportion of Males & Females that the Cargoe consists of, except the Spaniards, who sometimes give a great advance price to have nearly all Males." For more on the Spanish, as well as a good summary of the island's trade, see the Orde memorandum, 1 Sept. 1787, BT 6:41, PRO.

Governor Miró: entered 16 Jan. 1788, "Foreign Ships entered Inwards, Port of Roseau," [11 Jan.–11 April 1788], CO 76:4, PRO. Clark's cargo was listed as "four thousand dollars," a favorite import at Roseau. The ship measured fifty tons and had a crew of seven.

Clark: a former army captain, he was fifty-seven in 1788. Clinton N. Howard, *The British Development of West Florida, 1763–1769* (Berkeley, 1947), 81, 89. He is occasionally confused with his nephew of the same name, author of *Proofs of the Corruption of Gen. James Wilkinson and of His Connexion with Aaron Burr . . .* (Freeport, New York, 1970; orig. ed. 1809), who described him (p. 105) as a man "of considerable wealth and influence."

Jupiter Dawda: "Dowda" in Deed-Book B, 9, NAdCo. He was Clark's first slave and probably a Muslim. "We never knew that Jupiter did a base thing, told a falsehood, got intoxicated, or swore an oath," the deed reads.

Madam Pokata: it arrived on February 6, the first African slaver of the year, and it carried 190 people. "Account of Negroes Imported from Africa" [1784–1788], CO 71:14, PRO.

It might be expected . . . : Armytage, 56ff., 65–6.

News of Clark's coup . . . : "Account of Negroes Exported . . ." [1784–88], CO 71:14, PRO, reveals that the *Governor Miró* was the first vessel to leave Roseau for New Orleans with Africans in at least four years. However, by the first half of 1789 alone, five slave ships left the island for the city. CO 76:4, PRO.

Africa entered . . . : "Ships & Vessels Entered Inwards (Port of Roseau" [10 April–10 July 1788], CO 76:5, PRO. Harbor activity from the same. The Orde memorandum of 1 Sept. 1787, cited above, mentions the relationship of the road to the city.

Samuel Chollet and Company: identified in Thomas Irwin to Gerónimo Lachapella, power-of-attorney, 2 Dec. 1788, Acts of Pedro Pedesclaux, folio #1250, vol. 4 (1788), Notarial Archives, City of New Orleans.

sugar and cotton . . . : London *Daily Advertiser,* 28 May 1788.

It was customary . . . : "Examination of Heatley," cited above; MacPherson, *Annals of Commerce,* vol. 4, 146–7.

Navarro: arrived April 22. CO 76:5, PRO, mentioning also crew size and tonnage. The Farrar petition cited below describes the *Navarro* as a *goleta,* which could be either a barquentine or a schooner. Roseau port records identify it as a schooner.

Irwin: see below.

"the unforseen . . .": Irwin to Gen. William Irvine, New Orleans, 20 May 1789, Irvine Papers, PHi. The defaulter at Havanna was Joseph Francisco Vento.

leased the *Navarro* . . . : Joseph Connand of New Orleans owned the
vessel. Benjamin Farrar, petition, 20 May 1789, Document 2151,
Box 54, Louisiana State Museum, New Orleans. This document
was translated for me by Jack D. L. Holmes.
Irwin in Philadelphia: Tax-Assessor's Ledger, 1782, Dock Ward
South, p. 61, and Irvine (Irwin) to Peter Reeve (28 Aug. 1781,
Deed-Book D-4, 323–3) and to Mark Wilcox (18 March 1783,
Deed-Book D-5, 492–4), all Archives Division, City Hall, Phila-
delphia; Irwin, *et al.*, petition to the Pennsylvania House of Rep-
resentatives, 15 Feb. 1781, PHi; *The Philadelphia Directory* and
MacPherson's Directory for the City and Suburbs of Philadelphia,
issues of 1785. Lucinda Boyd, *The Irvines and Their Kin* . . . (Chi-
cago, 1908), 216–7, contains a short account of his brother
Matthew, who was Port Warden of Philadelphia.
"No person's . . .": Irwin to Washington, Philadelphia, 15 July 1791,
Washington Papers, DLC. For his revolutionary service and financial history, see his letter to Washington, Blair McClenahan to
Washington, Philadelphia, 15 July 1791, and William Patterson
to Washington, Brunswick, N.J., 11 Oct. 1791, all Washington
Papers; "Letters of Marque," 611–59, *Pennsylvania Archives,* 5th
Series, vol. 1 (Harrisburg, 1906). Among other ships he owned
was the twenty-six gun *Revolution* (1781).
Moroccans: Irwin to Washington, cited above, and Philadelphia *In-
dependent Gazetteer,* 28 May 1787.
"rather unfortunate": McClenahan to Washington, cited above.
New Orleans trade: Oliver Pollock to Gov. Thomas Nelson, New
Orleans, 4 May 1782, and Irwin to Gov. Benjamin Harrison,
Philadelphia, 18 June 1782, both Executive Department Letters-
Received, Virginia State Library, Richmond.
Irwin . . . immigrated . . . : the date is uncertain. In the deeds of June,
1788, cited below, he describes himself as a resident of New
Orleans. He was in Philadelphia in 1791, but back in New Orleans
in 1794. Alexander Fullerton to Baron de Rosenthal, Philadelphia,
4 Sept. 1794, *Pennsylvania Magazine of History and Biography,*
22 (#2, 1898), 257.
"honest . . .": Patterson to Washington, cited above.

page 34

to sell a sick . . . : liber E, 243ff., Translated Spanish Records, NAdCo.
(All subsequent "liber" citations refer to this set.)
to negotiate a bond: Liber G, 267.
cédula of 1782: Charles Gayarre, *History of Louisiana: The Spanish
Domination* (New York, 1854), 171; Carmelo Richard Arena,

"Philadelphia-Spanish New Orleans Trade: 1789–1803," (Ph.D. dissertation, University of Pennsylvania, 1959), 41ff., 65. The *cédula* is reproduced in Arthur P. Whitaker, ed., *Documents Relating to the Commercial Policy of Spain in the Floridas* . . . (Deland, Fla., 1931), 30ff.

winked at the business: they could hardly have been ignorant of this developing "free-port" trade. Yet–see the statement of Martin Navarro subsequently in the text.

Irwin purchased . . . : Irwin's 2 Dec. 1788 power-of-attorney to Gerónimo Lachapella, cited above, gives the date, figures and quotation used here. No copy of the bill of sale appears to have been preserved in the Archives of Dominica. S. A. W. Boyd of Roseau kindly searched for this particular deed among the records of the period, but it was not present.

Records indicating . . . : partial records, compiled from the New Orleans and Natchez bills of sale cited subsequently.

Jerome Fuiget: the *Catalán* entered April 28 with a cargo of eighteen thousand dollars bullion. CO 76:5, PRO. The same source indicates that the *Africa* landed 164 Africans; between themselves the *Navarro* and the *Catalán* carried away 157, nearly the entire cargo.

Nevin filled their . . . : his cargo is listed in the port records. The *Africa* left Roseau on May 13. CO 76:5, PRO.

Ibrahima left . . . : "Foreign Ships entered Outwards, Port of Roseau," 2 May 1788, CO 76:5, PRO.

Sir William Young: his *West-India Common-Place Book: Compiled from Parliamentary and Official Documents* . . . (London, 1807), a little-used gold mine of information. Here see 170.

"Foreigners only . . .": "Answers to Queries respecting . . . Slavery," enclosed in Orde's letter of 4 Oct. 1788, CO 71:14, PRO.

page 35

Judicial records . . . : document 1786, box 50, Louisiana State Museum. This was important to the traders because a slave, once sold, was returnable only for specified illnesses such as undeclared hernia (document 1751, box 50, Louisiana State Museum), epilepsy, "madness" (liber B, 186–7), or contagious diseases like leprosy (liber E, 223ff.). Venereal disease was not grounds (*ibid.*). By law all complaints on health had to be made within eight months of the sale to be considered (*ibid.*), although a shorter period could be specified (liber B, 186–7).

fourteen human beings: shipped fifty-seven (CO 76:5, PRO) and landed forty-three (Irwin to William Irvine, cited above). In the letter to Irvine, Irwin stated he had "made up a good part of the loss" at Havanna by the importation, but in the letter to George Washington, also cited above, he said the voyage had been financially "unfortunate."

fire: principal source for this paragraph is the London *Gentleman's Magazine*, 58 (Aug. 1788), 743. Also of use, the London *Chronicle*, 17–19 July 1788; the London *Daily Advertiser*, 1 July 1788; anon., letter headed New Orleans, 25 March 1788, in the Philadelphia *The Freemens' Journal*, 21 May 1788; Gayarre, *History of Louisiana: The Spanish Domination*, 203.

"The whole...": Clark to Thomas Fitzsimmons, New Orleans, 25 March 1788, Gratz Collection, PHi.

"The darkness...": Miró to Don Joseph de Ezpeleta, letters of 1 and 13 April 1788, "Dispatches of the Spanish Governors of Louisiana," typescript, Louisiana State University Library, Baton Rouge.

page 36

two hurricanes, etc.: *ibid.*

Epidemic fevers... : letter headed New Orleans, 25 Oct. 1788, in "The Letters of Padre Antonio de Sedella, Cura of the San Luis Cathedral, New Orleans," typescript, LSU Library.

Alexander Baldwin: captain of the frigate *Felix*. Document 1912, box 52, Louisiana State Museum. On December 2, 1788, Thomas Irwin bought from Oliver Pollock fifty slaves brought to New Orleans by Baldwin on this vessel. He paid Pollock in part with the bond that Thomas Foster gave him in August for Ibrahima. Liber B, 186–7.

Joseph Connand: he sold the vessel to Benjamin Farrar and William McFadden on August 1, 1788, for one thousand dollars in specie. Document 2151, Box 54, Louisiana State Museum.

Navarro voyaged to... : Irwin left Roseau on May 2 and was in the city by June 10.

three-mile apron... : Samuel S. Forman, *Narrative of a Journey Down the Ohio and Mississippi, in 1789–90* (Cincinnati, 1888), 62.

description: *ibid.;* Robertson, vol. 1, *passim*, quoting Paul Alliot, Victor Collot, and Berquin-Duvallon; *Account of Louisiana* (Washington, 1803).

"a total rising"... : letter headed New Orleans, [18 Oct. 1788?], "Letters of Sedella," LSU Library.

Ibrahima arrived... : date is approximate as indicated in the text, but Irwin (see below) was selling Africans from the *Navarro* by June 10.

5,300: Gayarre, 215–6.

The fire had spared . . . : *ibid.*, 203. A map appears in Robertson, vol. 1, between 58 and 59, showing the area of the fire.

page 37

"this colony . . .": Navarro, quoted in Gayarre, 187–8.

Ibrahima spent . . . : he was in the city at least through June 26, which is the date of folio 823–4 cited below.

a series of sales . . . : Irwin's slave trading is found in vol. 3 (fols. 756–8, 790–1, 815–7, 823–4), Acts of Pedesclaux, Notarial Archives. These were translated for me by Jack D. L. Holmes.

Samba: "a man who came with me from Africa." *WAR*, 4 (May, 1828), 81. He was to be purchased by Thomas Foster. See Chapter 3. For the name as an African word, see Henri Gaden, *Le Poular: Dialect Peul du Fouta Senegalais* (Paris, 1914), 165.

would be offensive . . . : "Sambo" and "Juba" both were opprobious to the Liberian colonist Edward W. Blyden as early as 1857. See Blyden, *Liberia's Offering* (New York, 1862), 52.

In the legends . . . : Sow, *Chroniques et Récits*, 91n.

captives now down . . . : seventeen of the forty-three landed were sold at New Orleans. The sale of about twenty can be accounted for easily at Natchez. Liber B, 150ff.

seagoing vessels . . . : NSG, 30 April 1829; Christian Schultz, *Travels on an Inland Voyage . . . Performed in the Years 1807 and 1808* (2 vols., New York, 1810), vol. 2, 137–8.

barge: time of travel from Anthony Haswell, *Memoirs and Adventures of Captain Matthew Phelps . . . Particularly in two Voyages from Connecticut to the River Mississippi, From December, 1773, to October, 1780* (Bennington, Vt., 1807), 200; anon., letter of 1807, #1658, LSU Library.

a group of Africans . . . : the brig *Jeune Felicité*, Captain Felipe Millot, which left Roseau on May 24, 1788, carried "four untrained negresses" sold by the New Orleans merchant Francis Mayronne in Baton Rouge on July 28. "Spanish West Florida Archives," vol. 1 (1782–9), typescript, LSU Library. No sales by Irwin in Baton Rouge are recorded.

page 38

Chamba, etc.: *ibid.*

The land was flat . . . : various travelers provide sketchy descriptions. See Haswell and Forman, cited above; also, John Pope, *A Tour Through the Southern and Western Territories of the United States of North-America . . .* (Richmond, Va., 1792), 34–6.

earth-and-wood fort . . . : Pope, 30ff.; Jack D. L. Holmes, *Gayoso: The*

Life of a Spanish Governor in the Mississippi Valley, 1789–1799
(Baton Rouge, 1965), 19–20, 164. Its ruins would later be a local
landmark. Edouard de Montule, *Travels in America, 1816–1817*
(trans. and ed. by Edward D. Seeber), (Bloomington, 1951), 94–7.
A road ran . . . : geography of site from Henry Tooley, *History of the
Yellow Fever* . . . (Natchez, 1823).
Natchez: period descriptions by Forman and Pope, cited above; Samuel S. Forman, "Reminiscences," New York Public Library, New
York; George Willey, "Natchez in Olden Times," in John F. H.
Claiborne, *Mississippi as a Province, Territory and State* (Jackson,
1880), 527–33. See also William B. Hamilton, "American Beginnings in the Old Southwest: The Mississippi Phase" (Ph.D. dissertation, Duke University, 1937), 142. Natchez at an earlier period is
described in "Autobiography of John Hutchens," Breckinridge Family Papers, Southern Historical Collection, University of North
Carolina Library.
eye of guards . . . : liber F, 176; Holmes, 110.
five boats, arriving . . . : incident in Forman, cited above.
long, unkept hair . . . : Griffin to Gurley, Natchez, 13 Dec. 1827, ACS-
DLC.
skin . . . copper-colored . . . : New York *Freedom's Journal,* 19 Sept.
1828.
"The prince . . .": Boston *Daily Commercial Advertiser,* 19 Aug. 1828.
young white man . . . : Thomas Foster. See notes to Chapter 3.

3. "A Common Slave"

Events in Natchez and the surrounding territory mentioned in Chapters 3, 4, and 5 can be followed in detail in Hamilton, "American
Beginnings in the Old Southwest"; D. C. James, *Antebellum Natchez*
(Baton Rouge, 1968); and Claiborne, *Mississippi as a Province, Territory and State.* For this chapter I also recommend Holmes, *Gayoso.*
Charles S. Sydnor, *Slavery in Mississippi* (Baton Rouge, 1933), although excellent in certain regards, is inadequate for the pre-1830
period.

pages 39–40

Foster origin and immigration: even Thomas Foster's grandchildren
were uncertain where he was born. Virginia and North Carolina
were mentioned, but the consensus was South Carolina. The only
eighteenth-century document commenting on the family's origin

gives the latter. It is James Foster's passport to travel in the Indian country in 1797. One reads there, "James Foster [brother of Thomas] is a native of South Carolina, and he has resided in the Natches since he was a boy." (See Mary G. Bryan, ed. *Passports Issued by the Governors of Georgia, 1785 to 1809,* Washington, 1959.) The second half of the sentence suggests that the Fosters migrated to the District prior to the Revolution, since James, born in 1752, was thirty-one in 1783, hardly a boy. *Biographical and Historical Memoirs of Mississippi,* vol. 1, 758, states the move occurred *during* the Revolution. The earliest reference to the Fosters in the Spanish records at Natchez is 1783.

Of chronological use are the tombstone inscriptions in the cemeteries at Foster Mound and "Greenwood Plantation," near Washington, Mississippi.

1784 petition: Mary Foster, Petition, 10 April 1784 (folio #57), vol. 6, Untranslated Spanish Records, NAdCo. See also John's petition, ? April 1784 (folio #81), *ibid.*

early Foster settlement: Matilda [Caroline Matilou] Bacon and Maude T. Burson (Thomas Foster descendants), "Family History (As I Remember It)," typescript, circa 1915, courtesy of Lillian Quinn, Setauket, New York; William D. Lum, [Martha Lum], and Nan Foster Schuchs, *Reunion of Descendants of James Foster at Foster's Mound . . . , 1965* (pamphlet, Jackson, 1965); conversation with T. J. Foster (a James Foster descendant), 22 Aug. 1972; Spanish censuses for 1784, 1787, and 1788, provided me by G. Douglas Inglis.

Sarah Smith: W. N. Foster, "The Family of Thomas Foster, of Natchez, Mississippi," typescript, n.d., generously furnished me by Martha Madeley, Conroe, Texas; hand-painted Smith Family Tree, circa 1819, made for Sinai Amelia Foster and now in possession of her descendant William D. Lum, Port Gibson, Mississippi. Quotation from Foster typescript.

page 41

Foster lands: claim #99, vol. A, 288–91, "Written Evidences of Claims West of the Pearl River," Civil Archives Division, RG49, DNA; liber A, 161–2, 240–1, 355ff.; liber B, 67–8, 242; liber C, 518.

Jesse: liber A, 380–1.

Gilbert: William Gilbert was the husband of Thomas's sister Nancy. See liber C, 441.

Spanish officer's quotation: Francisco Boulingy to Esteban Miró, Natchez, 22 Aug. 1785, in Lawrence Kinnaird, ed., *Spain in the Mis-*

sissippi Valley, 1765–1794 (3 vols. [vols. 2–4, American Historical Association, *Annual Report, 1945*], Washington, 1946–49), 136–42.

page 42

opinions about Africans: based on an assessment of the deeds in the Translated Spanish Records, NAdCo; Claiborne, 106; and Bryan Edwards, *The History, Civil and Commercial, of the British Colonies in the West Indies* (3 vols., London, 1793–4, 1801), vol. 2, 6off. William Dunbar wrote in 1807 that the Ibo nation "lies under a prejudice" at Natchez. See Dunbar to Tunno and Prince, [Natchez], 1 Feb. 1807, in Eron Rowland, *Life, Letters, and Papers of William Dunbar* (Jackson, 1930).

Higdon, McKnight, *et al.*: deeds of their purchases are found in vol. 15, Untranslated Spanish Records, NAdCo. The same records provide biographical details.

purchase of Ibrahima: Irwin to Foster, deed, 18 Aug. 1788 (folio #350), Untranslated Spanish Records, vol. 15, NAdCo.

rationale for service: Pedro Lartigue to William Dunbar, deed, 8 Aug. 1787, "Spanish West Florida Archives," vol. 1, typescript, Louisiana State University Library.

Samba: this man was a superannuated laborer on the plantation in 1830. See division of Thomas Foster's slave estate, Feb. 1830, Foster Probate Papers, NAdCo.

page 43

"Dunker's beard": Thomas Rodney to Caesar Rodney, Washington, Mississippi Territory [hereafter "MT"], 5 Dec. 1803, in Simon Gratz, ed., "Letters of Thomas Rodney," *Pennsylvania Magazine of History and Biography*, 43 (1919), 210.

"hut": Bacon and Burson, "Family History (As I Remember It)."

ransom attempt: N*YJC*, 16 Oct. 1828.

Mandinka neighbor: liber A, 271.

suspicion of pretentions to royalty: Aberdeen, Miss., *Monroe Democrat*, 25 April 1849. The "petty chief" personality was a troublesome one for authorities. See Vincente Manuel de Zespedes to Domingo de Badello, St. Augustine, Florida, 17 Oct. 1789, "Dispatches of the Spanish Governors of Louisiana," typescript, LSU Library.

page 44

name "Prince": Major Steve Power, *The Memento: Old and New Natchez, 1700 to 1897* (Natchez, 1897), 13–4; New Haven, Conn., *Religious Intelligencer*, 25 Oct. 1828. Of contextual interest is

Newbell Niles Puckett, "Names of American Negro Slaves," 471–94, in George P. Murdock, ed., *Studies in the Science of Society* (Freeport, New York, 1969).

haircut quotation: Griffin to Gurley, Natchez, 13 Dec. 1827, ACS-DLC. Also see Dr. Patenostre, "Le Coiffure chez Les Peuhls du Fouta-Djallon," *Outre-Mer*, 3 (Dec., 1931), 406–7; *Proceedings of the African Association*, I, 274ff. In regard to this chapter and the next I should mention James Register's *Jallon: Arabic Prince of old Natchez (1788–1828)*, (Shreveport, Louisiana, 1968), because it may contain Natchez traditions not available elsewhere. It gives a version of the haircut incident and resulting confinement.

pages 45–47

Fulbe opinion of agricultural labor: A. Levaré, "En Guinée Française Chez les Foulbé," Société de Géographie d'Alger et de l'Afrique du Nord, *Bulletin*, 1925, 126. Diallo, 83–100, writes, *"Le goût et les aptitudes physiques des Peuls ne les prédisposent en rien aux travaux agricoles. . . . Par fierté du nomade et par orgueil du pasteur, le Peul a toujours considéré le travail de la terre comme méprisable. Il ne consentait à courber le dos au soleil que s'il ne trouvait personne pour le faire à sa place."*

Watt quotation: "Journal," 14 March 1794.

resistance and flight: Power, *The Memento*, 13–4; conversation with T. J. Foster, 28 Aug. 1973. Power, reporting tradition, places this event about 1780 and locates it on Second Creek. He does not know the name of the plantation family involved. Here I have followed Edith W. Moore, a well-regarded Natchez historian, in identifying Power's "Prince" as Ibrahima. Mrs. Moore spoke on this subject in part at the first Foster family reunion, held May 3, 1964, near Washington, Mississippi. I could, unfortunately, locate no copy of her remarks. A second local historian, Amanda Geisenberger, informed me that Ibrahima fled the plantation very shortly after his arrival.

"bitter cup of poverty": New York *Freedom's Journal*, 29 Aug. 1828.

Tripoli: MacPherson, *Annals of Commerce*, III, 468.

Suicide . . . : Qur'an, sura 4:33; conversation with Thierno Diallo, Dakar, Senegal, 11 July 1974.

Ibrahima's return: quotations from Major Power.

spear thrust into the heart: Park, *Travels in the Interior Districts of Africa*, 343.

pages 48–49

"common slave": Gallaudet, in NY*JC*, 16 Oct. 1828.

"submitted to his fate without a murmur": Griffin to Gurley, Natchez, 14 Dec. 1827, ACS-DLC.

slavery in Futa: Noirot, *À Travers le Fouta-Djalon*, 211; Watt, "Journal," 14 March 1794; map inscription in Wadstrom, *An Essay on Colonization*. Negative opinions on Fulbe treatment of their slaves are found in O'Beirne, "Journal," 117, and Guébhard, "L'Etat social et politique du Fouta Dialon Autrefois et Aujourd'hui," Le Comité de l'Afrique Française et le Comité du Maroc, *Renseigments Coloniaux et Documents*, 1909, 179ff. Diallo, 106–110, thinks *"ni les esclaves de 'maison' ni les esclaves de 'champ' n'ont connu les durs travaux des esclaves . . . modernes transplantés par milliers aux Amériques."*

overview of the agricultural/technological interchanges: Oswald Durand, "Les Industries locales au Fouta," *B.CEHS*, 15 (1932), 42–71; M. Leprince, "Le Labé," *La Dépêche Coloniale Illustrée*, 31 Aug. 1907, 201–2; P. Fras, "Les Résultats Scientifiques de la Mission du Fouta-Djalon, 1887–1888," Société de Géographie Commerciale de Bordeaux, *Bulletin*, May, 1888, 385ff.; "Padron [Census] del Distrito de Natchez del Ano de 1792," Archivo General de Indias, Papeles Procendentes de la Isla de Cuba [AGI, PC], leg. 1441, photostat in possession of William Lum; Winthrop Sargent, Diary, *passim*, Massachusetts Historical Society; Andrew Ellicott to ?, 14 April 1797, to Sarah Ellicott, 27 June 1797, both Natchez, in Ellicott Papers, DLC; C. P. DeLasteyrie, *A Treatise on the Culture, Preparation, History and Analysis of Pastel, or Woad* (Boston, 1816), 111.

Ibrahima's opinions: "Miscellaneous Facts," John F. Watson, "Annals of Philadelphia," vol. I, 130, PHi; Boston *New England Palladium & Commercial Advertiser*, 12 Aug. 1828; NYJC (semiweekly edition), 21 Oct. 1828; NSG, 19 June 1828.

Wailes quotation: B. L. C. Wailes, Diary, 23 Feb. 1853, Perkins Library, Duke University.

"It killed . . .": Thomas Ashe, *Travels in America, Performed in 1806* (3 vols., London, 1808), vol. 3, 200.

pages 50–51

"The most ordinary mechanical arts . . .": NSG, 19 June 1828.

Watt: "Journal," 23 Feb., 5, 10 March 1794.

Wailes quotation: dairy, 23 Feb. 1853, Perkins Library.

tobacco culture: William Tatham, *An Historical and Practical Essay on the Culture and Commerce of Tobacco* (London, 1800), 6ff., based on the Virginia culture; liber B, 3.

Thomas Foster's 1789 harvest: addendum to Grand-Pré to Miró, 2 March 1790, AGI, PC, *leg.* 16, photostat at DLC.

politics of tobacco: both Burson and Clark give adequate accounts. Also, see Holmes, 90–9.

page 52

1790 petitions: document 1889, file 2632, 29 Oct. 1790, and document 2451, file 38, April 1790, both in Judicial Records, Louisiana State Museum.

Thomas Foster's 1791 harvest: "Padron . . . , 1792," cited above.

Dublan: Ross to Foster, deed, 8 Nov. 1791 (folio #300), Untranslated Spanish Records, vol. 24, NAdCo; Burson, *Miró,* 84–5.

page 53

Stark's 1790–91 trek: Washington, D.C. *United States Telegraph,* 22 June 1827.

Stark in the East: Mrs. Thomas Stark, Jr., to writer, Cedarow Farm, Amelia, Virginia, 28 May 1976, with genealogical data; "Westmoreland County, Virginia, Legislative Petitions," *The Virginia Genealogist,* 15 (Jan.–March 1971), 24; Rebecca Hogan to Robert Stark "the elder," Deed, 6 Feb. 1788, "Wills and Deeds, Edgefield County, South Carolina," typescript, 1942, copy at D.A.R. Library, Washington, D.C.

"a man of consideration . . .": Gayoso to Baron de Carondelet, Natchez, 6 Aug. 1793, AGI, PC, *leg.* 42, citation courtesy of G. Douglas Inglis.

Stark's land problems: claims #1273 (vol. 3, 769–70) and #1782 (vol. I, 346–8, and vol. 4, 1310–11), "Journal of the Board of Commissioners for Land-Claims West of Pearl River," RG49, DNA; *Stark's Heirs v. Mather* (1824), in R. J. Walker, *Reports of Cases Adjudged in the Supreme Court of Mississippi,* vol. I (Natchez, 1834), 181–94.

"disloyal expressions": both quotations in this paragraph are from *The King v. Robert Stark, et al.,* 16 Feb. 1794 and intermittent succeeding days, liber G, 181ff.

page 54

purchase of Isabella: Stark to Foster, deed, 23 April 1794 (folio #55), Untranslated Spanish Records, vol. 28, NAdCo. Stark to Flower follows this deed in the same volume.

Limerick: Griffin to Gurley, Natchez, 5 July 1828, ACS-DLC, men-

tions a stepson of Ibrahima's. Limerick was still living on the plantation in 1830. See division of Thomas Foster's estate, Real-Estate Record Book #1, NAdCo.
"an interesting . . . woman": Marschalk to ?, Natchez, 30 April 1828, in *PMFJ*, 21 Aug. 1828.

page 55

male-female proportions: comparison of census data.
marriage: New York *Spectator*, 21 Oct. 1828. The Marschalk letter cited above uses the word "wedlock." Cf., *Jallon*, 5. Also, Alcée Fortier, *A History of Louisiana* (4 vols., New York and Paris, 1904), vol. 2, 145.
Register states in *Jallon*, 5, that Isabella was "a Sabian, one of a group mentioned in the Qur'an as entitled to Muslim religious toleration." The source for this interesting statement appears to be the Spanish phrase "*a saver* [*saber*]," found before Isabella's name in the deed of sale from Stark to Foster. "*A saber*," however, far from translating "a Sabaist" or "a Mandean," means simply "that is to say" or "to wit."
Ibrahima's children: all those living in Adams County in Feb., 1830, are mentioned in Thomas Foster's estate account, Real-Estate Record Book #1, NAdCo. The age and paternity of Simon is established in "Emigration Register," series VI, vol. 17, ACS-DLC. Prince is mentioned in *NA*, 21 June 1828.

pages 56–57

Spanish interdiction of Muslims: Gonzalo Aguirre Beltrán, "The Slave Trade in Mexico," *Hispanic American Historical Review*, 24 (Aug., 1944), 412–31.
Ayuba Sulayman: Curtin, *Africa Remembered*, 41.
Wadstrom quotation: Wadstrom, *An Essay on Colonization*, 20.
"Big Jack . . .": "Inventory of George Proffitt," 18–19 Oct. 1790, "Archives of Spanish West Florida," vol. 1, typescript, LSU Library.
"fundamentalism": Paul Guébhard, *Au Fouta Dialon: Cent-Vingt Ans d'Histoire* (Paris, 1910), 71.
Thomas's tombstone: Greenwood Plantation cemetery, near Washington, Mississippi.
Mombéyâ: Mombéyâ (1755–1852) is featured in Sow, *Chroniques et Recits*, chapter 1.
"Mr. Foster . . . well knew . . .": NO*LA*, 25 Oct. 1828.
Thayer letter: Caroline M. Thayer to "a Methodist preacher," Wash-

ington, Miss., 28 Nov. 1827, in New Haven, Conn., *Religious Intelligencer*, 23 Feb. 1828.

Marschalk letter: Marschalk to "Miss Jane," Natchez, 7 April 1828, W*DNI*, 8 May 1828.

mutilation for theft: N*SG*, 5 June 1828. M. Leprince, 203, writing of the *jihaad* period, thinks, *"C'est l'époque ou l'exaltation religieuse se manifeste avec le plus de force."*

qadiriya brotherhood: P. Marty, "L'Islam en Guinée: Fouta-Diallon," *Revue du Monde Musulman*, 35/36 (1917–1918), 285.

Homer: Henri Gregoire, *An Enquiry Concerning the Intellectual and Moral Faculties and Literature of Negroes* . . . (Brooklyn, N.Y., 1810), 91.

absence of Islamic texts: when Marschalk showed Ibrahima some Arabic script in 1820 or 1821, the prince remarked "that it was the first of his country writing he had seen since he left home." *PMFJ*, 21 Aug. 1828. This incident is dealt with in Chapter Five.

tracing characters in the sand: Eliza F. Prentiss to George C. Shattuck, Boston, 29 Aug. 1828, Shattuck Papers, Mass. Historical Society.

pages 58–59

illiterates: Jesse Fin receipt, 5 Jan. 1788, John Bisland and Family Papers, LSU Library. Mary and Sarah Foster's marks are abundant in the NAdCo records.

Saugnier's quotation: *Voyages to the Coast of Africa, by Messrs. Saugnier and Brisson* (London, 1792), 40–1.

Thomas Foster's land acquisitions: liber C, 188, 363–5, 518–9; liber D, 150, 156; deed-book A, 31–4, 196–8, all NAdCo; claim #259, vol. A, 464–5, "Written Evidences of Claims West of the Pearl River," DNA.

Cotton at Natchez: Natchez *Green's Impartial Observer*, 14 June 1800; Daniel Clark to W. C. C. Claiborne, Clarksville, MT, 18 June 1800, in *Papers in Relation to the Official Conduct of Governor Sargent. Published by Particular Desire of His Friends* (Boston, 1801), 24; and James Hall, *A Brief History of the Mississippi Territory* (Salisbury, North Carolina, 1801), 29.

Cotton in Futa: see note earlier in this chapter, "Overview of the agricultural/technological interchanges."

Thomas Foster's livestock: "Padron . . . , 1792"; "Inventory of the Personal Estate of Thomas Foster Senior," circa 5 Nov. 1829, Foster Probate Papers, NAdCo.

"Nero": he appears between 1828 and 1834 in W. J. Ball, Plantation

Record-Book #3, Southern Historical Collection, University of North Carolina Library.

pages 60–62

strays: Natchez *Intelligencer,* 1 Dec. 1801; *Mississippi Herald and Natchez Gazette,* 15, 29 April 1807; N*A,* 12 May 1826.

Foster brand: deed-book B, 121, NAdCo.

"fabled Upas tree...": John G. Jones, *A Concise History of the Introduction of Protestantism into Mississippi and the Southwest* (St. Louis, 1866), 254. On racing see Laura D. S. Harrell, "Horse Racing in the Old Natchez District, 1783–1830," *Journal of Mississippi History,* 13 (July, 1951), 123–4; ? to Andrew Jackson, "Near Natchez," 9 Dec. 1801, Andrew Jackson Papers, DLC.

Ibrahima–Andrew Jackson: *Jallon,* 50–1.

Jackson in Natchez: "Sidney," in N*A,* 8 Sept. 1828; Irwin as creditor in liber D, 96; James Robertson to Gayoso, Nashville, 17 May 1790, AGI, PC, *leg.* 203, in Duvon C. Corbitt and Roberta Corbitt, trans. and eds., "Papers from the Spanish Archives Relating to Tennessee and the Old Southwest, 1783–1800," East Tennessee Historical Society, *Publications,* 23 (1951), 86.

Ibrahima's vending: NY*JC,* 16 Oct. 1828, mentions his selling sweet potatoes for himself.

pass: By Gayoso's order of 26 June 1792, it was forbidden to buy from or sell to any slave unless the slave had written permission to engage in such commerce from his or her owner. Liber D, 109.

"moss mattress": conversation with T. J. Foster, 28 Aug. 1973. These were common. For another example, see Natchez *Gazette,* 16 Nov. 1808.

"Abduhl Rahahman!" NO*LA,* 4 Nov. 1828.

Ibrahima's knowledge of events at home: N*SG,* 29 May 1828. This remarkable article, containing information Ibrahima gave Cyrus Griffin, mentions post-1788 developments in Fulbe politics (as well as giving the earliest printed statement of Karamoko Alfa's madness) that were not accessible in book form until long after Ibrahima's death. Laing, Gray and Dochard, and Mollien—all of whose books contain some remarks on the same characters and all of which were available in 1828—are obviously not the source for Ibrahima's information.

Ibrahima's account compresses in time the relationships of Saadu–Saalihu–Abd al-Qaadiri, as one expects from an oral report delivered years afterward.

death of Sori; Saadu: Watt, "Journal," 5–19 March 1794; Guébhard,

"L'Historie du Fouta Djallon et des Almamys," 56ff.; *cahier* 6, F. V. IFAN; Diallo, 41–2.

change of government and development of Natchez: James and Holmes both provide accounts of the departure of the Spanish and the development of Natchez above the bluff.

"religious element . . .": phrase from Hamilton, "American Beginnings," 474. For the Fosters' role in events, see James Truly, John Foster, *et al.*, petition, Natchez, 24 Oct. 1797, and Andrew Ellicott to the Secretary of State, Natchez, 26 Nov. 1797, both in Ellicott Papers, DLC.

page 63

"General is too high a rank . . .": Clark to Ellicott, [Clarksville, MT?], 8 July 1798, Ellicott Papers, DLC.

"perverseness . . . of the people": quoted in Claiborne, 208.

Ellicott quotation: Clarence Carter, ed., *The Territorial Papers of the United States,* vols. 5–6, *The Territory of Mississippi, 1798–1817* (Washington, 1937–38), vol. 5, 54.

Natchez Permanent Committee: *ibid.,* vol. 5, 10.

Sargent quotation: George B. Toulmin, "The Political Ideas of Winthrop Sargent," *Journal of Mississippi History,* 15 (Oct., 1953), 225.

John Foster: presentment of 6 June 1799, in Hamilton, "American Beginnings," 547. As early as 1789, John had served as *alguacil.* See Liber E, 166; F, 61; G, 178.

Thomas Foster: presentment of 18 Oct. 1805, in *Mississippi Messenger,* 5 Nov. 1805.

pages 64–65

Brazilian Muslims: chapter 9 (pp. 325–54), Pierre Verger, *Flux et reflux de la Traite de Nègres entre le golfe de Bénin et Bahia de todos os santos du dix-septième aux dix-neuvième siecle* (Paris, 1968).

"Negro's eleventh commandment": Peter Cartwright, quoted in William H. Milburn, *The Pioneers, Preachers, and People of the Mississippi Valley* (New York, 1860), 386.

Africans as bizarre: a good example of the feeling grandchildren had about their own grandparents is expressed in the interview with James Lucas of Natchez in W.P.A. Slave-Narrative Collection, vol. 9, 91ff., Rare Book Collection, DLC.

hauteur befitting a Pullo . . . : Griffin to Gurley, Natchez, 13 Dec. 1827, ACS-DLC.

Ibrahima's physical/moral description: *ibid.* See also N*SG,* 5 June

1828, which contains the quotation, "The privations incident . . ."
and N*SG*, 30 Oct. 1828.
never smiled: Geisenberger interview, 21 Aug. 1973, paralleling Philadelphia *Aurora and Pennsylvania Gazette,* 18 July 1828.

4. *Annus Mirabilis* and After

pages 66–67

Burr in the Territory: Thomas P. Abernathy, *The Burr Conspiracy*
(New York, 1954), 199–226. Also see James, *Antebellum
Natchez,* 107–8; Robert V. Haynes, "A Political History of the
Mississippi Territory," (Ph.D. dissertation, Rice Institute, 1958),
156.

Bruin characterization: John Smith to Thomas Jefferson, [Natchez?],
2 Feb. 1807, Carter, *Territorial Papers,* vol. 5, 510ff.

"a rough customer . . .": Joseph D. Shields, *Natchez: Its Early History* (written circa 1870), (Louisville, Ky., 1930), 57–8.

Jefferson quotation: Jefferson to Robert Williams, Washington, D.C.,
1 Nov. 1807, Carter, *Territorial Papers,* vol. 5, 573.

Dunbar fire: Thomas Rodney to Caesar Rodney, Washington, MT, 9
Dec. 1806, Gratz, "Letters of Rodney," 44 (1920), 298.

drought: H. Blennerhassett to Harmon Blennerhassett, Natchez, 26
Aug. 1807, in William H. Safford, *The Blennerhassett Papers . . .*
(Cincinnati, 1864), 283–6.

page 68

meeting with Dr. Cox: the conversation given here and all other
quotations and details are from the two principal-source accounts
of this meeting, N*YJC,* 16 Oct. 1828, and W*AR,* 4 (May, 1828),
81. Also used were Boston *Evening Chronicle,* 30 Aug. 1828;
Statement, 4; and *Biographical and Historical Memoirs,* vol. 1,
759–60.

Ibrahima's nineteenth-century biographers assign no date to this
meeting, but 1807 seems right to me for several reasons. For one
thing Dr. Cox did not move to the Territory until that year. On
April 18, 1807, he sold a slave in Rockingham County to his son-
in-law Tinsley Vernon; he was listed in the deed of sale as a
resident of Rockingham on that date. See deed-book O, 141, Rockingham County Register-of-Deeds Office, Wentworth, North Carolina. Papers relating to the case of *Arthur Scott v. Charles Mc-
Ginnis* (1805–08), Guilford County Courthouse, Greensboro,
North Carolina, contain Dr. Cox's signature of April 20, 1807, on
an appearance bond for McGinnis. In response to a subpoena
issued for him in 1808 by the Guilford County Superior Court,

however, Sheriff John Mattock of Rockingham County has written,
"Not hunted [because] John C. Cox don't live in the State & has
removed to the Mississipy Territory." (Miss Florence LeC.
Eisele of Natchez was kind enough to bring this document to my
attention.)

Dr. Cox had arrived in Natchez by August, 1807. In the Natchez
Mississippi Messenger of 27 Aug. 1807, we find that he attended
a banquet held in Washington two weeks earlier. He may have been
in the county early enough that year to plant and harvest a crop of
corn. See Thomas Rodney's account book, 6 Feb. 1808, New York
Public Library. As indicated subsequently in the text, he bought
a house and some land in the period October, 1807–February,
1808.

It appears, then, that Dr. Cox moved to the Territory in the
late spring or early summer of 1807. Most likely he met Ibrahima
at that time, and not on a previous visit to the state. Gurley (*WAR*,
4 [May, 1828], 81), has Ibrahima saying, "When I had been [in
Mississippi in slavery] sixteen years [1804], Dr. Cox removed to
Natchez." It has already been demonstrated, however, that 1804
was too early for the immigration. Gallaudet, less certain of the
date than Gurley, mentions sixteen *or* eighteen years (1804 *or*
1806). Fortunately, accounts of the meeting indicate that it occurred when Governor Robert Williams was present in the territorial capital. This is great news, since there was frequent complaint during his governorship that he was absent from the
Territory more often than not. Williams's term ran from May 10,
1805, to March 3, 1809. A land commissioner in 1804, he was
away much of that year (Isaac Briggs to Thomas Jefferson, New
Orleans, 27 Feb. 1804, Briggs-Stabler Papers, Maryland Historical
Society) and much of 1806 as well (Thomas Rodney to Caesar
Rodney, Washington, MT, 17 June 1806, "Letters of Rodney").
Deed records at Wentworth, moreover, show Dr. Cox present in
that county in both 1805 (book L, 146) and 1806 (M, 26–7).

1807, the demonstrated date of Dr. Cox's arrival, is strongly
indicated.

Of contextual interest are the Rodney account book, 27 Nov.
1808, 12 Jan. 1811, New York Public Library; interview with
George Drew, Pine Ridge, Mississippi, 28 Dec. 1974.

page 69

Cox shipwrecked: Griffin to Gurley, Natchez, 27 Dec. 1828, ACS-
DLC.
marriage: Cox–Inge family Bible, Ravenna, Natchez.

Cox in North Carolina: his activities traced in Books D-M, Register-of-Deeds Office, Wentworth. Cox witnessed a deed in the county on 18 Jan. 1790. For suits against him, including Lenox's, see N, 266ff.; O, 135–7; P, 265–7.

pages 70–71

spring "of curative properties": Miss Maude Reynolds (a Tinsley Vernon descendant) to writer, Wentworth, 18 Nov. 1974.
"fullness of his gratitude": *Statement*, 4.
Ibrahima quotation: *WAR*, 4 (May, 1828), 81.
one thousand dollars: *Statement*, 4.
"every possible exertion . . .": Boston *Massachusetts Journal*, 4 Sept. 1828.
Griffin quotation: Griffin to Gurley, Natchez, 13 Dec. 1827, ACS-DLC.
Gallaudet quotation: *Statement*, 4.
knew of "no other place . . .": Hartford, Conn., *Episcopal Watchman*, 4 Oct. 1828.
"He was so valuable . . .": *Statement*, 4.
Cox quotation: *WAR*, 4 (May, 1828), 81.
Cox land purchases at Washington: deed-book M, 287–9, NAdCo.
"party of exploration . . .": Griffin to Gurley, Natchez, 27 Dec. 1828, ACS-DLC.

page 72

Cox captured by Ibrahima: *Biographical and Historical Memoirs*, vol. 1, 759–60.
"a cannibal chief": conversation with the late Mrs. William A. Adams, Sr. (a Cox descendant), of Natchez, 11 Aug. 1972.
"Fancy that you see . . .": *NOLA*, 4 Nov. 1828.

page 73

Park quotation: Park, *Travels in the Interior Districts of Africa*, 59.
Griffin quotation: Griffin to Gurley, Natchez, 13 Dec. 1827, ACS-DLC.
"employed him . . .": Amanda Phipps, "History of the Methodist Church," project #2986, Adams County W.P.A. Source materials for Miss. history, MiDAH.
despotic African nobility: see, for example, W. A. Caruthers to Gurley, Lexington, Ky., 19 Jan. 1829, ACS-DLC.
Louisiana Advertiser charges: all quotations from *NOLA*, 25 Oct., 4 Nov. 1828. Levi Foster was in New Orleans often in 1828 attending legislative sessions and is a long-shot possibility as the source

for these stories. I doubt, however, if the author of the charges knew Ibrahima as well as he did.

page 74

Gallaudet quotation: *Statement,* 4–5.

"his kind . . . temper . . .": Boston *Christian Register,* 16 Aug. 1828.

"humanity of the Mohammedan . . .": N*SG,* 30 Oct. 1828.

Ibrahima never angry: Philadelphia *Aurora and Pennsylvania Gazette,* 18 July 1828.

runaways: deed-book B, 163–4, NAdCo; *Mississippi Herald and Natchez Gazette,* 1 Oct. 1805.

"truly amiable and worthy man": W*DNI,* 8 May 1828.

"Prince uniformly [spoke] . . .": NY*JC,* 16 Oct. 1828.

pages 75–76

Thomas's statement: Griffin to Gurley, Natchez, 13 Dec. 1827, ACS-DLC.

Foster economic development: the absence of farm records giving harvests, income and expenditures, slave censuses, etc., on a yearly basis, precludes a thorough understanding of Thomas's economic situation. The following sources were used to provide the outline given here: 1) territorial and state tax records, Adams County, 1802ff. (with intermissions), MiDAH; 2) Adams County Deed-Books, NAdCo; 3) The Bank of the Mississippi Papers, MiDAH; 4) Thomas and Sarah Foster Probate Papers, NadCo; 5) Mississippi censuses of 1816, 1820, and 1830, National Archives; and, 6) Natchez cotton prices in Robert C. Weems, Jr., "The Bank of the Mississippi" (Ph.D. dissertation, Columbia University, 1952).

Plantation through 1830: deed-books D, 189–93; F, 108–9; L, 164–5, 259; also, Real Estate Record Book #1, plat of Foster plantation on 211. The amount of land given in the deed books and in the tax records often do not agree. For 1802, computations using the former give 926 acres, the latter 1,254; in 1808, 1,302 and 1,535 acres, respectively. The tax records do not reflect Thomas's purchase of Levi's two hundred arpents in 1820, nor do they list Levi as a landowner in the county prior to that time. Obviously, Thomas considered this land his own and had been paying taxes on it before the formal transfer of title. The tax records do reflect, on the other hand, his sale of eighty-one acres that year to his brother James.

Natchez lots, 1810–18: indenture of 17 March 1810, Alexander Murray Probate Papers, NAdCo; also, deed-books G, 109–10; H, 291–4, 303; I, 76–7, 119–20, 397–401, 434–36; K, 30–1, 77–8, 113–5; will-book #1, 119–20, NAdCo.

Cole's Creek farm: deed-book H, 429ff., NAdCo.
cotton gin and grist mill: both are mentioned in Thomas Foster's
will, 22 Jan. 1829, Foster Probate Papers, NAdCo. G. Terry Sharrer, assistant curator of the Division of Manufacturing, Smithsonian Institution, in a letter from Washington, D.C., 24 Sept.
1973, gave me his impressions of the bill of L. and P. Zingline,
millwrights, 18 June 1837, Sarah Foster Probate Papers, NAdCo.
house: manuscript remarks and sketch of Mary Henderson Lambdin,
n.d., containing information provided by her father, Waldo P.
Henderson, who tore down the house in the 1870–1900 period,
kindly furnished me by Waldo P. Lambdin, Natchez. This item
contains the quotation, "looked like a cabinetmaker had built it."
Also of value were two letters from Waldo P. Lambdin to me,
Natchez, 24 Oct. 1973 and 11 Jan. 1974, giving recollections of
family members about the plantation area; Bess Alford's interview
of Thomas Henderson (son of Waldo P. Henderson), Greenwood,
Miss., 29 Oct. 1975; my interview with T. J. Foster, 22 Aug. 1972,
in which Mr. Foster reported the description of the house given by
his mother, who recalled seeing it from the Steamplant Road; and
Bacon and Burson, "Family History (As I Remember It)." Waldo
P. Henderson gave the date of 1808 for the house's renovation,
although there are no further data in the mansucript of his daughter to confirm it.

I made personal reconnaissances of the house site and plantation
in August, 1973, with T. J. Foster; in August, 1974, by myself; and
in December, 1974, with Mrs. Dalton Brown. Mrs. Brown and her
husband own the "old Henderson house," constructed (in 1872?)
a few yards north of where the Foster home stood. The Brown
home, built by Waldo P. Henderson and owned by the Henderson
family for many years, contains much original poplar from
Thomas's home.
Claiborne list: "List . . . ," Mississippi Territory File, PHi.
Rodney list: Thomas Rodney to Caesar Rodney, 4 May 1804, Washington, MT, Gratz, "Letters of Rodney," 43 (1919), 358.
National Intelligencer: received from 14 Sept. 1809 to 17 Aug. 1817.
See Foster Probate Papers, NAdCo.
tax assessor: Peter Walker to Thomas Foster, n.p., 5 Jan. 1801, Mis-
cellaneous Court Cases [and] Papers, Adams County, MT, MiDAH.
Bisland evaluation: John Bisland and James Stringfellow, "Agree-
ment," 22 Oct. 1811, Bisland and Family Papers, LSU Library.
Rodney: Natchez *Mississippi Messenger,* 4 Feb. 1808.
bail for Smith: James Smith to John Ellis, n.p., 26 Nov. 1800, and
Thomas's appearance bond, ? Feb. 1801, #162, W.P.A. typescript

of the "Minutes," General Quarter Session of the Peace for Adams County, 1799–1801, copy at MiDAH.

"Inspectors of Cotton": *Mississippi Herald and Natchez City Gazette,* 21 Jan. 1804.

pages 77–78

Thomas Foster's children: thirteen children, all adults, are mentioned in his will of 1829. My research indicates they are listed by order of birth.

Levi Foster: quotation from letter from Mrs. Paul Trowbridge to Sidney J. Romero, 27 June 1941, in Romero, "The Political Career of Murphy James Foster, Governor of Louisiana, 1892–1900" (M.A. thesis, LSU, 1941); Natchez *Weekly Chronicle,* 8 April 1811; Franklin, La., *Planters' Banner and Louisiana Agriculturalist,* 6 April 1848.

Ephraim Foster: Natchez *Mississippi Messenger,* 20 Jan. 1807, for his marriage.

Ellen and Barbara Foster: Ellen's husband was Isaac Nierson (Claiborne, 143); Barbara's, Colonel William Barnard (*Mississippian and Natchez Advertiser,* 8 May 1824; *Biographical and Historical Memoirs,* vol. 1, 343–4).

slave population: based on the Spanish censuses and the territorial and state tax records cited earlier.

Ibrahima's family: nine children are mentioned by number in both *WDNI,* 8 May 1828, and Baltimore *Genius of Universal Emancipation,* 10 May 1828. For Lee's paternity and age, see "Emigration Register," series VI, vol. 17, ACS-DLC.

Samba's family: inventory of Thomas Foster's slave estate, circa 5 Nov. 1829, Foster Probate Papers, NAdCo.

quarters: they are located on a map of the plantation in the Thomas Foster Probate Papers, NAdCo. An interview with George Drew, 28 Dec. 1974, provided some details about the site. Drew helped tear down the last remaining house on the bluff in the 1920s. Also helpful was Eleanor Brown to writer, Pine Ridge, 26 Jan. 1975.

William Foster: John G. Jones, *A Concise History,* 119–26, and Jones, *A Complete History of Methodism as Connected with the Mississippi Conference . . .* (2 vols., Nashville, 1887, 1908), vol. 1, 417ff. Gibson and slave-trade remarks from *Complete History.* Also, see Natchez *Mississippi Messenger,* 7 Oct. 1806; Natchez *Mississippi Republican,* 9 Nov. 1814.

William Foster's runaways: Natchez *Mississippi Messenger,* 8 Feb. 1805; Natchez *Mississippi Republican,* 12 June 1821.

letter to Thomas: Caleb King, *et al.*, to John Bisland, [Thomas Foster, *et al.*,] Natchez, 29 Dec. 1800, Bisland and Family Papers, LSU Library.

Salem Church: C. W. Grafton, "History of the Mississippi Synod," 49, 116ff., 320, typescript, n.d., MiDAH; Benjamin Williams, "The Introduction of Presbyterianism into the Southwest and a Brief History of the Pine Ridge Church," written Oct., 1854; and "A Record of the proceedings of The Washington Presbyterian Church Organized by and under the pastoral care of The Reverend James Smylie Feby 25th A.D. 1807" [Session Book, 1807–18], 4–5, 11, both in Pine Ridge Presbyterian Church Records, 1807–1961, microfilm copy at MiDAH. Quotation is from the Williams manuscript.

pages 79–80

Ibrahima at church meetings: Presbyterian (conversation with Amanda Geisenberger, Natchez, 21 Aug. 1973); Baptist (New York *Spectator,* 21 Oct. 1828, mentioning Isabella's affiliation with the Baptist church for thirty years); and Methodist (Phipps, "History of the Methodist Church," W.P.A. Source Materials, MiDAH.)

Blacks at church door: Walter B. Posey, *The Presbyterian Church in the Old Southwest, 1778–1838* (Richmond, 1952), 86.

"deal with [the slaves]...": quoted in Walter B. Posey, *The Baptist Church in the Lower Mississippi Valley, 1776–1845* (Lexington, 1957), 94.

Simon as speaker: Gallaudet to Gurley, New York, 14 Oct. 1828, and Griffin to Gurley, Natchez, 27 Dec. 1828, ACS-DLC.

"a man of genuine...": Boston *Christian Watchman,* 15 Aug. 1828.

Park: quotation from *Travels in the Interior Districts of Africa,* 60.

spirits source of the Niger River: New York *Freedom's Journal,* 29 Aug. 1828.

pages 81–83

Ibrahima on Christian beliefs: N*SG,* 12 June 1828. This article, and the Griffin letter cited below, prove illuminating when read with Edward W. Blyden, "Islam in Western Sudan," *Journal of the African Society,* 2 (Oct., 1902), 22, and Blyden, *Christianity, Islam and the Negro Race* (London, 1888), 13–8.

religion and race in Futa: Fisher and Fisher, *Slavery and Muslim Society in Africa,* 34; Derman, *Serfs, Peasants, and Socialists,* 42, 211–23.

Methodist ministers: for example, see William Winans to O. Winans, 14 April 1820, Winans Letterbooks, microfilm copy at MiDAH.

Griffin quotation: N*SG*, 12 June 1828; Griffin to Gurley, Natchez, 12 Dec. 1827, ACS-DLC, emphasis in original.

Ibrahima's statement: N*SG*, 12 June 1828, reproduced exactly as printed.

"a man of some eccentricity": Claiborne, *Life and Times of Gen. Sam Dale, the Mississippi Partisan* (New York, 1860), 90–1.

letter to Bisland: Cox to Bisland, n.d., n.p., photostat in Bisland and Family Papers, LSU Library.

Trask quotation: Worcester *Massachusetts Yeoman*, 1 Nov. 1828.

"surgeon"; "doctor"; "physician": James Flint, *Letters from America* ... (Edinburgh, 1822), in R. G. Thwaites, ed., *Early Western Travels*, vol. 9 (Cleveland, Ohio, 1904), 196.

"specialty was fevers ...": Thomas Rodney to Caesar Rodney, Washington, MT, 22 Aug. 1810, Rodney Family Papers, DLC.

Claiborne's characterization: *Gen. Sam Dale*, 90–1.

Shields's characterization: Shields, "A Historical Sketch of Adams County, Mississippi ...," 65, MiDAH.

"exports of the U.S. ...": Natchez *Mississippi Messenger*, 25 Aug. 1807.

"produce of the ... Territory ...": Natchez *Weekly Chronicle*, 10 Nov. 1810.

Cox appointments: Justice of the Peace, 27 Feb. 1811, "Register of Military Appointments, 1805–1812," series A, vol. M, Mississippi Territorial Archives, MiDAH; Jefferson College trustee, "Journal," Jefferson College Board of Trustees, 12 April 1810, Jefferson College Papers, MiDAH.

War of 1812: Cox signed letters to General Claiborne at Baton Rouge on 19 Nov. 1812 and 22 March 1813, both in J. F. H. Claiborne Papers, MiDAH.

birth of William Cox: Cox-Inge family Bible, Ravenna, Natchez.

William Cox at U.N.C.: information conveyed in letter of 18 June 1973 from T. G. Wolsalgel, General Alumni Association, University of North Carolina, and of 6 June 1975, from Archivist Michael G. Martin, Jr., Manuscripts Dept., University Library.

William Cox in War of 1812: General F. L. Claiborne to "The Officer Commanding at Liberty," "Near Fort Stoddart," 13 Aug. 1813, Claiborne Papers, MiDAH; *Washington Republican*, 8 Sept. 1813; Claiborne, *Gen. Sam Dale*, 102n; Shields, "Historical Sketch," 65.

"Doctr. William ...": Major Charles Kavanaugh and William R. Cox, "Articles of Agreement," Washington, MT, 25 March 1815, and receipts and statements of 25 April, 10 and 31 May, 1815, all Andrew Jackson Papers, DLC.

pen and paper for Ibrahima: *Jallon*, 56–7.

page 84

Cox as Bisland doctor: settlement of 27 March 1814, in John Bisland,
"Plantation Diary," 1814–18, Bisland and Family Papers, LSU
Library.

"le protecteur du Prince": phrase in New Orleans *Argus,* 23 Oct.
1828.

Gallaudet quotation: NY*JC,* 16 Oct. 1828.

Ibrahima statement: W*AR,* 4 (May, 1828), 81.

Williams: "A memorandum of what Dr. John C. Cox said to
me...," 15 Dec. 1816, will-book #1, 143, NAdCo. Bills in his
estate papers provided information on his reading interests.

Cox quotation: Williams's "memorandum," above.

Cox obituary: issue of 18 Dec. 1816.

5. "Unbroken in Body and Mind"

page 85

Ibrahima statement: W*AR,* 4 (May,1828), 80.

teeth: N*SG,* 30 Oct. 1828.

Everett phrase: "Rahaman," 188.

"The Negro [Ibrahima]...": NOL*A,* 4 Nov. 1828.

Ibrahima at market house: P*MFJ,* 21 Aug. 1828.

Cook statement: "To the citizens of Natchez, *Prince,* ... a slave to
a very respectable planter of this county, is well known." N*A,*
26 April 1828.

"Drug and Chemical Store": *Washington Republican and Natchez
Intelligencer,* 9 Aug. 1817. Cox continued this business at least
through 1820.

Cox description: based on his oil-on-wood portrait at Ravenna,
reproduced elsewhere in this book.

patients not charged: *The Natchez,* 14 Oct. 1831.

page 86

"His courtesies...": *ibid.*

Cox's practice: He began practice on Christmas Day, 1818. (Natchez
Mississippi Republican, 25 Dec. 1818.) For a sampling of his
patients, see *Mississippian and Natchez Advertiser,* 10 July 1824;
N*A,* 16 June 1826, 7 Sept. 1827.

interest in Ibrahima: *Statement,* 4, reading in part, "Since Dr. [John]
Cox's death..., his son has renewed the negociations for Prince's
freedom, but without success."

financial problems: father's estate (Natchez *Mississippi Republican,*
13 Aug. 1817; *Alexander Brown v. Deborah Cox, executrix of*

John C. Cox, in Natchez *Mississippi State Gazette,* 26 Feb. 1820; and deed-book M, 155–6, 245, NAdCo); Lyons's loan (deed-book L, 131, NAdCo.); lost money (Natchez *Mississippi Republican,* 28 Nov. 1820); borrowing (Cox note to John Minor, Natchez, 4 Jan. 1821, and protest for nonpayment, 7 Feb. 1821, Andrew Marschalk Papers, MiDAH); circuit-court cases (Adams County Circuit-Court Executions, box 497, NAdCo); bank (Bank of the Mississippi Papers, MiDAH).

Ibrahima's remark: *WAR,* 4 (May, 1828), 81.

Marschalk: Andrew Marschalk has not received the attention from historians that he deserves. The most substantial work on his life is Mary A. Welsh, "Andrew Marschalk, Mississippi's First Printer" (M.L.S. thesis, University of Mississippi, 1957), and Welsh has used previously published researches heavily. For the purposes of this book, I have had to go to the sources themselves.

runaway apprentice: Philadelphia *Pennsylvania Mercury and Universal Advertiser,* 10 Aug. 1787. This piece contains a physical description.

military service: Francis B. Heitman, *Historical Register and Dictionary of the United States Army, from Its Organization, September 29, 1789, to March 2, 1903* (2 vols., Washington, 1903), vol. 1, 690.

page 87

"patent medicine, cheap": Natchez *Mississippi Herald,* 10 Aug. 1802.

"a communicative temper": Natchez *Mississippi Messenger,* 7 April 1807, containing also "strange to tell. . . ."

Poindexter incident and quotation: Marschalk, complaint to R. H. Morrow, 17 Feb. 1815, series A, vol. 15, Governors' Records, MiDAH.

"the Col. was satisfied . . .": N*A,* 22 March 1828.

"The Galley Slave": Welsh, "Andrew Marschalk," which also retells the story of his impressment.

page 88

"a cruel and savage practice . . .": PMFJ, 21 Aug. 1828. His *Mississippi Herald* had always been open to attacks on the international slave trade (1, 14 Aug., 19 Oct. 1804, for example) and, more recently, he had printed favorable accounts of colonization (*Mississippi State Gazette,* 26 May 1819).

acquaintance with Ibrahima: PMFJ, 21 Aug. 1828, contains his statement of 1828 that he had known Ibrahima "upwards of 24 years."

Marschalk house: Marschalk House Data Sheet, 1937, Historical American Buildings Survey, series W, Federal Archives, MiDAH.
"Prince is really . . .": *WDNI,* 8 May 1828.
"I did not look . . .": *PMFJ,* 21 Aug. 1828.

page 89

"I produced to him . . .": *ibid.* This article contains all quotations and details on the incident.
Anderson: Thomas D. Anderson was appointed U.S. consul at Tunis on 10 May 1815 and served until his appointment as consul at Tripoli on 2 March 1819. He served there until 18 Dec. 1825.
"royal family of Morocco": Marschalk to Thomas B. Reed (copy), Natchez, 3 Oct. 1826, contained in Thomas Mullowny to Henry Clay, Tangier, 27 March 1827, "Dispatches from the United States Consuls in Tangier," vol. 4 (1819–30), State Department Records, DNA.
"The lie comes quickly . . .": this and the other two sayings are found in Henri Gaden, *Proverbes et maximes peul et toucouleur* (Paris, 1931), 163, 166.

pages 90–92

Griffin interview: discussed subsequently in this chapter.
"unwilling to believe . . .": *PMFJ,* 21 Aug. 1828.
"he had accumulated . . .": Bacon and Burson, "Family History (As I Remember It)."
"Foster Fields": phrase appears in family history papers belonging to Lillian Quinn, Setauket, New York. "Greenwood Plantation," frequently used on maps of this area, appears to be a more recent name, perhaps used by the Henderson family.
plantation affluence: *ibid.;* Irene B. Hotard (a Foster descendant) to writer, New Smyrna Beach, Florida, 1 April 1974; conversations with Mrs. H. J. Starr (a Foster descendant), Chattanooga, Tenn., 25 March 1974, 1 Jan. 1976; Thomas Foster's Adams County tax returns, 1825ff., MiDAH; Thomas's deposits in vols. 41, 45, Bank of the Mississippi Papers, MiDAH.
"Old Thomas Foster . . .": W. N. Foster to Martha Foster de la Houssaye, Conroe, Texas, 15 Oct. 1942, copy in possession of Thomas Kramer, Franklin, La.
Pennington statement: James Pennington, *The Fugitive Blacksmith* (London, 2nd ed., 1849), 69.
"The dog carried . . .": in Gaden, cited above.

beaver hat, etc.: inventory of Ephraim's effects, 21 Jan. 1825, Ephraim Foster Probate Papers, NAdCo.

truculent slaves: runaway George was "much marked with the whip," Ephraim noted in a newspaper advertisement, "having been very severely punished before I purchased him, but never since." *Mississippi State Gazette,* 12 Feb. 1820.

"whose parental kindness . . .": all quotations in this and the following two paragraphs are from *Cassandra Foster v. Ephraim Foster* (1824), Mississippi High Court of Errors and Appeals, case 452, drawer 73, MiDAH.

Ephraim's activities for Thomas: E. Foster to James Kempe, receipt, Natchez, 6 May 1815, has Ephraim describing himself as Thomas's "agent." Also, see marriage record #1 (1802–19), 293–4, NAdCo.

Ephraim in Wilkinson County: Natchez *Mississippi Republican,* 16 March 1814; deed-book B, 142–4, Wilkinson County Chancery Clerk's Office, Woodville, Miss.

Ephraim's plantation ambitions: traced in a complex series of deeds in deed-books L, M, and N, NAdCo.

Cassandra a runaway: *Mississippian and Natchez Advertiser,* 27 March 1824.

assault: E. Foster to Thomas McDannolds, promissory note, 27 Feb. 1824, Ephraim Foster Probate Papers, NAdCo. I could not find any particulars of this assault, as the papers of the case are not present in the NAdCc files for 1824.

illness, death: his last months were reconstructed from the bills and statements in his probate papers.

wills: E. Foster, wills of 8 Jan. and 7 Dec. 1824, both in will-book #1, 318, NAdCo.

Cassandra: her second husband was John Speed, for whom, see *Levi Foster et al., v. John Speed and Sarah Foster* (1832–6), Mississippi High Court of Errors and Appeals, case 230, drawer 70, MiDAH; and *Natchez Newspaper and Public Advertiser,* 11 Oct. 1826. According to her tombstone in "Greenwood Plantation" cemetery, she died 21 March 1831, at age forty-four.

pages 93–94

McIntosh: quotations and details from "Family History (As I Remember It)." Notice of his death appeared in Jackson *Southern Reformer,* 23 Aug. 1845.

James Foster described: F. L. Claiborne to Hiram G. Runnels, 20 March 1834, Governors' Records, MiDAH, citation courtesy of Bertram Wyatt-Brown.

"one of the finest . . .": *Natchez Courier & Journal,* 9 Jan. 1835.

Susan Alfhari: the spelling of her last name is uncertain, since the manuscript source, cited just below, is hard to read. I did not find any St. Mary Parish record of this name, although "Alfa" was present.

the murder: quotations and facts in this paragraph, including those about Ibrahima's son, are from *State of Mississippi v. James Foster* (1834), "Examination on a Charge of Murder before W. Wren, J.P." 28 March 1834, and undated statements, all in State Cases, June Term, 1834, Judgments and Dismissions, NAdCc.

"where Judge Lynch . . .": *Natchez Courier & Journal,* 9 Jan. 1835. Also of interest were Helen Gates Rossner, "There is always a black sheep in each family," typescript, n.d., copy in possession of Thomas Kramer, Franklin, Louisiana; Col. James Creecy, *Scenes in the South and Other Miscellaneous Pieces* (Washington, 1860), 52–6; and *Colonel Crockett's Exploits and Adventures in Texas* (Philadelphia, 1836), 100–3.

Thomas Foster, Jr.: born at Foster Fields, according to his grandson, W. N. Foster, in a letter from Conroe, Texas, 23 Nov. 1960, to Mrs. Floy Hume (copy provided me by Martha Foster Madeley, his daughter). The date is uncertain. The W. N. Foster letter of 1942, cited earlier this chapter, mentions his regard for Levi.

"his usual haunt": all quotations and details in this and the six paragraphs following are, unless otherwise designated, from *Susannah Foster v. Thomas Foster, Jr.* (1827–31), Mississippi High Court of Errors and Appeals, Case 683, Drawer 76, MiDAH.

marriage: *Mississippi State Gazette,* 1 July 1820.

Reverend Carson: Carolyn Carson Nugent (a descendant of the Reverend Carson) to writer, Rosalie, Natchez, 1 July 1975, giving facts from Henry G. Hawkins's "Methodism in Natchez."

page 97

naming relationship: a list of Simon's children is given in "Emigration Register," Series VI, Vol. 17, ACS-DLC.

ndiimaajo: these *captifs de case* enjoyed near-liberty and could own slaves themselves. See Guébhard, "L'Etat social et politique Du Fouta Dialon," 179ff.

pages 98–99

son in St. Mary Parish: Griffin to Gurley, Natchez, 5 July 1828, ACS-DLC.

Marschalk absorbed: *Natchez Newspaper and Public Advertiser,* 20

Sept. 1826. He was also in the process of preparing a *Natchez Printed Correct Almanac,* complete with "signs, omens, and long yarns."

letter: Marschalk to Reed, cited above.

Reed: see his obituary, N*SG*, 17 Dec. 1829, containing the editor's quotation. The banquet is covered in *Mississippian and Natchez Advertiser,* 8 Nov. 1826. Edwin A. Miles, *Jacksonian Democracy in Mississippi* (Chapel Hill, 1960), 14–24, places Reed in the context of state politics.

"to settle upon committing...": this quotation and the following one by Susan are both from *S. Foster v. T. Foster, Jr.,* MiDAH.

abandoned his family: in January, 1827, Susan stated in a petition in the case papers above that her husband had "given up all idea of ever again living with his family." She also informed the court that he was a resident of Adams County. However, Thomas appears to have left the county by then. A subpoena issued for him on February 1 was not served that entire year because he could not be found. In December, 1827, he was relieved as trustee of an estate because of his absence. Orphans' Court Minutes, vol. 5 (Dec. Term, 1827), 105, NAdCo.

Thomas is not mentioned in the Warren-County deed records, but he is listed as a landowner in Copiah County, where he lived from September, 1828 through March, 1830, at least. See Copiah County deed-book C, 17–8, 210, 280, 372, Chancery Clerk's Office, Hazlehurst, Miss. A deposition by Susan in the latter year indicates the estrangement was still complete.

This case was dismissed in January, 1831, for want of prosecution. The reason was Thomas's death, which seems to have occurred in late 1830. On July 21, 1831, Susan married Adelard Demaret of St. Mary Parish, Louisiana. She lived to a ripe old age. The fate of Susy is unknown.

Morocco: Henri Terrasse, *History of Morocco* (Casablanca, 1952), is useful for setting the domestic and international stage of the period.

Adams quotation: Adams to Mullowny, Washington, D.C., 15 July 1820, "Consular Instructions of the Department of State," microcopy M78, rolls 2–3, DNA.

page 100

"I received...": Mullowny to Clay, Tangier, 27 March 1827, cited above. Quotations in this and the following paragraph are from this letter.

Mullowny left Ibrahima's original document with the Moroccan government, keeping only a copy for the State Department files. The copy could not be located, and, despite the assistance of friends, I was unable to find the original in the Royal Library and Archives in Rabat.

Clay quotation: docket on Mullowny's letter.

page 101

Adams: Adams, diary, 10 July 1827, Adams Papers, originals at Massachusetts Historical Society, microfilm copy at DLC.

Brent letter: Brent to Marschalk, Washington, D.C., 12 July 1827, Adams Papers.

"I took the earliest . . .": *PMFJ*, 21 Aug. 1828.

"I immediately waited . . .": Marschalk to Henry Clay, Natchez, 20 Aug. 1827, Adams Papers. This letter also contains Thomas's feelings and his condition.

pages 102–103

"Notoriously a Jackson man": N*SG*, 30 Oct. 1828.

Dangerfield letter: Dangerfield to Marschalk, Natchez, 20 Aug. 1827, enclosed in Marschalk to Clay of the same date, cited above. "A young gentleman of the Bar . . ." is from Marschalk's letter.

Dangerfield had commenced the practice of law in July, 1825. *Mississippi State Gazette*, 9 July, 26 Nov. 1825. His family were neighbors to the Fosters, and on good terms with them.

"Although by birth . . .": Marschalk to Clay, Natchez, 20 Aug. 1827, cited above.

"Though sixty-five years . . .": Griffin to Gurley, Natchez, 13 Dec. 1827, ACS-DLC.

"He will be happy . . .": *ibid.*

"He expressed . . .": Marschalk to Clay, Natchez, 20 Aug. 1827, cited above.

pages 104–105

Thayer statement: Thayer to "a Methodist preacher," Washington, Miss., 28 Nov. 1827, in New Haven, Conn., *Religious Intelligencer*, 23 Feb. 1828.

"In a recent conversation . . .": Marschalk to Clay, Natchez, 20 Aug. 1827, cited above. This letter also contains Ibrahima's reply.

Statesman quotations: N*A*, 29 March 1828, quoting his issues of 23 and 30 Aug. 1827.

Griffin and family: *Vital Records of Andover, Massachusetts, to the end of the Year 1849* (2 vols., Topsfield, 1912), *passim;* Old South

Church Parish Treasurer's Book (1763–1835), entries of 1 Nov. 1794, 3 March 1795, 16 April 1799, 5 March 1807, from microfilm copy, Merrimack Valley Textile Museum, North Andover, Mass.; "Town and Country Tax Lists, Andover," 1821, East District, South Parish, located at the Town Hall, Andover; deed-book vols. 176–242, as appropriate, for Jonathan, Zerviah and Cyrus Griffin, Vault Room, Essex County Register-of-Deeds Office, Salem, Mass.; Essex County Probate Records, O.S. box 85 (N.S. box 385), 393–6, inventory dated 7 March 1816, *ibid.;* Charlotte Helen Abbott, comp., "Early Records of the Grainger, Graves, Green, Griffin, Grow, and Gutterson Families of Andover," typescript, n.d., Memorial Hall Library, Andover.

"unsteady habits," etc.: see his unhappy autobiography in *The Natchez,* 10 July 1830.

Patridge statement: I. M. Patridge, "The Press in Mississippi—Historical Sketch," *DeBow's Review,* O.S., vol. 29 (Oct., 1860), 504.

Cook: N*A,* 14 March 1829.

"Mr. Griffin was a gentleman...": obituary notice, *Vicksburg Register,* 11 Oct. 1837.

Cyrus's office: N*A,* 5 Jan. 1828.

shooting of runaways: N*SG,* 9, 23 Oct. 1828.

"Born and educated...": N*SG,* 26 June 1828.

"a peculiar interest...": Marschalk to Clay, Natchez, 20 Aug. 1827, cited above.

Everett phrase: "Rahaman," 193.

"We have all...": N*SG,* 29 May 1828.

"At my own request...": Griffin to Gurley, Natchez, 13 Dec. 1827, ACS-DLC.

page 106

"[Ibrahima] was sent...": N*A,* 25 Oct. 1828.

"I address you...": Griffin to Gurley, Natchez, 13 Dec. 1827, ACS-DLC.

page 107

Clay letter: Clay to Marschalk, Washington, D.C., 12 Jan. 1828, Domestic Letters, M40, State Department Records, DNA.

deed in trust: Foster to Marschalk, deed-book Q, 83–4, NAdCo.

pages 108–109

"It is impossible...": sentence from New Haven, Conn., *Religious Intelligencer,* 25 Oct. 1828, containing a version of Gallaudet's New York address.

slave from North Carolina . . . : Lunsford Lane, *The Narrative of Lunsford Lane, Formerly of Raleigh, N.C.* (Boston, 1842), 17–8.

"I immediately . . . set . . .": *PMFJ*, 21 Aug. 1828.

Ibrahima "looked at the old companion . . .": *WDNI*, 8 May 1828.

"Cheering as his [own] . . .": *NYJC*, 16 Oct. 1828.

"What was to be done?": *WDNI*, 8 May 1828.

"I applied again . . .": *ibid.*

"obstetrick practitioner . . .": *PMFJ*, 21 Aug. 1828.

"Yet he could not . . .": *ibid.*

"a very small sum . . .": *WDNI*, 8 May 1828. Marschalk remarked that this sum was not one third her value.

"The kindness of Mr. Foster . . .": *Statement*, 8. I could not locate a copy of the subscription paper.

"so great was the respect . . .": Griffin to Gurley, Natchez, 6 April 1828, ACS-DLC.

"Several gentlemen gave . . .": *WDNI*, 8 May 1828.

"This fact alone . . .": *Statement*, 4.

Isabella deeded: Foster to Marschalk, deed-book Q, 132–3, NAdCo.

certificates of recommendation: *Statement*, 8, lists the writers and summarizes the contents.

page 110

Ibrahima Marschalk's guest: N*A*, 25 Oct. 1828, contains Griffin's statement, "I believe there is no doubt that Prince was entertained at Col. M.'s house during some days previous to his departure. I also heard the Colonel remark that, were he at leisure, he would accompany him to the Seat of Government."

"The Colonel absolutely *bored* . . .": N*A*, 1 Nov. 1828, emphasis in original.

public dinner, parchment document: N*A*, 25 Oct. 1828, which also contains "It is scarcely necessary for me to say . . ."

route to Washington: *ibid.*

"Perhaps by doing so . . .": *ibid.*

two-hundred-dollar authorization: Clay to Marschalk, Washington, D.C., 12 Jan. 1828, cited above. The draft was sold for only $185. N*A*, 25 Oct. 1828.

"His master's indulgence . . .": *PMFJ*, 21 Aug. 1828.

page 111

outfit described: Boston *Patriot and Mercantile Advertiser*, 12 Aug. 1828; Sarah Tuttle (supposed authoress), *Claims of the Africans* (Boston, 1832), 143–4; and Boston *Daily Commercial Advertiser*, 11 Aug. 1828.

"A tawdry dress . . .": N*A*, 25 Oct. 1828.

"The indulgence of appearing . . .": P*MFJ*, 21 Aug. 1828.

weather: John B. Nevitt, Diary, 6–8 April 1828, Southern Historical Collection, University of North Carolina Library.

"It was indeed . . .": N*A*, 26 April 1828.

"bid them a final adieu": *ibid.*

"but realize his prospects . . .": W*DNI*, 8 May 1828, which also contains Marschalk's closing remarks.

6. A Northern Campaign

It is a difficult task to select a few books that give the flavor of the people, movements, and time in Chapters 6–8. Standard references, however, should always include Merton L. Dillon, *Benjamin Lundy and the Struggle for Negro Freedom* (Urbana and London, 1966); Philip S. Foner, *History of Black Americans from Africa to the Emergence of the Cotton Kingdom* (Westport, Conn., 1975); P. J. Staudenraus, *The African Colonization Movement, 1816–1865* (New York, 1961); and Bertram Wyatt-Brown, *Lewis Tappan and the Evangelical War Against Slavery* (New York, 1971).

pages 112–113

Neptune: W.P.A. Survey of Federal Archives, "Ship Registers and Enrollments of New Orleans, Louisiana," vol. 2 (1821–30), #625, copy at DLC. John Francis McDermott, *Before Mark Twain: A Sampler of Old, Old Times on the Mississippi* (Carbondale and Edwardsville, Ill., 1968), gives an excellent description of the sounds of these early boats. Also see E. W. Gould, *Fifty Years on the Mississippi* (St. Louis, 1889).

weather: Nevitt, Diary, cited above.

flood of spring, 1828: well described in Una Pope-Hennessy, ed., *The Aristocratic Journey* (New York, 1931), 264.

"superior accommodations . . .": N*SG*, 9 Oct. 1828.

Nathaniel Ware selected: W*DNI*, 8 May 1828. The Boston *Massachusetts Journal*, 4 Sept. 1828, contains his statement, "I have lived in the neighborhood of [Thomas] Foster ten years. . . ."

Ware described, family history: Mary T. Tardy, *Southland Writers* (2 vols., Philadelphia, 1870), vol. 1, 26–40; Julia D. Freeman, *Women of the South* (New York, 1860), 114–7.

Ware's African slaves: *Washington Republican and Natchez Intelligencer*, 11 Sept. 1816.

"It is a singular . . .": Ware's novel, *Harvey Belden; or, a True Narrative of Strange Adventures* (Cincinnati, 1848), 93–4.

"I know the . . .": *Statement*, 8.
"a tub of soap-suds . . .": Thomas L. Nichols, *Forty Years of American Life* (2 vols., London, 1864), vol. 1, 168.
Neptune at Louisville: Louisville *Public Advertiser*, 19 April 1828.
Neptune at Cincinnati: Cincinnati *Daily Gazette*, 19, 21 April 1828. This paper's issue of the twenty-second mentions Ibrahima's arrival the previous day, but *WDNI*, 8 May 1828, quoting the Cincinnati *Republican*, gives the nineteenth as the day of his appearance.
Cincinnati described: Henry Tudor, *Narrative of a Tour to North America* (2 vols., London, 1834), vol. 2, 432ff.; Richard T. Farrell, "Cincinnati in the Early Jackson Era, 1816–1834: An Economic and Political Study" (Ph.D. dissertation, Indiana University, 1967), is likewise valuable.

page 114

"The grave looking . . .": Cincinnati *Republican*, quoted in *WDNI*, 8 May 1828.
two other newspapers . . . : *Daily Gazette*, 22 April 1828; *National Republican and Ohio Political Register*, 25 April 1828.
cost of costume: Marschalk stated (*PMFJ*, 21 Aug. 1828) that the costume had cost "about $70," which left $115 for the trip.
"No provision is made . . .": issue of 22 April 1828.

page 115

"romantic and extraordinary . . .": *ibid.*
"Prince of Timbuctoo": *WDNI*, 8 May 1828, reprinting the remarks of a Washington, Pennsylvania, editor on the passage of Ibrahima through that town on May 1.
Griffin letter: "The Unfortunate Moor," *WAR*, 3 (Feb. 1828), 364–7, is drawn from Cyrus Griffin's letter to the Colonization Society, Natchez, 13 Dec. 1827, ACS-DLC. This number of the *WAR* reached the public in mid-March.
"He is entitled . . .": issue of 29 March 1828.
"a great zealot": Providence, R.I., *Literary Cadet*, 16 April 1828.
Lundy: Marschalk had directed Ibrahima to leave Isabella with Lundy before proceeding to Washington. Marschalk to Adams, Natchez, 4 April 1828, Adams Papers.
Lundy attacked: *Genius of Universal Emancipation*, 20 Jan. 1827.
Lundy absent/Swaim: Dillon, 133, 141.

page 116

"Though this victim . . .": *Genius of Universal Emancipation*, 10 May 1828.

"abstraction from . . .": Clay to Adams, Philadelphia, 8 May 1828, and Adams, diary, 13–4 May 1828, both Adams Papers.

Clay in Baltimore: Baltimore *American & Commercial Daily Advertiser,* 14 May 1828.

Clay described: "Biographical Sketch of Henry Clay," Philadelphia *Casket,* 1 (April, 1828), 145–7, and Tudor, *Narrative of a Tour,* Vol. 2, 461.

"He is highly . . .": John Kennedy to Gurley, Washington, 15 May 1828, ACS-DLC.

"wore a miserable . . .": James Fenimore Cooper, *Notions of the Americans, Picked up by a Travelling Bachelor* (2 vols., New York, 1963 [original ed., 1828]), vol. 2, 4–5.

pages 117–120

Washington described: *ibid.,* vol. 2, 11; Edward T. Cooke, *A Subaltern's Furlough: Descriptive Scenes of in Various Parts of the United States* . . . (London, 1832), chapter 4; Nathan Sargent, *Public Men and Events* . . . (2 vols., Philadelphia, 1875), vol. 1, *passim.*

"quiet and economical": W*DNI,* 10 June 1828.

"I have been . . .": N*A,* 21 June 1828.

mistress of the governor-elect: L. C. Adams to Charles F. Adams, Washington, 30 May 1828, Adams Papers.

"The public will be . . .": Bennington, Vt., *Journal of the Times,* 28 Nov. 1828.

Cash!! Cash!! . . . : *Genius of Universal Emancipation,* 24 Dec. 1825, emphasis in original.

mood of May: Elizabeth F. Ellet, *The Court Circles of the Republic.* . . . (Hartford, 1869), 137–8; L. C. Adams to A. B. Adams, Washington, 18 May 1828, Adams Papers.

"Rain": Adams, diary, 15 May 1828, Adams Papers.

White House described: In addition to those works on Washington already cited, see also James Boardman, *America and the Americans* (London, 1833), 235; "The John Quincy Adams Administration," in the series "Reminiscences of Washington," *The Atlantic Monthly,* 45 (March, 1880), 289–99.

Adams described: Rufus R. Wilson, *Washington: The Capitol City and Its Part in the History of the Nation* (2 vols., Philadelphia, 1901), vol. 1, 225.

"I found him . . .": Tudor, *Narrative of a Tour,* vol. 2, 461.

President's office: it was on the second floor of the mansion, although the exact room is unknown. Clement E. Conger to writer, White House, 17 July 1972.

Howell quotation: R. B. C. Howell to H. Keeling, postscript to letter,

Norfolk, 29 Jan. 1829, in *Richmond Religious Herald*, 13 Feb. 1829.

"Abdel Rahman . . .": Adams, diary, 15 May 1828, Adams Papers. Another in the variety of spellings of his name.

"he expressed a . . .": Clay to Mullowny, Washington, 17 Jan. 1829, State Department Records, DNA.

"The President thought . . .": *ibid.*

"He says . . .": Adams, diary, 15 May 1828, Adams Papers.

page 121

letters pleading his case: They were Marschalk to Adams, Natchez, 4 April 1828, and Thomas B. Reed to Adams, Natchez, 6 April 1828, both in Adams Papers.

"Mr. Clay was . . .": N*A*, 21 June 1828. Ibrahima's meeting with Clay on the fifteenth is mentioned in Kennedy to Gurley, Washington, 15 May 1828, ACS-DLC.

Griffin letter: Griffin to Gurley, Natchez, 6 April 1828, ACS-DLC. An extract was published in W*AR*, 4 (May, 1828), 77–8.

American Colonization Society: see Staudenraus.

page 122

"Massa Clay . . .": Boston *Columbian Centinel,* quoted in N*A,* 1 Nov. 1828. I checked the file of the *Columbian Centinel* semi-weekly edition without finding the original.

"We have chosen . . .": Boston *Liberator,* 23 March 1833.

"Nothing appears . . .": New York *Rights of All,* 12 June 1829.

"an insidious attack . . .": *Mercury* quoted in Archibald Alexander, *A History of Colonization . . .* (Philadelphia, 1846), 349.

Society office: mentioned in New York *Freedom's Journal,* 29 Aug. 1828. For Gurley and Kennedy, see [Elliott's] *Washington Directory* (Washington, 1827), 36, 46. Kennedy should not be confused with Andrew T. Kennedy. Both sold books in the city.

Liberian coffee: NY*JC,* 20 Jan. 1829.

page 123

Gurley, Key absent: Board of Managers, Proceedings, 28 April 1828, and Gurley to John Kennedy, Brunswick, N.J., 7 May 1828, both ACS-DLC; New York *Advertiser,* 13 May 1828. Gurley's letter reads in part, "I am informed that the Unfortunate Moor is actually on his way to Washington, &, of course, will expect the advice & aid of the Board."

"It affords . . .": Griffin to Gurley, Natchez, 6 April 1828, cited above.

"To day the Moor . . .": Kennedy to Gurley, Washington, 15 May 1828, ACS-DLC.

Laurie: William B. Sprague, *Annals of the American Pulpit* (9 vols., New York, 1857–69), vol. 4, 314ff.; Washington *Star,* 15 Nov. 1903; conversations with Mrs. James N. Peale (a Laurie descendant), Washington, D.C., 17 July, 9 Sept. 1970; Mrs. Allen Newman (a Laurie descendant) to writer, Hendersonville, N.C., 6 Sept., 1 Nov. 1970.

Gurley: Albert E. Gurley, *The History and Genealogy of the Gurley Family* (Willimantic, Conn., 1897), *passim;* R. R. Gurley, *Mission to England* (Washington, 1841), 239.

page 124

"We have repeatedly . . .": W*AR,* 4 (May, 1828), 78.

"Teembo, the . . .": Boston *Massachusetts Journal,* 4 Sept. 1828.

Ibrahima's letter: N*A,* 21 June 1828.

Board meeting: Board of Managers, Proceedings, 19 May 1828, ACS-DLC. Others present included Dr. Thomas Henderson, professor of medicine at Columbian College (now George Washington University); the Reverend William Hawley, pastor of St. John's Episcopal Church, Washington; the Reverend Stephen B. Balch, of the Bridge Street Presbyterian Church, Georgetown; and the Reverend Obadiah B. Brown, one-time president of Columbian College and then pastor of the First Baptist Church of Washington.

Key: described in this period in Henry S. Foote's *Casket of Reminiscences* (Washington, 1874), 12–3. Foote is also the source for the quotation beginning, "would have done. . . ."

page 125

"He told me . . .": Kennedy to Gurley, Washington, 15 May 1828, ACS-DLC.

"wait upon the . . .": Board of Managers, Proceedings, 19 May 1828, cited above.

his expenses . . . city . . . : Proceedings, 26 May 1828.

United States Telegraph: the entire issue of 7 May 1828 was devoted to criticism of the Department's expenditures.

page 126

forget his children . . . : "Prince, before leaving Natchez," wrote Griffin, "expressed an ardent wish that his children might follow him. I then advised with him upon the subject and stated to him what I thought to be the impracticability of the scheme." Griffin to Gurley, Natchez, 5 July 1828, ACS-DLC.

"He entertains . . .": Kennedy to Gurley, Washington, 15 May 1828, ACS-DLC.

"If the other cities . . .": Ibrahima to Thomas H. Gallaudet, Washington, 7 June 1828, *The Philadelphian*, 20 June 1828.

"He seems to think . . .": Kennedy to Gurley, Washington, 15 May 1828, ACS-DLC.

"write Mr. Foster . . .": motion by the Reverend Hawley. Board of Managers, Proceedings, 19 May 1828, ACS-DLC.

page 127

"He has the . . .": statement dated Washington, 22 May 1828, in Boston *Massachusetts Journal*, 4 Sept. 1828.

Ibrahima's inscription: *ibid.*

"We are requested . . .": W*DNI*, 20 May 1828.

"The Falls": Boston *Daily Advertiser*, 23 Aug. 1828, commenting on the opening of the panorama in Baltimore. W*DNI*, 23 June 1828, identifies the artists and prints several letters of high praise for the work.

half the gate . . . : Washington *National Journal*, 21 May 1828.

ladies who saw him . . . : "Rahaman," 188.

pages 128–129

opening sura of the Qur'an: Ibrahima's al-Fatihāh is found in Miscellany Box 37, Peter Force Papers, DLC.

"It must be . . .": New York *Freedom's Journal*, 29 Aug. 1828.

"his deportment . . .": "Rahaman," 189.

"the Arabic character . . .": quoted in *Address of the Hon. Edward Everett, Secretary of State, at the Anniversary of the American Colonization Society, 18th Jan., 1853* (Washington, 1853).

"I must allude . . .": *ibid.* Everett was impressed enough with Ibrahima to write a lengthy account of his life in 1851 for the Albany *Journal and Telegraph*. It has been cited throughout this book under the short title "Rahaman." See the notes to Chapter 1 for a full citation on the source.

"The African Prince . . .": Everett, diary, 25 May 1828, Massachusetts Historical Society, copy on microfilm at DLC.

"Abduhl Rahaman brought . . .": Adams, diary, 22 May 1828, Adams Papers. This entry in the manuscript diary was suppressed by Charles Francis Adams when he edited his father's journals in the *Memoirs of John Quincy Adams* (12 vols., Philadelphia: 1874–1877).

Clay's recommendation: Boston *Columbian Sentinel*, 13 Aug. 1828.

"I observe . . .": *Genius of Universal Emancipation*, 10 May 1828.

page 130

Voices from Africa: Boston Recorder and Religious Telegraph, 9 May 1828.

Harper: for Harper and Latrobe, see John E. Semmes, *John H. B. Latrobe and His Times, 1803–1891* (Baltimore, 1917), 118, 168. Letter quoted is from this source.

"If what I have . . .": Harper to Gurley, Baltimore, 10 June 1828, ACS-DLC.

"He is quite . . .": *ibid.*

"Mr. Latrobe and I . . .": *ibid.*

page 131

$420: Ibrahima to Marschalk, Philadelphia, 13 July 1828 in *NS&G,* 23 Oct. 1828.

"a grave decorum": Henri Wikoff, *Reminiscences of an Idler* (New York, 1880), 5.

statues mutilated: Caleb Atwater, *Remarks Made on a Tour to Prairie du Chien; Thence, to Washington City, in 1829* (Columbus, 1831), 239.

Gerard Ralston: many of his letters appear in ACS-DLC.

John Hanson: "Viator," 7 July 1829, in Philadelphia *Poulson's American Daily Advertiser,* 8 July 1829, mentions that Hanson had the vessels *Liberia* and *J. Ashmun* in the Liberian trade and notes his gold dust, ivory, and camwood imports in the summer of 1828.

John Mitchell: Alexander Henry to Roberts Vaux, 5 April 1827, Vaux Papers, PHi.

"but on consulting . . .": Mitchell to Gurley, Philadelphia, 13 June 1828, ACS-DLC.

page 132

"convinced of the . . .": Boston *Massachusetts Journal,* 4 Sept. 1828.

"We join . . .": *ibid.*

Ware endorsement: *ibid.*

"Prince will get . . .": James Nourse to Gurley, Princeton, N.J., 25 June 1828, ACS-DLC. Mitchell had written Gurley on June 13, "You will gratify me by sending a letter to me by Rahahman."

haunting the Coffee House: Philadelphia *Poulson's American Daily Advertiser,* 18 July 1828.

Indians . . . his tongue: Philadelphia *United States Gazette,* 4 July 1828.

"with much facility . . .": John F. Watson, "Annals of Philadelphia," vol. 1, 130, PHi.

"he appeared . . ." and "a dignified . . .": both *ibid.*

"a tall genteel . . .": Philadelphia *Aurora and Pennsylvania Gazette,* 27 June, 18 July 1828.

Sixth Presbyterian Church meeting: *United States Gazette,* 1–3 July 1828. This notice, a paid advertisement, mentions Lewis.

page 133

John H. Kennedy: M. Brown, "Memoir of the late Rev. John H. Kennedy" [1840], 368, in Joseph Smith, *History of Jefferson College* (Pittsburgh, 1857), treats his interest in colonization. Philadelphia *Christian Advocate,* 6 (April, 1828), 187, mentions his chairmanship of the "Young Men of the City of Philadelphia Associated for the Distribution of the Holy Scriptures." Philadelphia *American Sentinel,* 6 March 1828, contains a related item. Philadelphia *Saturday Evening Post,* 29 Nov. 1828, has a reference to his presidency of the "Young Mens' Association for the Suppression of Intemperance."

"Mr. Kennedy is . . .": Alexander R. Plumley to Gurley, New York, 19(?) July 1828, ACS-DLC.

July 4 described: Philadelphia *American Sentinel,* 7 July 1828.

call for Christian benevolence . . . : all quotations from Kennedy are taken from his sermon, which was published in 1828 under the title given in the text. A copy is located at the Presbyterian Historical Society, Philadelphia.

page 134

African Observer: see its obituary in the *Genius of Universal Emancipation,* 26 April 1828.

page 135

"the contributions this . . .": Ralston to Gurley, Philadelphia, 22 July 1828, ACS-DLC.

"Prince Abduhl . . .": *ibid.*

"I was very much . . .": Plumley to Gurley, New York, 19(?) July 1828, ACS-DLC.

"I am inclined . . .": William B. Davidson to Gurley, Philadelphia, 7 Aug. 1828, ACS-DLC.

"The case of the old man . . .": Plumley to Gurley, cited above. Plumley wrote Gurley from New York on June 24 about the tour mentioned.

Ibrahima's departure: New York *Commercial Advertiser,* 2 Aug. 1828, mentions his presence in that city.

writing of book: mentioned in *Independent Chronicle and Boston Patriot,* 13 Aug. 1828, which further stated that the writing had been done "at his ease."

pages 136–137

"a scholar of no . . .": Boston *Evening Bulletin,* 11 Aug. 1828.

illness: "The old man has somewhat of a fever on him," John Kennedy wrote Gurley in May. "I have advised him to keep his room, which he promises to do." Letter from Washington, 17 May 1828, ACS-DLC.

development of Boston: chapters 3–4, Walter Muir Whitehill, *Boston: A Topographical History* (Cambridge, Mass., 1968).

"a high moslem-looking . . .": Basil Hall, *Travels in North America in the Years 1827 and 1828* (3 vols., Edinburgh, 1829), vol. 2, 111.

Boston blacks: all quotations from Donald M. Jacobs, "A History of the Boston Negro from the Revolution to the Civil War" (Ph.D. dissertation, Boston University, 1968).

Charles Tappan: *The Boston Directory* (Boston, 1828), 264–5. Wyatt-Brown delineates his character well.

"fallacious . . .": Boston *Courier,* 11 Aug. 1828.

"Abdullah Mohammed": *Norfolk and Portsmouth Herald,* 19 Aug. 1829.

"Almourad Ali": NYJC, 1 Dec. 1828; Boston *New England Palladium & Commercial Advertiser,* 14 Nov. 1828. Unfortunately, newspaper editors seem to have gotten "Almourad" and "Abdullah" confused at times. Both imposters were also called "the Turk." Accounts of their activities were common.

"People now-a-days . . .": *New England Palladium & Commercial Advertiser,* 14 Nov. 1828.

"tall, venerable . . .": Boston *Jackson Republican,* 13 Aug. 1828.

"a striking face . . .": Boston *Statesman,* 12 Aug. 1828.

"We had the pleasure . . .": *Evening Bulletin,* 11 Aug. 1828.

pages 138–139

Ibrahima ill: Boston *Patriot & Mercantile Advertiser,* 12 Aug. 1828.

his appearance: *ibid.,* 13 Aug. 1828. Eliza F. Prentiss to George C. Shattuck, Boston, 23 Aug. 1828, Shattuck Papers, Mass. Hist. Soc., mentions the cape thrown over the arm.

"His dress gave . . .": Boston *Columbian Centinel,* quoted in N*A,* 1 Nov. 1828.

children at corners: *ibid.* "His affected stateliness, his glassy eye, his

Turban and Crescent, and the singular costume which he wore, was a matter of surprise and amusement to the group of boys which gathered at the corners and the public squares to look at him as he passed along."

"the most of our . . .": *Evening Gazette,* 16 Aug. 1828.

"We have as a people . . .": "Gambia," in *Evening Chronicle,* 30 Aug. 1828.

"I felt ashamed . . .": *Claims of the Africans,* 143–4.

Blacks with Ibrahima on the Mall: *Columbian Centinel,* quoted in NA, 1 Nov. 1828. "He walked on the Mall, attended by several decent coloured people, who seemed to view him with anxious pity, more than with pride or pleasure." The latter part of this sentence, as the subsequent dinner indicates, is false. But it is no more curious than the same writer's attempt to pass the dinner toasts off as Harvard lampoons. See Chapter 6.

"The day of my . . .": Peter Butler, quoted in *New England Palladium & Commercial Advertiser,* 29 Aug. 1828.

"enthusiastic feeling": "A Friend to the African Race" [i.e., a white man], in *Evening Bulletin,* 26 Aug. 1828.

"the Bostonians . . .": Providence, R.I., *Patriot,* 21 June 1828.

the celebration: the most complete description of the day's activities is in the *Nantucket [Mass.] Inquirer,* 6 Sept. 1828, which reprinted it from the *American Traveller.* The *New England Palladium & Commercial Advertiser,* 29 Aug. 1828, should also be consulted. All quotations and details are from these two sources.

The banquet had been announced in the *Daily Commercial Gazette,* 19 Aug. 1828, and in other newspapers in the city.

page 140

"the whole ceremony . . .": Boston *Courier,* quoted in *Norfolk and Portsmouth Daily,* 3 Sept. 1828.

David Walker: Jacobs, "History of the Boston Negro," 63, places him in the context of the city. Walker's occupation and that of the other diners was determined by reference to *The Boston Directory* for 1828 and 1829.

Might not the fact that *Walker's Appeal in Four Articles . . .* (1829) was addressed to "the Colored Citizens of the World" have been encouraged by his acquaintance with Ibrahima, among others?

"Our worthy guest . . .": *Nantucket Inquirer,* 6 Sept. 1828.

"May the Slave-Holders . . .": *ibid.*

"Brethren, the token . . .": *ibid.*

page 141

"excited the indignation . . .": *New England Palladium & Commercial Advertiser*, 29 Aug. 1828.

7. "The Almoner of His Bounty"

pages 142–143

Southern Galaxy: vol. 1, no. 1, appeared on May 22, 1828, and the newspaper was issued regularly every Thursday for the next two years. In a letter to Gurley (Natchez, 5 July 1828, ACS-DLC), Griffin mentioned that he was sending the minister a newspaper featuring an article on Ibrahima. "The paper containing it," he wrote, "is one conducted by myself during my leisure from professional pursuits. It contains generally matter of small import. . . ."

Joseph Griffin: he printed many items for Bowdoin College and subsequently wrote a history of the press in Maine.

New-England Galaxy: Isaac Pray, in his biography of James Gordon Bennett, wrote of the *Galaxy* in the 1820s, "No one could live in Boston then, and not know that the *Galaxy* and Saturday were of equal importance. That paper was desired more eagerly than the sermon on the Sabbath."

"No gentleman . . .": *New England Galaxy*, 20 June 1828.

four hundred subscribers: N*SG*, 10 July 1828.

"What a happy . . .":*New-England Galaxy*, 20 June 1828.

"You no pray . . .": issue of 12 June 1828, mentioned in the text in Chapter 4.

"It may be thought . . .": N*SG*, 29 May 1828.

"He states . . .": Griffin to Gurley, Natchez, 5 July 1828, ACS-DLC.

"Every letter . . .": N*SG*, 30 Oct. 1828.

"in relation . . .": Griffin to Gurley, Natchez, 5 July 1828, ACS-DLC.

summer of 1828: N*SG*, 24 July 1828, which also contains the phrase "overrun by Negroes. . . ."

page 144

"Stand back . . .": all quotations and details of the "duel" and its aftermath are from N*A*, N*S&G*, and N*SG* for this period. See particularly N*SG*, 14 Aug.–25 Sept.

"I consider . . .": N*S&G*, 23 Oct. 1828.

pages 145–146

"I write you . . .": Griffin to Gurley, Natchez, 19 Sept. 1828, ACS-DLC.

sold himself . . . : in February, 1827, Marschalk had taken charge of the pro-Jackson *Statesman & Gazette,* a new newspaper that resulted from the merger of his own newspaper and Jackson's local campaign organ. He shared editorial control of the newspaper with a Jackson group that bankrolled the venture.

Routine attacks on the Adams-Clay administration were printed in *Statesman & Gazette* in 1827, but, when the colonel was stripped of the federal printing by the Secretary of State early in 1828 (*NS&G,* 6 March 1828), he bombarded the coalition fiercely, calling Clay "dangerous in a free government," etc. (*ibid.*) This may have been the principal reason why he did not reply directly to Clay upon receipt of the Secretary's letter authorizing Ibrahima's manumission, but replied only to Adams, whom he considered less culpable.

The colonel was quite sensitive to the charge that he had "sold himself" or compromised his integrity by association with the Jackson partisans (who were, it is only fair to say, doing much of the editorial work of the *NS&G* in 1828), and such taunts as *"They* have *commanded,* and *he* must *obey"* (*NA,* 25 Oct. 1828) made him livid.

Ibrahima's letter: Boston, 10 Sept. 1828, in *NS&G,* 23 Oct. 1828.

page 147

"Mr. Adams and . . .": I have not located a copy of this handbill, so relied on the text printed in *NS&G,* 16 Oct. 1828.

page 148

Cyrus's reaction: *NA,* 25 Oct. 1828. Though his newspaper was nominally nonpartisan, he was a thoroughly political character himself. He was a member of an Adams committee that drafted a statement proclaiming "a total dereliction of honorable principles" in Andrew Jackson. *NA,* 2 Feb. 1828. Moreover, he was, Marschalk alleged, "the author of a speech against General Jackson so abusive that many of his own party condemned it." *NS&G,* 23 Oct. 1828.

"The apprehension . . .": *NA,* 25 Oct. 1828, emphasis in original.

"hypocritical . . .": New Orleans *L'Abeille,* 30 Oct. 1828.

"Who would . . .": *NA,* 25 Oct. 1828.

page 149

"The undersigned . . .": the text of the "extra" was reprinted in the *Ariel* of the twenty-fifth. "Gentlemen of the Ariel extra," Marschalk replied to the threat of indictment, "we have borne imprisonment and persecution once for the liberty of the press and we can bear it again." *NS&G*, 23 Oct. 1828.

Off to the Alligators . . . : N*A*, 18 Oct. 1828.

pages 150–151

"the arrogance . . .": *NS&G*, 23 Oct. 1828.

"a personage . . .": *NS&G*, 30 Oct. 1828.

"it is believed . . .": *NS&G*, 23 Oct. 1828.

lampoons: N*A*, 1 Nov. 1828.

"With what . . .": N*SG*, 30 Oct. 1828.

pilfered letter: *ibid.*

"unjustifiable . . .": *ibid.*

"Louisianans!": New Orleans *Louisiana Advertiser*, 25 Oct. 1828.

"A more daring . . .": New Orleans *Argus*, 23, 25 Oct. 1828.

"Long live . . .": *L'Abeille*, 27 Oct. 1828.

page 152

"*libelle* . . .": *Argus*, 23 Oct. 1828.

"Had an . . .": *Argus*, 28 Oct. 1828.

"*le sang* . . .": *Argus*, 25 Oct. 1828.

"The people . . .": *Louisiana Advertiser*, 25 Oct., 3 Nov. 1828.

"I have come . . ." R. R. Gurley, *Life of Jehudi Ashmun* (New York, 1835), 390–1.

page 153

last days: New Haven *Religious Intelligencer*, 30 Aug. 1828.

funeral: Harry Crosswell, diary, 27 Aug. 1828, Bienecke Library, Yale University; Hartford *Episcopal Watchman*, 6 Sept. 1828.

"A correspondent . . .": *Episcopal Watchman*, 6 Sept. 1828.

black armbands: Board of Managers, Proceedings, 1 Sept. 1828, ACS-DLC.

"I came to . . .": Ibrahima to Marschalk, Boston, 10 Sept. 1828, in *NS&G*, 23 Oct. 1828.

"This escorting . . .": *Evening Bulletin*, 26 Aug. 1828.

page 154

idea dropped: *ibid.*, 1 Sept. 1828.

"This aged Moor . . .": *New-Bedford Mercury*, 19 Sept. 1828.

One venerable Quaker . . . : Providence *Microcosm*, 19 Sept. 1828.

"appears too . . .": *Rhode-Island American & Providence Gazette*, 16 Sept. 1828.

"The Prince . . .": New Haven *Connecticut Journal*, 14 Oct. 1828.

Hartford described: Tudor, *Narrative of a Tour*, vol. 2, 514ff.; John

Bigelow, *Retrospections of an Active Life* (5 vols., New York, 1909–13), vol. 1, 28–32.

Sterling: Boston *New England Palladium & Commercial Advertiser,* 10 Oct. 1828, containing all quotations on the incident, though not supplying Sterling's name. That is provided by Gallaudet in NY*JC,* 16 Oct. 1828.

page 155

Gallaudet: this individual is ready for a modern biographer, although the older ones, Heman Humphrey (New York, 1857) and Edward M. Gallaudet (New York, 1910), are still serviceable. Both contain his letter to Ibrahima, written from Hartford, 15 May 1828.

Gallaudet described: Samuel G. Goodrich, *Recollections of a Lifetime* (2 vols., New York, 1856), vol. 1, 126–7.

"Gallaudet never...": Henry Bernard, *Tribute to Gallaudet...* (Hartford, 1852), 27.

the Asylum: an excellent short description appeared in the *Vermont Statesman,* reprinted in the Boston *American Traveller,* 28 Nov. 1828.

pages 156–158

"Mr. Gallaudet's...": Mrs. Hall's remark was provided me by Maxine Tull Boatner, director of historical research for the American Schools for the Deaf, West Hartford, who favored me with several letters in 1971 concerning Gallaudet and the school.

"The field...": Horace Hooker to William B. Sprague, Hartford, 23 Oct. 1851, in Sprague, *Annals of the American Pulpit,* vol. 2, 613.

"He selects...": Gallaudet, *A Discourse Delivered at the Annual Meeting of the Hartford Evangelical Tract Society in the Baptist Meeting-House, in Hartford, January 5, 1820* (Hartford, 1820), 7.

attack of fever... : Board of Directors, "Minute-Book, 1816–58," 25 Sept. 1828, Papers of the Connecticut Asylum for the Education and Instruction of Deaf and Dumb Persons, examined courtesy of Ben Hoffmeyer, American School for the Deaf, West Hartford. Also, Hartford *Connecticut Courant,* 30 Sept. 1828.

"Are you fully...": Gallaudet to Gurley, New York, 14 Oct. 1828, ACS-DLC.

"I think...": W*AR,* 4 (Oct., 1828), 246.

Center Church meeting: Hartford *Connecticut Observer,* 6 Oct. 1828; *Episcopal Watchman,* 4 Oct. 1828.

$156: Worcester *Massachusetts Spy,* 8 Oct. 1828.

"It is somewhat...": Gallaudet to Griffin, New York, 14 Oct. 1828, ACS-DLC.

"It is most . . .": same to same, Guiford, Conn., 8 Nov. 1828.
"The finger of . . .": W*AR*, 4 (Oct. 1828), 246.
"Age has . . .": *Statement*, 5.
"We see . . .": W*AR*, 4 (Oct., 1828), 246.
"Blessed be God . . .": *ibid.*
Cushing quotation: "New York memoranda," undated but circa 1828, Cushing Papers, DLC.
construction: Boston *Bower of Taste,* 9 Aug. 1828. The flavor of life in the city at this period is from Charles H. Haswell, *Reminiscences of an Octogenarian of the City of New York, 1816–1860* (New York, 1896); John Sartain, *The Reminiscences of a Very Old Man, 1808–1897* (New York, 1969); and Horace Greeley, *Recollections of a Busy Life* (New York, 1868).
Wainwright: he delivered an address at the forming of the school at Hartford in August.
"the most respectable . . .": Gallaudet to Gurley, New York, 14 Oct. 1828, ACS-DLC.

page 159

committee-of-arrangement: New York *American*, 13, 14, Oct. 1828.
"We all believe . . .": Gallaudet to Gurley, New York, 14 Oct. 1828, ACS-DLC.
Tappan: see Wyatt-Brown.
"poor": so says "Walter Barrett" [Joseph A. Scoville] in an unsympathetic reflection in *Old Merchants of New York City* (4 vols., 1863–66), vol. I, 229.
"I regard myself . . .": Tappan to Benjamin Tappan, New York, 5 March 1829, Lewis Tappan Papers, DLC.

page 160

"Money was his . . .": quotation from Wyatt-Brown.
Journal of Commerce: a rival editor observed that the *Journal of Commerce* was begun "for the express purpose of having a daily paper conducted upon Christian principles, and whose hands, editors, &c., shall not work on Sundays. . . . The Proprietor of that paper has expended thousands upon it without hope of gain." New York *National Advocate,* 6 Oct. 1828.
"Abdual Rahaman . . .": Lewis Tappan, *The Life of Arthur Tappan* (New York, 1870), 141–2.
"some coloured youths . . .": Gallaudet to Gurley, Guilford, Conn., 8 Nov. 1828, ACS-DLC.
Ibrahima a trader: Boston *New England Palladium & Commercial Advertiser,* 12 Aug. 1828.

page 161

Schroeder: see the memoir by his son that appears in Samuel Orcutt, *History of the Towns of New Milford and Bridgewater, Connecticut, 1703–1882* (Hartford, 1882), 806–11. Dix Morgan, ed., *A History of the Parish of Trinity Church in the City of New York,* vol. 4 (New York, 1906), 197–200n, 502–3, remarks on his personality and his career with that institution. I have benefited from conversations with three of his descendants: 1) Helen Wright, New Milford, Conn., 13 July 1973; 2) Walter Wright, Great Barrington, Mass., 13 July 1973; and 3) Joan McDaniel, Washington, D.C., 15 July 1973.

"with correctness . . .": Schroeder to "Rev. & dear Sir [Gallaudet?], New York, 21 Oct. 1828, ALS drafts in the possession of Joan McDaniel.

"I have *hopes* . . .": Gallaudet to Gurley, Guilford, Conn., 8 Nov. 1828, ACS-DLC.

"I saw in . . .": Gallaudet to McLain, Hartford, 11 May 1848, Gallaudet Papers, DLC.

page 162

"the most . . .": Boston *Amaranth, or Masonic Garland,* 1 (April, 1828), 1.

Thomas Servoss: John Pintard to Mrs. Richard Davidson, 16 Oct. 1828, John Pintard Letters, New-York Historical Society.

"Mr. Chairman . . .": NY*JC,* 16 Oct. 1828, contains the speech. Quotations for the balance of the chapter, unless noted below, come from it.

"the hearer . . .": Horace Hooker to William Sprague, cited above.

communicate to a deaf-mute . . . : New Brunswick, N.J., *Fredonian,* 19 Nov. 1828.

Henry Inman: his picture of Ibrahima is the only one known to me. Theodore Bolton, "Henry Inman, An Account of His Life and Work," *The Art Quarterly,* 3 (Autumn, 1940), 353–73, and 3 (Supplement), 104–18, catalogues the work under "Portraits in Oils," but fails to date it or locate a copy. I doubt if more than a crayon sketch was made, however. See *New-York Statesman for the Country,* 22 Oct. 1828. A stipple-point engraving of the drawing by Thomas Illman was offered for sale shortly afterward. It is found prefixed to the first and only volume of the Boston *Colonizationist and Journal of Freedom,* 1833.

For Inman, see Samuel L. Knapp, *Sketches of Public Characters* (New York, 1830), 199–200, and C. Edwards Lester, *The Artists*

of America ... (New York, 1846), which devotes a chapter to
him.
"quite black": New York *Statesman,* 16 Oct. 1828.

page 164

"excited repeated applause": *ibid.*
hall difficult for speakers: Lewis Tappan, "Journal," 10 Oct. 1828,
Lewis Tappan Papers, DLC.
"A powerful ...": *New-York American,* 16 Oct. 1828.
"to obtain ...": *ibid.,* which also gives a list of the committee
members.

8. A Single Plank

pages 165–166

Randall biography: "Portraits of African Colonizationists," PHi, and
WAR for 1829.
Foote statement: Andrew Foote, *Africa and the American Flag* (New
York, 1854), 141–2.
Mechlin: Board of Managers, Proceedings, 17 Oct. 1828, ACS-DLC.
As was usual in these years, Randall and Mechlin were also ap-
pointed agent and assistant agent, respectively, for the reception
of recaptured Africans. Samuel L. Southard to Randall, 1 Oct.
1828, and to Mechlin, 18 Oct. 1828, both from Washington, on
roll 1, microcopy 205, Correspondence of the Secretary of the
Navy Relating to African Colonization, RG45, DNA.
Shark: New York *Statesman,* 29 Nov. 1828, quoting the Charleston
Courier.
Tappan's company: "He will be prepared to invest $10,000 in this
trade and has expressed his belief that he can easily raise a capital
of $50,000," the Society's board understood. Proceedings, 13
April 1829, ACS-DLC.
"my project ...": Tappan to Gurley, 27 March 1829, ACS-DLC.
Ibrahima to write a letter: "Resolved that the Colonial Agent be authorized and requested to confer with Prince Abduhl Rahaman
with regard to opening communications with Almamy Abduhlka-
dre, his brother, King of Foota Jalloh, and, if judged expedient,
that he obtain letters from Prince, and also a translation into Arabic of one written by himself, in the name of the Society, stating
the circumstances and prospects of Prince and transmit them by
special messengers to Teembo." Proceedings, 22 Oct. 1828, ACS-
DLC.
colonist from Sierra Leone ... : *WAR,* 4 (Oct., 1828), 245. This

colonist told Ibrahima that Abd al-Qaadiri ("Abduhl-Garde") had been dead twenty years and that Bubakar ("Boorbarkar") had succeeded him. He also said that Ibrahima's son al-Husayn had declined being made *almaami* because of the insecurity of the job.

Ibrahima's letter: a translation of this remarkable letter was made at Monrovia in December, 1828, and this copy returned to the United States in a letter from Randall to Arthur Tappan, Monrovia, 3 Jan. 1829. Tappan published it in NY*JC,* 27 March 1829.

"Do instruct . . .": Gallaudet to Gurley, Guilford, Conn., 8 Nov. 1828, ACS-DLC.

"We are doing . . .": Tappan to Gallaudet, New York, 1 Nov. 1828, Gallaudet Papers, DLC.

page 167

Benjamin Paul: New York *Freedom's Journal,* 20 Dec. 1828. A collection of twenty-five dollars was taken for Ibrahima following a sermon preached by Paul in December.

John Murphy: *Freedom's Journal,* 12 Dec. 1828.

Cornish quotation: New York *Rights of All,* 17 July 1829.

African Free School: Charles C. Andrews, *The History of the New-York African Free-Schools, from Their Establishment in 1787, to the Present Time . . .* (New York, 1830), 23–4, 116. Pp. 69–70 detail Cornish's relationship as agent.

"Their conversation . . .": Andrews to Gurley, New York, 6 Nov. 1828, ACS-DLC.

John Russwurm: Russwurm, like many characters mentioned in this book, awaits his biographer. Mary Sagarin, *John Brown Russwurm: The Story of Freedom's Journal, Freedom's Journey* (New York, 1970), is a step in the right direction.

"opposed to the . . .": *Freedom's Journal,* 25 Jan. 1828.

"Abide in the . . .": New York *Colored American,* 13 May 1837.

"the friends of . . .": *ibid.,* 12 Dec. 1828, emphasis added.

listening to him pray: Russwurm to Alexander Plumley, Monrovia, 18 Nov. 1829, in *Boston Recorder and Religious Telegraph,* 28 April 1830.

pages 168–170

"I consider it . . .": Russwurm to Gurley, New York, 24 Feb. 1829, ACS-DLC, and *Freedom's Journal,* 14 Feb. 1829, announce his enlistment into the Society.

"I want . . .": Tappan to Gallaudet, New York, 30 Dec. 1828, Gallaudet Papers, DLC.

"The Committee . . .": Gallaudet to Gurley, Hartford, 22 Nov. 1828, ACS-DLC.

Society faced the winter . . . : Gurley to Leonard Bacon, Washington, 7 Sept. 1828, Bacon Family Collection, Sterling Library, Yale University.

"We only . . .": Gurley to "a gentleman in Philadelphia," Washington, n.d., in *Boston Recorder and Religious Telegraph,* 29 Aug. 1828. The financial situation was freely discussed in the press. See NY*JC,* 1 July, 15 Nov. 1828; New Haven *Religious Intelligencer,* 6 Sept., 18 Oct. 1828.

loan from Key: made 15 Jan. 1829 and noted in "Register of Payments, 1820–32," ACS-DLC.

"Prince Abduhl . . .": Tappan to Gurley, 9 Dec. 1828, ACS-DLC.

"Abduhl Rahaman . . .": *Freedom's Journal,* 20 Dec. 1828.

Isabella: "His aged wife . . . is at Philadelphia." Springfield *Republican,* 8 Oct. 1828.

From Dr. Mitchell . . . : Ralston to Gurley, Philadelphia, 10 Jan. 1829, ACS-DLC, lists several contributors.

"The old man . . .": *ibid.*

"Prince is not . . .": Tappan to Gurley, New York, 9 Dec. 1828, ACS-DLC.

"Prince Abduhl . . .": manuscript dated 29 Dec. 1828, American Philosophical Society Library.

opening sura . . . : William Brown Hodgson, the first American Sudanist, translated it for the Society in 1837. He remarked that "it is correctly written, in Mauretanic characters."

parade: Philadelphia *Democratic Press,* quoted in NY*JC,* 20 Jan. 1829; Philadelphia *Poulson's American Daily Advertiser,* 1 Jan. 1829.

stores for ship: Harper to Gurley, Baltimore, 19 Jan. 1829, ACS-DLC.

Ibrahima's provisions: Harper to Gurley, Baltimore, 21 Jan. 1829, ACS-DLC.

Virginia: Baltimore *American and Commercial Daily Advertiser,* 21 Jan. 1829. The boat left from Cordery's Wharf; the regular fare to Norfolk was eight dollars.

weather: Henry Thompson, Diary, 21 Jan. 1829, Maryland Historical Society.

"provided by . . .": Harper to Gurley, Baltimore, 17 Jan. 1829, ACS-DLC.

"I have this . . .": Latrobe to Gurley, same, 21 Jan. 1829, ACS-DLC.

page 171

William Draper: see Draper to William Maxwell, [Liberia], 17 Aug.

1837, printed in Philip Slaughter, *The Virginian History of African Colonization* (Richmond, 1855), 88.
Margaret Mercer: the daughter of Revolutionary War general John Francis Mercer. John H. B. Latrobe, *Maryland in Liberia* (Baltimore, 1885), 25n.
"would infuriate . . .": Latrobe to Gurley, Baltimore, 17 Jan. 1829, ACS-DLC.
"The Norfolk . . .": Harper to Gurley, Baltimore, 17 Jan. 1829, ACS-DLC, emphasis added.
Captain Ducrot: Margaret Mercer to Gurley, [near Annapolis,] 23 Jan. 1829; Harper to Gurley, Baltimore, letters of 24 and 25 Jan. 1829; and Latrobe to Gurley, Baltimore, 24 Jan. 1829, all ACS-DLC.
"So shall all . . .": all quotations and Harper's observation from Harper to Gurley, Baltimore, 25 Jan. 1829, ACS-DLC.

The reference to the "boat-load for Georgia" was prompted perhaps by the departure the previous month of the *Lafayette* for New Orleans with a cargo of about two hundred blacks chained in pairs in the hole. Benjamin Lundy remarked that it was the largest number of slaves he knew of ever to be congregated in a domestic slave ship. *Genius of Universal Emancipation,* quoted in Salem, Mass., *Observer,* 13 Dec. 1828.

page 172

Harriet: registrations at Bath, Maine (1 Dec. 1819, 21 June 1823, 14 June 1824, 7 Dec. 1827) and New Orleans, Louisiana (6 March 1830), RG41, DNA.
troops: Charleston *Courier,* 4 Dec. 1828; Charleston *City Gazette & Commercial Daily Advertiser,* 3 Dec. 1828.
ship history: Stonington, Conn., *Telegraph,* quoted in Bennington, Vt., *Journal of the Times,* 3 Oct. 1828; *State v. Dexter Adams,* #96, New London County, Conn., Superior Court, "Record of Trials," vol. 5, Conn. State Library, Hartford. The *Harriet* had been anchored off Old Point Comfort since December 15.
drowning: New York *Spectator,* 10 Oct. 1828.
"that a long . . .": Board of Managers, Proceedings, 8, 22 Dec. 1828, ACS-DLC.
Nautilus: when this vessel was offered to the Navy Department in June, 1829, for use in transporting 120 Africans from St. Augustine, Florida, to Monrovia, it was found to be unseaworthy by the Norfolk naval agent. Jonathan Branch to Miles King, Washington, 30 July 1829, Letters sent by the Secretary of Navy to Commandants and Navy Agents, microcopy 441, roll 2, DNA.
John McPhail: Thomas Rowland Scrapbooks, vol. 1, 208; 2, 264,

325; and 3, 338, Norfolk Public Library; William S. Forrest, *Historical and Descriptive Sketches of Norfolk and Vicinity* (Philadelphia, 1853), 282.
"zeal, energy ...": Alexander, *History of Colonization*, 361–2.
house frame: Tappan to Gurley, 20 Dec. 1828, ACS-DLC. "I hope you will see that he is provided with a frame and other materials for a house and suitable furniture; also garden tools and garden seeds. My idea is that five hundred dollars will supply all these.... Prince will also need some clothing and something to live on for a time after they arrive in Liberia.... Do see that he is made comfortable." Also, see Board of Managers, Proceedings, 12 Jan. 1829, ACS-DLC.

page 173

sixteen-by-eighteen ... : McPhail to Gurley, Norfolk, 27 June 1829, ACS-DLC.
"well known and honest": Norfolk *American Beacon*, 12 Dec. 1828.
"of a very ...": *American Beacon*, quoted in Baltimore *Patriot & Mercantile Advertiser*, 20 Jan. 1829.
"emotional farewells ...": anon., letter headed Richmond, 18 Jan. 1829, printed in *Freedom's Journal*, 7 Feb. 1829. Also, see Benjamin Brand to Gurley, Richmond, 20 Jan. 1829, and McPhail to Gurley, Norfolk, 19 Jan. 1829, both ACS-DLC.
"I wish to ...": J. B. Taylor, *Biography of Elder Lott Carey* (Baltimore, 1837), 16.
"Lord, save me!": Baltimore *Patriot & Mercantile Advertiser*, 26 March 1829. By February 1, 1829, no letters had been received from Liberia later than those dated August of the previous year.
"They all ...": McPhail to Gurley, Norfolk, 27 Jan. 1829, ACS-DLC.
"Amongst them ...": anon., letter headed Norfolk 26 Jan. 1829, in New Haven *Religious Intelligencer*, 14 Feb. 1829.

pages 174–176

"They are spoken ...": Baltimore *Niles' Weekly Register*, 7 Feb. 1829.
"I am *very* ...": Clay to Gurley, Washington, 3 Jan. 1829, ACS-DLC, emphasis added.
"A reasonable ...": Board of Managers, Proceedings, 12 Jan. 1829, ACS-DLC.
passport text: Clay to Randall, with enclosure, Washington, 17 Jan. 1829, and Clay to Mullowny, same, State Department Records, DNA.

loading: McPhail to Gurley, Norfolk, letters of 6, 15, and 27 Jan. 1829, all ACS-DLC.

Ashmun's suggestion: Board of Managers, Proceedings, 12 Jan. 1829, ACS-DLC.

"at a meeting . . .": *ibid.,* 9 Feb. 1829, containing all quotations.

departure: *Norfolk and Portsmouth Herald,* 9 Feb. 1829; *American Beacon,* 11 Feb. 1829.

Great changes had taken place . . . : Ibrahima's state of mind may be deduced from the following. Washington *United States' Telegraph,* 21 May 1828: "He says that he is old [and] that great changes may have taken place during his absence. . . ." *Statement,* 5: "Prince . . . has no wish to be a king. He has seen too much of the vanity of human life to wish to wear a crown of thorns in his declining days." Springfield *Republican,* 8 Oct. 1828: Ibrahima "returns to his native country with no ambitious projects." *Genius of Universal Emancipation,* 10 May 1828: "He says that forty years' slavery have subdued his ambition for power."

cabin: McPhail to Gurley, Norfolk, 27 Jan. 1829, ACS-DLC.

fifty berths: same to same, Norfolk, 15 Jan. 1829, ACS-DLC.

smallpox vaccination: Board of Managers, Proceedings, 26 May 1828, ACS-DLC. It was a "standing condition" of emigration.

"continued healthy . . .": Boston *Daily Advertiser,* 25 June 1829.

"There were no . . .": Kennedy to Gurley, n.p., 20 June 1829, ACS-DLC.

"fine, pleasant gales . . .": Amelia Roberts to "a resident of Petersburg," Liberia, 26 April 1829, in *Baltimore Gazette and Daily Advertiser,* 9 July 1829. This letter is especially valuable as it was written by the mother of the future President. She continued, "I see everything carried on here as it is in the United States. I am, Sir, much pleased, and have not the least desire to return to Virginia." The editor of the *Gazette* described Mrs. Roberts as a woman of "honest and artless mind."

page 177

"In this . . .": anon., "Sketch of the History of Liberia," circa 1852, series VI, container 10, ACS-DLC.

Roberts: complete list of the passengers is found in "Emigration Register," series VI, vol. 17, ACS-DLC. See above the note on his mother.

"Except for . . .": quoted in Slaughter, *The Virginian History of African Colonization,* 109–10.

moored: "We arrived here in 38 days from Cape Henry, and moored under the guns of Monrovia, all in good health at our arrival."

Beverly P. Yates, Monrovia, 14 April 1829, to a correspondent in Richmond, in Baltimore *Patriot & Mercantile Advertiser,* 3 July 1829.

Monrovia described: in presenting the colony in 1829 I have attempted to use letters written by the colonists themselves, preferably those who sailed in the *Harriet.* They are widely scattered and difficult to obtain, but I have succeeded in locating some. In addition to the Yates and Roberts letters cited above, and the Shiphard and Cheeseman letters below, also see Samuel Richardson, Monrovia, 1 April 1829, in Norfolk *American Beacon,* 13 July 1829; James B. Lund, Monrovia, 10 April 1829, in *Daily Richmond Whig,* 20 June 1829; John Barbour and Frederick Lewis, both Monrovia, 6 May 1829, to Gurley, ACS-DLC; Remus Harvey to John H. B. Latrobe, Monrovia, 26 May 1829, Maryland State Colonization Society Papers, Maryland Historical Society; Ibrahima's letters, cited below; and Remus Harvey's earlier letter, Monrovia, n.d., excerpted in *Genius of Universal Emancipation,* 28 June 1828.

Of further interest are Septimius Arabin, "Western Coast of Africa, Colony of Liberia, 1828," CO 267:101, PRO; report of Captain Johnson, in the *American Beacon,* reprinted in Philadelphia *Church Register,* 5 Sept. 1829; Richard Randall to a correspondent in Annapolis, Liberia, 5 Jan. 1829, in *Richmond Religious Herald,* 3 April 1829; and Gurley, *Life of Ashmun,* 122ff.

fugitive English debtor . . . : "Petition of Charles Reynolds," Monrovia, 24 July 1829, CO 267:99, PRO.

"This country is . . .": letter of James Shiphard, Monrovia, 16 April 1829, in *Norfolk and Portsmouth Herald,* 19 June 1829.

"I assure you . . .": letter of Abraham Cheeseman, Monrovia, n.d., in *Norfolk and Portsmouth Herald,* 24 June 1829, emphasis added.

pages 178–181

"most of the . . .": Shiphard letter, cited above.

"Comfortable shelters . . .": G. S. Stockwell, *The Republic of Liberia* (New York, 1868), 112.

Randall collapsed: *Daily Richmond Whig,* 18 July 1829.

Mandinka from . . . : Randall to the Board of Managers, Monrovia, 25 Dec. 1828, ACS-DLC, containing all quotations. Randall to Arthur Tappan, Monrovia, 3 Jan. 1829, in *NYJC,* 27 March 1829, describes him as "a Mandingo or Mahometan Priest." It is not clear if the writer intends to say the Mandingo was a *marabout.* More likely, the writer was simply following a contemporary confusion that made every Mandinka a "Mahometan priest," since many

Mandinka in Africa and the West Indies were, by this time, Muslims.

second letter: mentioned in Ibrahima to Tappan, Monrovia, 13 April 1829, in NYJC, 27 June 1829.

passport circulated: Clay to Randall, Washington, 17 Jan. 1829, cited earlier in this chapter, contains in part; "The chief motive for the interest which has been taken in this affair [with Ibrahima] was to make a favorable impression, in regard to the United-States, on the Emperor of Morocco and the people in Africa. It is desirable, therefore . . . that you will cause a knowledge of what has been done by direction of the President . . . to be diffused as extensively as practicable."

"broke from . . .": *Daily Richmond Whig,* 18 July 1829.

death: *Poulson's American Daily Advertiser,* 10 July 1829; *Claims of the Africans,* 149.

mortality: well traced in the letters of the colonists cited above.

"the oldest settlers . . .": Mechlin to the Board of Managers, Monrovia, 31 Aug. 1829, ACS-DLC.

Ibrahima ill: *ibid.,* containing quotations used.

tragic oversight . . . : *13th Annual Report of the American Society for Colonizing the Free People of Colour of the United States. With an Appendix* (Washington, 2nd ed., 1830), 7.

"I beg you . . .": Ibrahima to Paul, Monrovia, n.d., in *Rights of All,* 17 July 1829.

"You speak of . . .": Frederick Lewis to Gurley, Monrovia, 20 March 1830, ACS-DLC.

"I believe . . .": Russwurm to Gurley, New York, 24 July 1829, ACS-DLC.

passengers' grumblings . . . : Gurley to ?, Washington, 7 Nov. 1829, in *Poulson's American Daily Advertiser,* 9 Nov. 1829.

"I cannot . . .": Benjamin Brand to Gurley, Richmond, 18 Nov. 1829, ACS-DLC.

"I am sorry . . .": Ibrahima to Gurley, Monrovia, 5 May 1829, ACS-DLC. It is impossible to determine which Cooper this was; five adult male Coopers were on the *Harriet.*

"We had progressed . . .": McPhail to Gurley, Norfolk, 27 Jan. 1829, ACS-DLC.

"I shall . . .": Ibrahima to Gurley, cited above.

"I . . . shall . . .": *ibid.*

trade: Beverly Yates and James Lund's letters, cited above, give the prices current in April. American ships then trading were the schooner *Hannah* and brigs *Jehudi Ashmun* and *Liberia,* all of Philadelphia, and the brig *Hope* of Boston.

Harvey quotation: *Genius of Universal Emancipation,* 28 June 1828.

"A man coming . . .": Lund quoted in *Norfolk and Portsmouth Herald,* 19 June 1828.

Baltimore-built vessels: Newport, R.I., *Mercury,* 14 Nov. 1829.

"to be bearded . . .": an 1825 issue of the Freetown *Sierra-Leone Gazette,* quoted in W*AR,* 4 (Oct., 1828), 247.

Abd al-Qaadiri's scruples: O'Beirne, Journal, 140. It was the *almaami's* opinion, he wrote, "that he would be brought to account in the next world, for disposing of his fellow creatures in [the slave trade], but hoped at the same time, God would accept the excuse of the impossibility that formerly existed of procuring the necessities of life in such abundance, or resisting the inducements held out at that time by the white people that came to purchase them."

page 182

"to lend his . . .": *Statement,* 6.

death of Abd al-Qaadiri: Guébhard, "L'Histoire du Fouta-Djallon et des Almamys," 84.

"My brother . . .": Ibrahima to Tappan, Monrovia, 13 April 1829, in NY*JC,* 27 June 1829. For Yaya, see Diallo, 44.

"I found one . . .": Ibrahima to Gurley, Monrovia, 5 May 1829, ACS-DLC.

five hundred dollars: Clay to Randall, Washington, 17 Jan. 1829, cited above.

"I am unwell . . .": Ibrahima to Gurley, cited above.

"attacked with . . .": Mechlin to the Board of Managers, Monrovia, 31 Aug. 1829, ACS-DLC.

"An overflow . . .": "A very highly respectable colonist" to ?, Monrovia, 24 Aug. 1829, in *Baltimore Gazette and Daily Advertiser,* 6 Nov. 1829.

manuscripts to Timbo: Russwurm to "a young man of colour," Monrovia, n.d., in W*AR,* 6 (April, 1830), 60.

page 183

"He had every . . .": letter of "A very highly respectable colonist," cited above. The Mechlin letter of 31 Aug. gives the date of Ibrahima's death.

never returned to Futa: there is even some question if he heard from Timbo before he died. N*A,* 18 July 1829, citing a Baltimore newspaper, states that "Prince transmitted by travellers and *received* letters in 15 days from his brother, who says he is the present king and was enthroned three years since." Emphasis added. This does not appear to be true, however. The source of the Baltimore article must have been the NY*JC,* 27 June 1829, piece, which printed part of Ibrahima's letter to Tappan, written at Monrovia, 13 April 1829. This article reads in part, "[Ibrahima] is able by means of travellers to transmit or receive communications in the space of 15 days. 'My brother,' he says, 'is the present King, having been enthroned three years since....' " G. S. Stockwell, *The Republic of Liberia*, 113, seems to be correct in stating that Ibrahima died awaiting word from Futa.

recommenced the practice of Islam: the "very highly respectable colonist" cited above adds, "I was informed that he took up his Mohametan principles as soon as he got in sight of this land, and he died with the same." He died "in full belief" of Islam, according to a writer in the Worcester *Massachusetts Spy*, 18 Nov. 1829. Gurley understood the same from his sources. See William McLain to Gallaudet, Washington, ? May 1848, ACS-DLC. In "Rahaman," 191–2, Everett attempts an apologia.

"He died in...": Baltimore *Niles' Weekly Register*, 14 Nov. 1829.

Epilogue

pages 184–185

caravan at Boporo: Russwurm to "a young man of colour," Monrovia, n.d. [1829], W*AR*, 6 (April, 1830), 60. *Claims of the Africans*, 165–6, seems based on this letter.

"their emancipation...": Ibrahima to Tappan, Monrovia, 13 April 1829, cited above.

"Poor fellow!...": Tappan to Gallaudet, New York, 30 June 1829, Gallaudet Papers, DLC.

new will, etc.: items from Thomas Foster Probate Papers, NAdCo. His tombstone in Greenwood Plantation cemetery provided the date of death.

Ibrahima's children divided: Thomas Foster Estate, Real Estate Book #1, NAdCo.

trashy cotton: Thomas's agent was Reynolds, Ferriday, & Co. See their items in his probate papers.

Tappan's doorstep: Tappan to Gurley, New York, 30 July 1830, ACS-DLC, contains "in a pious family in Brooklin [*sic*]..."

theft: two letters from Tappan to Gurley, Sept. 1830, ACS-DLC.

pages 186–187

"Satan sometimes...": Boston *Liberator*, 6 July 1833.
Cox: obituary in *The Natchez*, 14 Oct. 1831.
Griffin: obituary in Vicksburg *Register*, 11 Oct. 1837.

Marschalk: obituary in Woodville, Miss., *Republican,* 25 Aug. 1838.

Sarah Foster: "Died on Saturday evening last, at Pine Ridge, Mrs. Sarah Foster." *Mississippi Free Trader and Natchez Gazette,* 7 April 1837.

"the old house . . .": miscellaneous family history papers in possession of William Lum.

Prince: living when mentioned in the testimony of Nancy Foster Wood, n.d. [March, 1834], *State of Mississippi v. James Foster,* NAdCo.

Bridget and family: Sarah Foster Probate Papers, NAdCo. Sarah's estate was divided in March, 1838.